T0212594

Lecture Notes in Computer Science 9588

Commenced Publication in 1973
Founding and Former Series Editors:
Gerhard Goos, Juris Hartmanis, and Jan van Leeuwen

More information about this series at http://www.springer.com/series/7410

Adrien Bécue · Nora Cuppens-Boulahia
Frédéric Cuppens · Sokratis Katsikas
Costas Lambrinoudakis (Eds.)

Security of Industrial Control Systems and Cyber Physical Systems

First Workshop, CyberICS 2015 and First Workshop, WOS-CPS 2015
Vienna, Austria, September 21–22, 2015
Revised Selected Papers

 Springer

Editors
Adrien Bécue
Airbus Defence & Space Cybersecurity
Elancourt
France

Nora Cuppens-Boulahia
Télécom Bretagne
Cesson-Sévigné
France

Frédéric Cuppens
Télécom Bretagne
Cesson-Sévigné
France

Sokratis Katsikas
Center for Cyber and Information Security
Norwegian University of Science and
  Technology
Gjøvik
Norway

Costas Lambrinoudakis
Department of Digital Systems
University of Piraeus
Piraeus
Greece

ISSN 0302-9743   ISSN 1611-3349   (electronic)
Lecture Notes in Computer Science
ISBN 978-3-319-40384-7   ISBN 978-3-319-40385-4   (eBook)
DOI 10.1007/978-3-319-40385-4

Library of Congress Control Number: 2016941300

LNCS Sublibrary: SL4 – Security and Cryptology

Printed on acid-free paper

This Springer imprint is published by Springer Nature
The registered company is Springer International Publishing AG Switzerland

Preface

This book presents the revised and selected papers of the First Workshop on Cyber-security of Industrial Control Systems (CyberICS 2015) and the First Workshop on the Security of Cyber-Physical Systems (WOS-CPS 2015), held in Vienna, Austria, September 21–22, 2015, co-located with the 20th European Symposium on Research in Computer Security (ESORICS 2015). The volume contains six full papers and two short papers from the submissions to CyberICS and three full papers from WOS-CPS.

The two events aim to address the increasing number of cyber threats faced by cyber-physical systems operators around the world. Cyber-physical systems range in size, complexity, and criticality, from embedded systems used in smart vehicles, to SCADA and industrial control systems like energy and water distribution systems, smart transportation systems etc. The papers that have been accepted cover topics related to the management of cyber security in these systems including security monitoring, trust management, attack execution models, forensics, economics, and training.

April 2016

Adrien Bécue
Nora Cuppens-Boulahia
Frédéric Cuppens
Sokratis Katsikas
Costas Lambrinoudakis

Organization

First Workshop on Cybersecurity of Industrial Control Systems (CyberICS 2015)

General Chair

Adrien Bécue   Airbus Defence and Space, France

Program Committee Co-chairs

Nora Cuppens-Boulahia   Télécom Bretagne, France
Frédéric Cuppens   Télécom Bretagne, France

Program Committee

Ari Takanen   Codenomicon, Finland
David Espes   University of Brest, France
Ernesto Damiani   University of Milan, Italy
Jean Leneutre   Telecom ParisTech, France
Joaquin Garcia-Alfaro   Telecom SudParis, France
Jozef Vyskoc   VaF, Slovakia
Khan Ferdous Wahid   Airbus Group Innovations, Germany
Mauro Conti   University of Padua, Italy
Michele Bezzi   Sap, France
Mourad Debbabi   Concordia University, Canada
Radu State   University of Luxembourg, Luxembourg
Reda Yaich   IMT-Telecom Bretagne, France
Safaa Hachana   IMT-Telecom Bretagne, France
Samiha Ayed   IMT-Telecom-Bretagne, France
Waël Kanoun   Alcatel-Lucent Bell Labs, France
Yves Roudier   EURECOM, France

First Workshop on the Security of Cyber-Physical Systems (WOS-CPS 2015)

Program Committee Co-chairs

Sokratis Katsikas	Center for Cyber and Information Security, Norwegian University of Science and Technology, Norway; University of Piraeus, Greece
Costas Lambrinoudakis	University of Piraeus, Greece

Program Committee

Alcaraz Cristina	University of Malaga, Spain
Debar Hervé	Télécom SudParis, France
Gollmann Dieter	Hamburg University of Technology, Germany
Lopez Javier	University of Malaga, Spain
Mauw Sjouke	University of Luxembourg, Luxembourg
Mitchell Chris	Royal Holloway, University of London, UK
Petit Jonathan	University College Cork, Ireland
Röning Juha	University of Oulu, Finland
Samarati Pierangela	Università degli Studi di Milano, Italy
Song Houbing	West Virginia University, USA
Wolthusen Stephen	Royal Holloway, University of London, UK
Zanero Stefano	Politecnico di Milano, Italy

Contents

CyberICS 2015 Papers

The Economics of Cybersecurity: From the Public Good to the Revenge
of the Industry 3
   Danilo D'Elia

Teaching Industrial Control System Security Using Collaborative Projects . . . 16
   Thuy D. Nguyen and Mark A. Gondree

Trust Establishment in Cooperating Cyber-Physical Systems 31
   Andre Rein, Roland Rieke, Michael Jäger, Nicolai Kuntze,
   and Luigi Coppolino

Security Monitoring for Industrial Control Systems 48
   Alessio Coletta and Alessandro Armando

WirelessHART NetSIM: A WirelessHART SCADA-Based Wireless
Sensor Networks Simulator 63
   Lyes Bayou, David Espes, Nora Cuppens-Boulahia,
   and Frédéric Cuppens

Remote Attestation for Embedded Systems 79
   Markku Kylänpää and Aarne Rantala

WOS-CPS 2015 Papers

LiMon - Lightweight Authentication for Tire Pressure Monitoring Sensors . . . 95
   Cristina Solomon and Bogdan Groza

Umbra: Embedded Web Security Through Application-Layer Firewalls 112
   Travis Finkenauer and J. Alex Halderman

Towards Standardising Firewall Reporting 127
   Dinesha Ranathunga, Matthew Roughan, Phil Kernick,
   and Nick Falkner

CyberICS 2015 Short Papers

Forensics in Industrial Control System: A Case Study 147
   Pieter Van Vliet, M.-T. Kechadi, and Nhien-An Le-Khac

An Attack Execution Model for Industrial Control Systems Security
Assessment 157
   Ziad Ismail, Jean Leneutre, and Alia Fourati

Author Index 169

CyberICS 2015 Papers

The Economics of Cybersecurity: From the Public Good to the Revenge of the Industry

Danilo D'Elia[✉]

University of Paris VIII Vincennes-Saint Denis, Paris, France
deliadanilo@gmail.com

Abstract. In the aftermath of Edward Snowden's intelligence revelations, many governments around the world are increasingly elaborating so-called «digital sovereignty» policies. The declared aim is to develop trusted technologies to protect the more sensitive networks. The ambition of this article is to turn over the complex- and often contrasting- motivations and interests behind the industrial policy movements, explain how the dominant representation of cybersecurity as public good is impacting the public policy and analyse the dynamics between private and public players.

Keywords: Cyberspace · Public policy · Risk analysis · Critical infrastructures

1 Introduction

We live in the information age; everyone knows the advantages we enjoy from that. What is still blurred is the cost and the risk of our dependence upon the online life. As aptly stated by the philosopher Floridi, with the development and the massive penetration of ICTs in all advanced economies, people and engineered machines are now continuously connected with digital network and part of the same global environment made of information: the infosphere [1].

In addition, the same information infrastructure underpins the assets and services considered as vital to the essential functioning of industrialised economies, and make them interdependent. From power grids to banking systems, from traffic light controller to water distribution, the information assurance of data, networks and protocol of those infrastructures has become the central nervous system of our society. The internet of things (50 billion of devices to be connected to the internet in 2030) and the concept of smart city show the complexity of this interdependence that knows no sign of slowing.

Now, if the pervasiveness of ICTs in our daily life has many advantages because facilitate social and economic activities, there is also a downside. The infosphere has come with new risks that are changing the nature of cybersecurity from a technical issue for a restricted expert-community to a social-political one.

In fact at the origin, security was not a priority for the ICT's developer and this has led to two interrelated levels of risk. The first one is the danger of systems failure and the cascading effects. Due to the interdependence of critical infrastructures (CIs), the impact of an incident won't be limited to the original sector of activity nor to a national

© Springer International Publishing Switzerland 2016
A. Bécue et al. (Eds.): CyberICS 2015/WOS-CPS 2015, LNCS 9588, pp. 3–15, 2016.
DOI: 10.1007/978-3-319-40385-4_1

border. For instance, in November 2006 a shutdown of a high-voltage line in Germany resulted in massive power failures in France and Italy, as well as in parts of Spain, Portugal, the Netherlands, Belgium and Austria, and even extended as far as Morocco, affecting ten million customers in total.

The second risk is given by the potentially malicious actors exploiting technical vulnerabilities. Beyond the hacktivism (politically motivated) and criminal (monetization earning) threats, the major challenges come from the espionage - both political and economic- and sabotage. These threats raise a wide range of questions linked to national security (critical infrastructures protection), economic prosperity (security of business secrets) and privacy issues (data protection).

Over the course of the last decade, the increasing sophistication of attacks, the disclosure of large intrusions to corporate, and the latest revelation to the global public the massive network exploitation by Western intelligence agencies have considerable changed the threat perceptions. As a result, the cybersecurity has become a complex political question and is increasingly perceived as a public good by many governments [2].

Of the various consequences of this situation, one particular trend has emerged, especially in Europe: the need to implement industrial policy in order to develop national-base technologies to protect independently the critical information networks from the challenges aforementioned.

Rather than attempting a theoretical analysis, the ambition of this research is to start from a specific case study (the French experience) in order to point out some key trends and future challenges for the global debate on cybersecurity. In fact, over the past years academics from economics and public policy have already investigated theories on public good and cybersecurity[1]. Based on the concepts borrowed from such disciplines we analyze the recent dynamics on industrial policy through the multidisciplinary approach developed by the French Institute of Geopolitics [3]. This is based on two main features: the study of conflicting perceptions used to reinforce or defy an established order and the power competition over territories between rival forces.

In the following, the arguments unfold as follows. First, we will outline the conceptualization approach: the meaning of the cybersecurity as representation of public good. We identify the changes in how, in the post-Snowden era, the cybersecurity discourse and the cyber security market are perceived.

Then, through the in-depth analysis of the French case, we analyze the rivalries challenging the emergence of the national market on cybersecurity. We point out the conflicts between sovereignty, business interests and privacy. Dealing with national industrial policy of cybersecurity is ambitious because it means understanding the points of view of various players acting at different layers (local, national, global). Find the good path is thus complex and this article aims to help the understanding. In conclusion, we reflect on the definition of efficient public-private partnership and the new role of the citizen on the economics of cybersecurity.

---

[1] Some of main references in ecomics of cybersecurity are: Moore, Tyler et al. "The Economics of Online Crime," Journal of Economic Perspectives, 2009; Anderson, Ross, "Why Information Security is Hard: an Economic Perspective," Proceedings of the 17th Annual Computer Security Applications Conference, 2001.

2   The Cyberspace as "Open-Bar Market" for Some Brothers

There is a common refrain about the cybersecurity origin: Internet and the information systems were not designed with security in mind. Therefore, this has led to the risk given by the potentially malicious actors exploiting vulnerabilities. These actors comprise generally four categories: state or state-sponsored actors, insiders, organized or individual criminals and politically motivated non-state actors.

2.1   The Risk of the Online Life

The sabotage and espionage are widely considered as the major challenges for the nation states [4].

For the former one, the growing interconnection with the Internet and the IP convergence result in the shift from largely proprietary isolated systems to highly interconnected and based on commercial-of-the-shelf hardware and software. That has left CIs vulnerable to cyber attacks. So far, Stuxnet malware in 2010 and the recent attack against a German steelworks remain the only publicly-acknowledged destructive attacks and unexpected disruptions of normal life are still more likely to come from accidents or natural hazards than from deliberate sabotage[2]. However, over the last five years, the number and the sophistication of the attacks doesn't stop to increase[3], thus the most demanding scenario is that where the risk is systemic: again, the hyperconnectivity of our society and existence of vulnerable supply chains raise the prospect of disruption having impact on the society as a whole.

Cyber espionage is the second serious threat. Here the main concern is on long-term consequences of massive exfiltration of trade secrets and confidential data for activities that are at the core of advanced economic development such as defence, finance, energy and high technology sectors. Moreover, the intelligence services worry because the information collected through targeted network attacks could facilitate a large scale attack during a conflict situation. Finally, the issue is not just economic but becomes of national security nature.

Beyond the vulnerability exploitation but strictly related to the risk of espionage, two additional features have to be detailed here: the contradictory roles of national authorities and the ambiguous role of tech-corporations handling personal data. Both of them have come to the foreground in June 2013 when the former NSA contractor Edward Snowden's revelation disclosed the Internet surveillance programs established by U.S. intelligence agencies and in cooperation whit their closer allies.

---

[2] According to the 2014 German IT Security Report released by Federal Office for Information Security, a cyber-attack that caused significant damage in an steel facility in Germany. For a detailed analysis see Robert M. Lee, ICS Cyber-Attack on German Steelworks Facility and Lessons Learned, 17 December 2014.

[3] According to research conducted by US ICS-CERT, in 2012, 197 cyber incidents were reported by asset owners or trusted partners to the US Department of Homeland Security. In 2013, the incidents were 257. Moreover, at every security conference, information technology experts disclose new vulnerabilities and demonstrate how sabotage of ICS got easier.

Protecting against the cyber threats has led to a contradictory practice and has revealed the schizophrenic conduct of national security authorities. In many countries (35[4]), intelligence services and defence agencies are developing offensive capabilities: to achieve that, they buy and exploit zero-day vulnerabilities in current operating systems and hardware. In addition, as revealed by Snowden, the US government, either cooperating with domestic internet companies or secretly, cracked existing and contributed to new vulnerabilities in widespread encryption systems. All these initiatives, launched for national security interests, are making cyberspace more insecure for everyone: the exploitation of vulnerabilities has the potential to undermine trust and confidence in cyberspace overall as backdoors could be identified and exploited by malicious actors and thus reduce the resilience of the entire system. This situation makes the cyber risk assessment clearly more complex.

In addition, the disclosure of June 2013 highlighted the political role of the big American platforms in collecting and retaining user's entire online life. We know as personal data have become the "crude oil" for the economy of the information society. As aptly analysed by the INRIA research team [5], the American giants in search engine, social networks, clouds, etc. have developed a business model based on network effect (both direct and indirect) and private data as "virtual currency" in exchange for services.

Thanks to their increasing ability to collect, store, analyse personal information, the most important internet services (like Google, Facebook, Twitter, Amazon, etc.) raised a dominant business position transforming users' data into added value: often in selling targeted online advertising reaching a global audience.

But what it isn't always clear is that beyond the economic effects, there are also important strategic consequences. These corporate know more that anyone about people's commercial interest, their political and societal preferences, their networks of friends and wishes…and all that without any security clearance. For this reason, intelligence services that are generally prohibited by law from asking private data without a judicial authorisation, are extremely interested in enjoying the same network effects of the internet companies and thus in having access to the users' data. The sale rationale is behind the proliferation of surveillance programs like those revealed in June 2013 [7].

If seen on the political level, it's clear if one nation relies mostly on foreign Internet platform, this leads to let a large amount of their data be exploited outside their jurisdiction. According to the INRIA research (Fig. 1), the result is strong information asymmetries between those who (U.S.) import the "raw material" and transform in gold and those who (European countries) sell for free their resources.

This explain why the information advantage on data harvesting make the domination of US-based companies a threat to sovereignty and why the topic has come under scrutiny by European states.

2.2 June 2013 as Starting Point for Shaping an Industrial Policy

In addition to the European dependency on ICT developed and based elsewhere for the data gathering, another important risk came up in the last years. Many consulting

---

[4] This is the analysis made by the McAfee expert, Jarno Limnéll, NATO's September Summit Must Confront Cyber Threats, 11 August 2014.

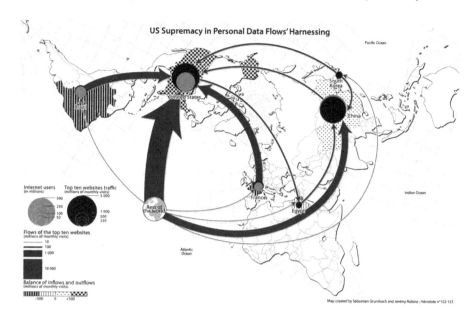

Fig. 1. Geopolitical Map on US Supremacy in personal data flow's harnessing (S. Frénot and S. Grumbach, Les données sociales, objets de toutes les convoitises, in Hérodote, n° 152–153, Paris 2014.)

studies (Table 1) confirm global suppliers, mainly form U.S., Asia and Israel, are dominating the cybersecurity supply chain market while European nations are straggling behind.

At the political level this problem has been addressed as a strategic issues by national and European documents[5]. If securing critical infrastructures networks is essential to protect lives (from sabotage) and privacy of citizen (from surveillance) and to boost the market prosperity (against economic espionage), the dependency on foreign technologies without full confidence that the devices do not include built-in backdoors or are applying the same level of quality requirement is a strategic issue.

Now what changed with Snodwen's affair is the increasing perception that technology control means sovereignty. On one hand, the disclosures of three particular NSA programs (PRIMS, MUSCULAR and TEMPORA) revealed an embarrassing relationship between the major U.S. internet corporates and the American national security agencies providing the NSA with access to the data of their services. The result, confirmed by many political declarations, was a loss of confidence in U.S. based companies. According to some reports, a first economic consequence was the lost revenues (22–35 billion of dollars) in cloud outsourcing business for many American

---

[5] According to the 2013 European communication on «Cybersecurity Strategy of the European Union: An Open, Safe and Secure Cyberspace» "there is a risk that Europe not only becomes excessively dependent on ICT produced elsewhere, but also on security solutions developed outside its frontiers".

Table 1. Red color means "totally dependent on", yellow color means Whit low position within the global market <10 %; green color means with good position within the global market >10 %. The table takes in consideration the regional origin (EU-US-ASIA-ISRAEL) of the leading companies and their stakes for each market segment. The data come from a cross-analysis of several studies: Magic Quadrant for Global MSSPs, The Cyber Security Market 2012–2022 – Visiongain; «La cybersécurité Enjeux et perspectives d'un marché en pleine mutation», Xerfi, 2012; «Forecast: PCs, Ultramobiles, and Mobile Phones, Worldwide, 2010–2017, 4Q13 Update», Gartner, 2013, IC insights, Major 2013 IC Founderies, 2013; Marché des smartphones: Samsung n°1, Apple n°2 au Q3 2013 ~ IDC, Eco Conscient; Industrial Control Systems (ICS) Security Market Market Forecast and Analysis (2013–2018), Market and Market, 2013; «La Cybersécurité Europeenne: de l'importance d'une politique industrille», Jeremy Labarre report to the Council of the European Union 2014.

LEVEL OF EUROPEAN DEPENDENCE ON FOREING TECHNOLOGY	
Sector	Level
Desktop computing applications	
Graphics processors	
PC motherboards	
Semi-conductor	
Mobile computing	
Industrial Control Systems	
Routers	
Networking switches	
Computing servers	
Data and Content Security	
Application Security	
Endpoint Security	
Network security	
System Security	

companies[6]. The political reaction from European countries was focusing on data localization policies: many proposals were on national e-mail, undersea cables, localized routing and data storage, aiming to limit the harvesting and processing of digital data to specific U.S. companies and jurisdiction.

While those technical and legal initiatives have already been analysed [7, 8], we would highlight another trend: the dynamics on industrial policy seeking to promote cyber-security sector. The leak about the adoption by RSA, a major cyber security company, of two encryption tools developed by the NSA in order to increase its ability to eavesdrop on Internet communications, was a wake-up call for the need to strengthen the industrial security capabilities.

How a country aiming to be independent on cyber-security can provide cyber security facing a market dominated by foreign and strong competitive companies? What are the obstacles? In order to answer these questions, the second part of the article will focus on the French experience developed over the last years.

---

[6] An in-depth analysis was made by Danielle Kehl, *Surveillance Costs: The NSA's Impact on the Economy, Internet Freedom and Cybersecurity*, New America's Open Technology Institute, 2014.

3 Structuring a Complex Dialogue

In accordance with the strategic objective to become a world power in cyberdefence, France has put many resources in and launched numerous initiatives aiming at ensuring independently its security. Industrial policy is part of the toolbox used in order to "master and develop (…) a range of guaranteed 'trusted products and services" [9].

3.1 Trusted Solution Wanted

The definition of trusted solution can thus be found through the reading of official documents[7]. A sovereign solution is firstly synonymous with integrity: namely, the assurance of the absence of built-in backdoors ensuring the protection of sensitive information and systems. For that, the public powers require " an evaluation process under the control of the National Network and Information Security Agency (ANSSI)". But the integrity and high-grade requirements are not sufficient criteria for assuring the commercial success of the solutions.

As discussed above, the cyber security demand has evolved with the commercialisation of Internet and the pervasiveness of the information systems in the industrial world. Since the current demand consists mainly of civilian infrastructures, a twofold need, therefore, has arisen. The customers are requiring ergonomically designed solution compatible with operational technology and simultaneously marketed at competitive price. As result, the offer of trusted solutions needs to be suitable for the new demand. The difficult is thus achieving the right balance between commercial solution and high-grade technology solution.

For doing that, the French authorities developed a policy based on four pillars: the conventional rulemaking, the organization of the public-private partnership, the R&D funding campaign, and the certification process.

3.2 A Coordinate Public Procurement Policy

In 2013 the government passed a law (*Loi de Programmation Militaire-LPM 2014–2019*/LPM) and imposed mandatory measures on public and private critical infrastructures. The rules consist of mandatory cartography of the critical information systems, mandatory and regular audits of information systems and networks by certified third parties; mandatory declaration of cyber incidents; implementation of certified detection sensors. In parallel, the government released an internal circular to impose the purchase of trusted solution on the public agencies.

The aim of those moves is to boost the internal demand to consume national solutions and thus to promote the development of a broad offering and limit the

---

[7] Three are the reference documents: Loi de Programmation Militaire 2014–2019, art. 22.; Programme d'Investissements d'Avenir 2013 – Développement de l'Économie Numérique, «Cœur de filière numérique-Sécurité numérique», Octobre 2013; Le guide pour la qualification de Prestataires d'audit de la sécurité des systèmes d'information (PASSI).

dependence on foreign suppliers. This move was carefully supported by the nation industrial base consisting of a few big corporates (Airbus, Thales, Orange, Sogeti, Bull-Atos) and a large SME complex (600). For these players the emergence of an internal market estimated to be 1.5 billion of euros and projected to grow at a 15 % to 20 % rate per year has been hailed as an Eldorado. What should be noted is that the market growth (globally estimated at $73 billion[8]) is happening in an environment of financial crisis and large cuts across the public administration in France as well as in Europe. Thus, helping in the structuring the market is seen as an economic opportunity for both the public and private sector [10].

3.3   Structuring the Public-Private Partnership

The democratization of information systems and the interdependence of the networks infrastructures have risen the need- for the government- to develop a coordinated approach between the different players involved in cyber security: private infrastructure operators, industrial control systems (ICS) providers, maintenance firms security companies, etc. [10].

The French authorities were aware of that already in 2008, when the White Paper on Defence and Security Policy recognizes the State no longer has all the essential levers it could need to take action against the threats it faces and it needs to develop better relationships with the private sector. In 2010, ANSSI conducted a series of interviews on ICS security with CI operators, security suppliers and ICS vendors. A long process was thus initiated in order to address the following question: how to develop and maintain a trusted information system based on (a few) national and international technological bricks?

The aim of the interviews was to draw a shared understanding of the limits of the current solutions and where the best practice was to be found. Thus, the information sharing within the selected players contributed to the understanding of the future requirements, so that national authorities can establish new standards and industry can work to offer tailored solution for CIs.

However, during the first year, the differences of language and culture emerged and strengthened the need for a permanent exchange. In 2011 ANSSI was aware of that and created a department fully dedicated to foster cooperation with the private sector around the twelve sectors defined as critical and an office dedicated to the industrial policy. Additionally, to move beyond the different languages and interests, in 2012 a permanent exchange platform was established with 25 players (SCADA Working Group). On a voluntary basis, ANSSI brought together the main stakeholders from government (ANSSI and MoD representatives) and industry (SCADA providers, national CIs and security suppliers) to develop supply chain risk management best practices that can apply to CIs. The long term goal of the SCADA WG is to be able to label the next ICS and prepare the CIs for the standards imposed in 2013.

---

[8] The Future of Global Information Security, Gartner Security Scenario Research 2014.

On the same level, and shaped by the aim to encourage the cooperation and the dialogue between public and private players, another initiative should be mentioned: the establishment of the Council of Security Industrial Base (*Comité de la filière des industries de sécurité-COFIS*, 30). Strongly wanted by the private sector, the Prime Minister launched the COFIS in 2013. This initiative brings together all the stakeholders involved in security industry from government agencies to trade federation and CI representative in order to match the needs of the offer and the demand and so to structure the security supply chain.

The latest initiative is the Cybersecurity Industrial Roadmap dubbed "Cyber Plan": a broad policy program consisting of seventeen actions around four strategic goals: boosting the national demand of trusted solutions, development of a national offer, structuring the export approach, consolidating the national industrial complex. The working group aiming at the implementation of the plan was led by ANSSI but composed of the representatives of private and public sector. Again the main goal was to bring together the whole spectrum of players interested in the industrial policy: providers, users, shareholders, regulators, customers, and investors.

The common achievement of these moves is the mutual understanding of various interests and thus the convergence of opinions in adopting minimum-security standards. In doing that, these initiatives reduce the gap between the government lack of technological path and the operators lack of security path and contributes to better assess future needs for security providers.

3.4   The Certification Process

The certification process, led again by ANSSI, is seen as a strategic way to ensure confidence on trusted solutions. In order to help the public authority to state how well CIs have implemented the new legal framework passed in 2013, the labelling process assesses the audit companies as independent evaluators. In addition, it tests also the integrity of security solutions and vendors aiming to bring transparency to the suppliers that should be embedded in the CIs. In this way, ANSSI through the expertise acquired on-the-field of incident-response and recovery, promotes the development of trusted suppliers evaluating products and services should be commercialized. Thus, potential customers could choose their trusted solutions among the catalogue established by the national authority. With these trends in play, the public authority aims to structure the offer available on the national market. Moreover, in order to promote the certificated solutions, ANSSI established a label "MADE in FRANCE" that will facilitate the marketing toward the customers.

The outcomes of these initiatives directly impact the risk factors: elaborating the secure design of new solutions leads to reduce the technical vulnerabilities. On the other hand, the implementation of trusted products, as detection sensors, generates more countermeasures and a broader view of frequency and gravity of cyber attacks. Finally, this means fundamentally less risks for the network infrastructure.

3.5 Orienting the R&D

To ensure continuous investment in R&D, the state has increased its efforts in both the civilian and military investments. The Minister of defence has tripled in two years the research credit (€30 million in 2014). In parallel, in the framework of the *Program for the Future Investments* 2013 a call for projects entitled "Digital Security" has received 18 proposals. Through a fund of €20 million, this initiative aims to guide investment in R&D and thus promote the development of an offer so far absent. This will include the implementation of capacity requested by the LPM 2014–2019. In continuation of this strategy, the Cyber Plan envisages a new wave of call for projects for 2015 in order to develop two to three new ranges of deals per year.

In addition, a flagship project was announced and funded by the Minister of Defence in 2013. The project aims to structure a regional cluster focused on the cyber defence in Brittany and based on the concept of triple helix. Private company from telecom sector as well as from security and defence will jointly cooperate with the main research laboratories and MoD agencies in promoting innovation and technological development. On the one hand, the private sector will drive scientific developments; on the other hand, the public sector will shape the innovation through supporting policies and relevant research. In fact, a comprehensive approach cannot disregard the academia contribution: cyber-security needs continuous research and education, mission and task normally belonging to the academia. In parallel, training of future experts will find an important place in the Cyber Defence Cluster: private servants are participating with national authorities in drafting the cyber-security syllabus for national cyber defence centre of excellence. In doing that, the impact on the cyber risk is clear: the public-private cooperation aims to reduce the vulnerabilities (in process and human action) and to develop (human) countermeasures.

4 The Limits of the High-Tech Colbertism

The analysis of the initiatives launched in France stress how industrial policy depends on many variables that public and private players can impact only through a coordinated approach. Therefore, a comprehensive policy is needed. That means the implementation of various actions at different level in order to structure the market: the law to boost the demand, the education and R&D to structure the expertise, the organization of the dialogue and the certification process to support a trusted offer.

In addition, as demonstrated by the evolution undertaken by ANSSI in 2009–2013, dealing with the evolution of cyber security means to be adaptive: being the police man (conducting the inspection), the conventional rulemaker (boosting the demand and helping the market to understand the measures to be implemented) or the facilitator (to develop the technical solution). However, a more in-depth analysis reveals important tensions that might be potentially damaging the implementation of the industrial policy.

4.1   Sovereignty Versus Business Interests

On the private side, increasing critics have been heard condemning the regulatory-based approach without taking in account the market drivers.

Due to the deregulation process of many public sectors in the 80s and the globalization of 90s, the private sector is now owning or controlling the majority of vital infrastructures many of them with multidomestic sites. Thus the primary interest of CI operators is to employ solutions broadly adequate for their multinational plants.

At the same time, for security suppliers their concern is more for developing solutions able to be sold on the international market and amortize R&D costs. Now here is where corporate interests clash with national security and highlight the need of more international cooperation. Since cyber-security is defined as matter of national sovereignty, public powers are imposing new constraints to CIs. In addition, they are influencing the development of national technologies that should fulfill national standards with high-grade requirements demanding a lot of investment. The consequences are relevant for private sector: limitation of foreign investment, increasing cost to implement a multitude of national standards and more constraints on the development of national solutions.

Given that the national demand and R&D budget are a fraction of the multibillion-dollar budget of the American and Asian market, the security vendors are complaining for less regulations and a more business-oriented, balanced and neutral regulation framework.

That leads to the question of the right scale of international cooperation: how to define a good partner? The European Unions is the most appropriate level or it would be more valuable to establish a trusted group of partners on the basis of mutual acceptance of national standards? Nevertheless, cyber-security of national strategic assets remain a national responsibility: in sensitive domains like cryptography, this would mean to continue developing country-specific solutions. Hence, there is a strong link between cyber-security solutions and sovereignty matters for the Member States which result in lack of cooperation and lead to increased market fragmentation. The issue is complex, and the debate is still on-going in Europe.

4.2   When the Size Market Matters

SMEs are the engine of innovation in cyber domain: due to their structure and innovative culture, they are an essential element to face the extremely rapid evolution of threats and technologies. This reason explains the importance of the relationship between SME and big corporate in building the ecosystem of cyber-security. Although it is not a specific to the cyber domain, this point becomes important for the French case because of the current critical situation and the fierce competition in international markets.

However, the national market is too tight and although the presence of many innovative SMEs, these are not able to reach a critical mass because of lack of the demand. Moreover, the absence of a culture adapted to the new market is at the heart of the difficulties of coordination between SME and big corporations to bid jointly: times and methods of development, sales channels and culture management are not the same on cyber-security market. In addition, more complexities rise in case of acquisition or merger of an SME: French large industries have difficulty in managing the integration of staff and maintain innovative technologies for SMEs. The result is that many SMEs are acquired by foreign competitors or they stop investing.

4.3 The Paradox of a Schizophrenic World

On the political side, there are also some complications. As the Snowden affair revealed to the global public, the State organization suffer schizophrenia: promoting and implementing defences while actively attacking is no longer sustainable with the concept of resilience. This applies to the U.S. as well as to the other states developing offensive capabilities like France. Keeping secret vulnerabilities, cracking encryption standards and installing backdoors means increasing technical vulnerabilities for everyone and thus mining the trust of society in the global information infrastructure and the public authorities.

However, the schizophrenia is also on the citizen's side: we accept that the State needs pre-emptive intelligence in order to anticipate the major threats as the terrorism [11]. This explains the reaction of law enforcement agencies such as the FBI and the GCHQ to the strengthening of encryption technology by social network companies[9]. For intelligence agencies adding extra layers of security that prevent national authorities from gaining access to information stored by service providers means more difficulties in the fight against threat using these technologies.

5 Conclusion

In conclusion, the French case is striking for a least two reasons. First, there are a number of reasons behind the implementation of industrial policies: market fragmentation, corporate interests, and national security are coupled with the ever-increasing issues of technological independence and privacy protection. It is important to keep in mind the different and often conflicting arguments supporting such actions.

Secondly, the dynamics analysed reveal on the one hand the willingness of public authorities to control the cyber-security mechanism and, on the other hand, they underscore the need to find the balance between national sovereignty, business interests and privacy. Given that the industrial policy needs to take in account market driven objectives (to be competitive) and equally important objectives linked to societal (data protection) and technological independence concerns (the protection of CIs through trustworthy technology), the research of the balance is hard task. It is even more complicated because businesses operate across borders while law enforcement agencies are national based.

We are now only at the very beginning of the important international debate about the dynamics within the infosfere. As the Online Manifesto has observed, "the

---

[9] For the official declarations see: R. Hannigan, *The web is a terrorist's command-and-control network of choice*, The Financial Times, November 3, 2014, and A. Thomson and A. Satariano Silicon Valley Privacy Push Sets Up Arms Race With World's Spies, Bloomerg, Nov 5, 2014.

repartition of power and responsibility among authorities, corporate agents, and citizen should be balance more fairly" [12]. This situation pushes States and especially law enforcement agencies to openly explain their activities –without revealing security recipes- to the citizens and work more closely with personal data protection agencies. We need to move from what Bruce Schneier names "corporate-government surveillance partnership" to the public-private debate partnership [13]: in order to continuously entrust the security to public powers, the citizen, whose confidence is fundamental for the resilience, has to be involved in the cyber-security equation.

Acknowledgements. This work is funded by *Airbus Defense and Space-CyberSecurity* and supported by the *Chaire Castex de Cyberstratégie*. Any opinions, findings, and conclusions or recommendations expressed in this publication are those of the author and do not necessarily reflect the views of Airbus.

References

1. Floridi, L.: Information: A Very Short Introduction. Oxford University Press, Oxford (2010)
2. Dunn Cavelty, M.: From cyber-bombs to political fallout: threat representations with an impact in the cyber-security discourse. Int. Stud. Rev. **15**(1), 105–122 (2013). Friedman, A.: Economic and Policy Framework for Cybersecurity Risks. Brookings, July 2011
3. Lacoste, Y.: La géographie ça sert d'abord à faire la guerre. La découverte, Paris (2014)
4. Rid, T.: Cyberwar Will Not Take Place. Oxford University Press, Oxford (2013)
5. Castelluccia, C., Grumbach, S., Olejnik, L.: Data Harvesting 2.0: from the Visible to the Invisible Web. Presented at the 12th Workshop on the Economics of Information Security, Washington, DC, United States, June 2013. https://who.rocq.inria.fr/.../WEIS13-CGO.pdf
6. Anderson, R.: Privacy versus government surveillance: where network effects meet public choice. Presented at the 13th Workshop on the Economics of Information Security, Pennsylvania State University, United States, June 2014. http://weis2014.econinfosec.org/papers/Anderson-WEIS2014.pdf
7. Hill, J.F.: The Growth of Data Localization Post-Snowden: Analysis and Recommendations for U.S. Policymakers and Industry Leaders. Lawfare Research Paper Series, vol. 2–3 (2014)
8. Maurer, T., Morgus, R., Skierka, I., Hohmann, M.: Technological sovereignty: missing the point? In: An Analysis of European Proposals after 5 June 2013
9. White Paper on Defence and National Security, La documentation Fransaise, Paris, p. 174 (2008)
10. D'Elia, D.: Public-private partnership: the missing factor in the resilience equation. The French experience on CIIP. In: Stefanowski, J., Panayiotou, C.G., Ellinas, G., Kyriakides, E. (eds.) CRITIS 2014. LNCS, vol. 8985, pp. 193–199. Springer, Heidelberg (2016). doi:10.1007/978-3-319-31664-2_20
11. Omand, D.: Securing the State. Hurst, London (2010)
12. Floridi, L.: The Online Manifesto, Being Human in a Hyperconnected Era. Springer, Berlin (2015)
13. Schneier, B.: A Fraying of the Public/Private Surveillance Partnership. https://www.schneier.com/blog/archives/2013/11/a_fraying_of_th.html. Accessed 30 November 2013, The Battle for Power on the Internet, The Atlantic. http://www.theatlantic.com

Teaching Industrial Control System Security Using Collaborative Projects

Thuy D. Nguyen$^{(\boxtimes)}$ and Mark A. Gondree

Department of Computer Science, Naval Postgraduate School,
Monterey, CA 93943, USA
tdnguyen@nps.edu, mgondree@nps.edu

Abstract. In this work, we discuss lessons learned over the past three years while supporting a graduate capstone course centered on research projects in industrial control system (ICS) security. Our course considers real-world problems in shipboard ICS posed by external stakeholders: a system-owner and related subject matter experts. We describe the course objectives, format, expectations and outcomes. While our experiences are generally positive, we remark on opportunities for curricula improvement relevant to those considering incorporating realistic ICS topics into their classroom, or those working with an external SME.

Keywords: ICS · SCADA · Ship-board ICS · Education · Capstone project

1 Introduction

As mandated by Executive Order 13636, "Improving Critical Infrastructure Cybersecurity" [6], the National Institute of Standards and Technology (NIST) published its *Cybersecurity Framework* document to provide guidelines for managing security risks that could affect the national critical infrastructure [18]. This NIST framework recognizes that information technology (IT) systems and industrial control systems (ICS) differ in term of operational environment and potential risk. It also identifies cybersecurity education as a core requirement to protect the critical infrastructure services.

The insecurity of industrial control systems (ICS) is a pressing and tangible problem, prompting the formation of the Industrial Control Systems Cyber Emergency Response Team and various working groups on critical infrastructure protection, like the Critical Infrastructure Partnership Advisory Council. In the security education community, several groups have proposed curricula to address the needs to educate students and professionals about critical infrastructure protection and ICS security [7,8,15]. SCADA (supervisory control and data

---

The views expressed in this material are those of the authors and do not reflect the official policy or position of the Department of Defense or the U.S. Government.

A. Bécue et al. (Eds.): CyberICS 2015/WOS-CPS 2015, LNCS 9588, pp. 16–30, 2016.
DOI: 10.1007/978-3-319-40385-4_2

acquisition) security is a knowledge unit highlighted as contributing to the academic requirements for the designation as the Center of Academic Excellence in Cyber Operations from the U.S. government [19].

In keeping with the broader goal of preparing our graduates for real-world challenges, we introduced a capstone course that aligns with the observation that IT security and ICS security are different and thus teaching ICS security needs to be tailored for the ICS domain and taught as a separate course [13]. Our capstone course focuses on shipboard ICS because of its relevance to the mission of our institution.

The pedagogical approach of *learning by doing* assumes that the learner can work independently, leveraging on prior experience, to develop an effective solution to a complex problem. *Collaborative learning* and *problem-based learning* are two synergistic instructional methods in which learners work in small groups to solve real-world problems, utilizing knowledge, skills and abilities learned prior in the classroom. Our course follows these teaching strategies, while involving participation of a shipboard ICS system owner (i.e., the stakeholder) and ICS subject matter experts (SME).

In the remaining sections, we discuss previous work on ICS security education and describe the objectives and structure of the capstone course. We then enumerate the class projects that addressed a number of shipboard ICS security concerns, ranging from a comparative analysis of version control systems for ICS development to a table-top vulnerability assessment of a notional ICS target system. We highlight lessons learned and recommendations for future course enhancements.

2   Related Work

Several educators describe the need for security curricula leveraging practical laboratories for ICS security, as a motivating context for undergraduate education and for professional development. These prior efforts include the discussion of curricula [4,7,9], the design of teaching laboratories [10,16,22] and the development of various teaching modules [8,11,13]. For example, McGrew and Vaughan describe a set of exercises demonstrating software vulnerabilities associated with a commercial HMI product [14]. Generally, education research related to industrial control security has focused on the description of a specific laboratory environment or the potential hands-on course exercises using this environment. In contrast, we do not describe a target, instructional laboratory environment or exercises for use in direct-instruction courses. The course described here explores very different intentions, audiences and delivery strategies.

3   Course Description

The course presents a capstone experience in which students are immersed in an operational or policy challenge of interest to an external stakeholder. Student teams develop courses of action (COA) that address legal, ethical, political, technical, tactical, operational and strategic implications. At the end of the course, the recommended COA is presented by students to the stakeholders. The outcome of this research is a solution to the stakeholder's technical problem. Students draw upon their classroom knowledge and research skills to analyze the problem space, derive potential solutions, and communicate these to subject matter experts and stakeholders. However, the stakeholder's problems require students exercise critical thinking in a problem domain with which they have no prior curricular experience, i.e., industrial control systems.

Program Context. Our capstone course is an upper-division class in the Cyber Systems and Operations (CSO) curriculum at the Naval Postgraduate School. The CSO program is an 18-month (six-quarter) multidisciplinary graduate program covering a broad range of cyber operations [12]: computer network attack, defense, and exploitation; cyber analysis, operations, planning and engineering; and cyber intelligence operations and analysis. The program is very practically-focused, employing site visits, wargaming exercises, seminars, guest speakers and practical workshops to complement traditional instruction. The program is designed for students with diverse, non-CS backgrounds: entrance requirements are based on a bachelor's degree in some STEM discipline.

Prerequisites. Prior to enrolling in this capstone course, students have completed most CSO program requirements including basic courses on computer security and network security. It is expected that students can use virtual machines, trial-install unfamiliar software, employ penetration testing tools and reason about systems from an adversarial perspective. Students have already started their Master's thesis projects prior to the capstone course, and are familiar with many on-campus resources for performing background research and literature reviews.

Learning Objectives. Prior courses require both individual and group work, while student thesis projects emphasize individual research; in contract, our capstone course emphasizes collaborative research for an external stakeholder. At the end of the course, students will be able:

- to collaborate on research in self-directed teams;
- to communicate in-progress research results to a technical audience;
- to interpret and respond to outside technical feedback;
- to prepare COA design alternatives;
- to evaluate alternatives from an operational perspective;
- to synthesize final technical recommendations; and
- to communicate technical recommendations to a stakeholder.

These learning objectives are understood to be quite advanced, falling in the highest levels of Bloom's taxonomy (i.e., applying, analyzing, evaluating, creating). Compared to prior group coursework, this capstone project requires significant time management (on the scale of months rather than weeks) and coordination outside the classroom (nearly all group work is performed outside of class).

4   Course Format

The capstone is offered as a four-credit class twice a year. It follows a resident course format with in-class meetings each week. Significant course work occurs in group meetings outside class time and via the course website and forums. The expected time commitment for out-of-class course work is approximately eight hours per week. By the end of the course, students demonstrate an in-depth understanding of project-related material. Grading is based on team accomplishments, SME evaluation of the final COA report and each individual's technical contribution to project tasks including oral presentations and written deliverables (e.g., correspondence with the SME, written reports).

Through a guided inquiry learning process facilitated by the instructor, students work together in small teams to develop a recommended COA to solve a problem provided by the external sponsor or SME. The course is divided into several phases (see Table 1), with phase 0 occurring approximately three months before class begins. Phases 1–5 occur over a ten-week period. Throughout phases 3 and 4, the instructor works with the SME to guide students in research and to oversee interactions between the students and the SME.

Table 1. Course schedule overview.

Phase	Purpose	Primary participants
Phase 0	Project creation	SME, instructor
Phase 1	Technology familiarization	Students, instructor
Phase 2	Initial engagement with SME	SME, students, instructor
Phase 3	Interim progress review	SME, students
Phase 4	Final progress review	SME, students
Phase 5	Project conclusion	Students

4.1   Phase 0 – Project Creation

Prior to each class, the instructor solicits real-world ICS problems from stakeholders, stated in relatively general terms. Additionally, stakeholders and SMEs may propose specific research ideas for certain problem areas. Iteratively, the SME and instructor refine the scope of work to better align with the students' technical background and the course timeframe. The final outcome of this iterative process is a project assignment.

Each project assignment has four key components: a problem statement, including the needs and goals expressed by the SME; a description of the research activities to be performed; the guidelines for team formation; and the expected deliverables from each team. Students are asked to organize their own teams, with some guidelines and final approval from the instructor. To promote the development of new student leadership and project management skills, students who served as group leaders in prior coursework cannot serve as project team leaders. The instructor approves team membership and leader selection to ensure a balanced distribution of experience, and a good alignment between individual skills and those required for success in the team's project. This strategy has been successful: over three years, only one team (of 12 total teams) has had interpersonal conflict that required some instructor intervention.

4.2   Phase 1 – Technology Familiarization

During the first two weeks, students learn about ICS technology through a relatively traditional lecture-oriented approach, with homework and lab exercises.

Lectures. There are two introductory course modules. The ICS Fundamentals module covers system types (e.g., Distributed Control System and SCADA), components (Human Machine Interface, Programmable Logic Controller, etc.) and industrial protocols. This module explains the *security zone* and *conduit* concepts defined by the ISA/IEC-62443 (formerly ISA-99) security standards, and introduces students to shipboard control systems (e.g., steering, propulsion, electrical plant). The ICS Vulnerabilities module focuses on select ICS attacks. The main objective is to show students the similarities and dissimilarities of cyber exploits between a traditional IT systems and industrial control systems.

Homework. Module homework assignments consist of about 5–6 assigned readings, including academic papers, trade articles, SME-provided background materials and video recordings on ICS security research. For each assignment, students are asked to provide a written synopsis, including a constructive evaluation discussing the material's strengths and weaknesses in terms of reasoning, logic and evidence. A 90-minute video on PLC vulnerabilities and exploit tools [24] is a class favorite since it explains how ICS security researchers uncover design and implementation deficiencies in popular PLC products, e.g., Rockwell Automation ControlLogix and MicroLogix.

Laboratory. Students learn about ICS vulnerabilities using a "SCADA-in-a-box" lab environment [21] simulating a realistic natural gas compression system. It includes a commercial PLC, HMI software, a commercial ICS firewall and malware demonstrating a ModBus-based PLC exploit. Student exercises using this environment consist of two activities. First, students conduct an attack on the unprotected PLC using a malicious payload delivered via opening a PDF on the HMI system. Second, students add and configure a firewall for the system, allowing only select ModBus traffic between HMI and PLC to block attack traffic. Although introductory in nature, the exercise provides hands-on experience with different components and operational aspects of a SCADA system—i.e., as an operator using the HMI, as an attacker and as a security administrator. Students develop a short report explaining their understanding of the ICS components in the environment, the protection mechanisms, any problems they encounter during the activities and how they solve these. Student feedback on the exercise has been positive, and the lab report provides an opportunity for formative feedback, to correct misunderstandings or confusions.

4.3   Phase 2 – Initial Engagement with SME

In this phase, the class assignment work begins, with team formation and background research to prepare for the first meeting with the SME. This meeting is either in-person or via video teleconference. At this meeting, students interview the SME to collect information and ask questions about scope and expected outcomes. Early interaction with students allows the SME to clarify research needs, ratify assumptions, provide insights on the operational setting and gauge students' technical strengths.

During this phase, the instructor and SME coordinate a ship tour for students to learn about the inner workings of shipboard control systems. Guided by a SME, the students can see the physical layout of various ICS equipment and gain additional knowledge on how these systems are operated and maintained. Although most students are U.S. Navy officers who have served on ships, very few have managed these types of systems. Information obtained from the trip is documented in individual trip reports, used as a basis for in-class discussions to clarify misunderstandings relevant to the project assignments. Seeing ICS systems in context during a tour is extremely valuable, highlighted in nearly all course feedback.

4.4   Phase 3 – Interim Progress Review

Students begin an iterative research process to develop the COA following a traditional prototyping systems development methodology, i.e., working versions of the COA are developed, deliberated and refined cyclically. Project management uses web-based tools through the course website. In particular, each team maintains a wiki that contains a work plan and a set of individual activity logs. Communication with the SME is via email and teleconference. This phase ends with a progress review in which students present emerging ideas and potential approaches informed by the on-going research.

Team Work Plan. This is a lightweight, free-form artifact (as opposed to the traditional work breakdown structure) describing tasks assigned to each team member, the objectives and outcomes that the team plans to accomplish weekly, and the research methodology used to complete the identified work items (interviewing the SME, reaching out to professional contacts, etc.). It is the responsibility of the team leader to update the work plan regularly to reflect changes as the project progresses. Naturally, the level of detail and freshness of this artifact depend on the project management experience of the team leader. A common trend that has been observed is that the work plan tends to lag behind actual work.

Individual Research Log. Each student maintains a running log describing their weekly accomplishments and research findings. The log acts as evidence and an agenda for required in-class briefs where students discuss their activity and open issues. In their log, students describe the status of each assigned task, the time spent on each task, and the outcomes of each task. Students also keep track of problems encountered during the implementation of each work item, the resolution to these problems, and any rationale for technical decisions made. The soundness of the technical discussion is partially judged based on the supporting materials attached to the contents, e.g., web links to reputable sources, citation to academic papers and technical articles.

Given the variety of assignments and tasks, there is no formal rubric for the evaluation of this log. At a minimum, however, students must demonstrate the following: their understanding of the tasks, any issues to resolve, interactions with the SME, and how they respond to or incorporate advice from the SME. An interesting observation is that, for some classes, the quality of the research log was related to team competition: friendly team rivalry caused activity logs to be more complete and in-depth.

Interim Review. The class is structured to include checkpoints for the SME to review interim results and provide guidance on challenges encountered. Typically, there is only one interim review; however, if problems affect the assignment goals or research direction, an additional review of subsequent findings take place, if deemed necessary. When multiple feasible COA alternatives exist, the team and SME confer to select the most promising path.

For each review, students prepare a written report to the SME and, immediately following this, a formal presentation to the SME based on the report. Before submission to the SME, each team's report is reviewed by all members of the other team. From the regular in-class briefs and activity logs, most students have an adequate understanding of the other team's work to provide constructive comments during peer review.

4.5   Phase 4 – Final Progress Review

Teams have established their research direction by this phase, and students can concentrate on generating the final COA. The predominant activity in this phase is COA refinement, where questions to the SME are more detailed and the analyses are more focused. If the project requires implementation of some selected technology, students must demonstrate a working prototype before the final progress review with the SME.

This phase culminates in a draft final report from each team for review by the SME. The report describes the recommended COA for the team assignment and rationale for its selection over any alternatives. Procedures to build and operate the prototype are fully documented in this report. The rubric to assess the report includes the following characteristics:

- Content: purpose, literature review, technical content, critical thinking, and organization;
- Communication: tone and writing mechanics; and
- References: usage and quality.

This phase ends with a final progress review in which the SME examines the validity and feasibility of the actionable recommendations. Recommendations with solid technical analysis or prototypes will be considered for implementation while ideas that are relevant to the problem but are not fully developed will be considered for future work.

4.6   Phase 5 – Project Conclusion

During the final week, teams finalize their COA report and perform peer assessments of their own team's members. The objective of this peer assessment is to review and evaluate each team member's effort, contribution to the project and interaction with the team. The peer-assessment rubric employs a 4-point Liekert-scale, with each item accompanied by a justification explaining the score. The peer assessment is feedback to the instructor only, used as an aid in course grading decisions. The completed assessment is itself evaluated based on its fairness and usefulness to the instructor.

5   Project Description

To date, our capstone course has been offered six times across three years, involving three different SMEs at different times over this period. We provide synopses of past projects to illustrate the variety of ICS security aspects—from developmental security to operational security—addressed in the course.

5.1   Software Subversion via Portable Memory Devices

This project addressed the threat of inappropriate use of portable memory devices to introduce malicious code into a shipboard ICS environment. The threat landscape of modern shipboard ICS architectures has grown significantly because of the dissimilarity in ICS hardware and software technologies used in different ship designs. Hence, two different ships were used as case studies for this project. The assigned tasks included:

– Review existing policies and operational practices for using portable memory devices on shipboard control systems; and
– Propose changes to allow the use of these devices while safeguarding the integrity of the system.

One team examined the list control system and the other team studied the ventilation control system. The selection of these two systems exposed students to different system architectures and ICS technologies; the list control system used Allen Bradley equipment while the ventilation control system utilized Siemens equipment.

5.2   Network Security

This project investigated technologies for network isolation to control unauthorized traffic between an ICS network and the external shipboard network. The project used the same ventilation control and list control systems employed in the prior project (see Sect. 5.1) as case studies. The project assignment tasks included:

- Survey existing DMZ architectures and perimeter control technologies (e.g., firewall and intrusion detection systems) used in land-based SCADA systems;
- Propose a relevant shipboard ICS design that incorporates these technical measures; and
- Propose a concept of operations on security incident response, including detection and analysis, containment, eradication and recovery.

Teams reviewed best practices for implementing perimeter control as recommended by ICS-CERT and NIST. Students learned about preprocessors and signatures for the Snort IDS that were designed to support industrial protocols such as DNP3, Modbus and Ethernet/IP [5, 20].

5.3   Protection of Multicast IPsec Messages

This project investigated the use of IPsec with manual keying to provide message authentication and replay protection for multicast communications. The target ICS used IP multicast to conserve bandwidth, i.e., status update messages could be sent to pre-defined groups of HMI systems instead of broadcasting them to all HMI systems. The tasks included:

- Survey IPsec products that support multicast;
- Make recommendations for a bump-in-the-wire (BITW) appliance;
- Make recommendations for a bump-in-the-stack (BITS) appliance;
- Propose an IPsec-based ICS design that can provide integrity and anti-replay protection for data transiting the ICS network; and
- Propose a key management design that addresses the entire life cycle of cryptographic keys and other keying material, and is resilient to unauthorized key disclosure.

Students were divided into three teams: two teams focused on BITW and BITS implementations and the third team worked on key management. A number of functional requirements were levied on the BITW implementation: fast Ethernet support (at least two ports), memory (256 MB), physical size (6" × 6" × 8"), cost ($2000), operating temperature (0–65 degrees Celsius), power (12–24V), DIN rail mountable, ruggedized. A candidate BITW appliance must also conform to the IETF RFC 5374 which extends IPsec to support multicast addressing [23].

5.4 Continuous Monitoring

This project examined the use of two security information and event management (SIEM) and network monitoring tools—OSSIM [1] and Zabbix [2]—to provide continuous monitoring and real-time analysis of a shipboard ICS environment. The project assignment tasks included:

– Acquire a full understanding of the tools being investigated. This includes installing the tools and running experiments to gain insight on each tool's capabilities, system architecture, software design, and dependencies. This task also includes a survey of comparable commercial products; and
– Propose how the tools can be used in a shipboard ICS. The proposed design must identify the modules (plugins) that must be developed or customized for the afloat environment.

This was a hands-on project in which students built two test environments and ran a series of functional tests on the target tools. One environment was an isolated "practice network" for learning about the tools, and the other was a mock ICS environment modeled after an actual ICS network provided by the SME. Packet captures provided by the SME were replayed to test the tools.

5.5 Smart Card Authentication

This project explored the use of PKI-based smart cards for user authentication in shipboard control systems. Both contact and contactless smart card technologies were investigated. The assigned tasks were:

– Survey existing smart card technologies and products, including their utilization in ICS domain.
– Develop a concept of operations for PKI-based user authentication in a land-based ICS architecture, informed by DoD regulations on using smart cards for Personal Identity Verification (PIV); and
– Recommend a smart card product for use in an ICS on ships.

The recommendation also addressed: operational scenarios including different classes of users, e.g., operators, maintainers, security administrators; system life cycle management from initial deployment through retirement or disposal; and system boundaries and interconnections.

5.6 Code Repository Security

This project investigated security threats and defenses related to revision control systems for ICS software. Two revision control systems were examined: Apache Subversion (SVN) and Git. The assigned tasks included:

- Survey known threats against revision control systems;
- Survey known attacks against SVN and Git services, including how such attacks could theoretically damage the life cycle maintenance of ICS software artifacts;
- Recommend how to secure an SVN server and a Git server for use in ICS development, including eliciting functional and security requirements from ICS software developers; and
- Recommend a revision control system and methods for configuring and hardening it for use in ICS.

It was important to the SME that the recommended system addressed challenges for using a revision control system in a disconnected development environment, i.e., the revision control system resides in a disconnected laboratory and the corporate LAN is where non-developers (systems engineers, managers, auditors, etc.) view related artifacts.

5.7   Backplane Intrusion Detection

Modern PLCs are modular, consisting of multiple modules that communicate via a backplane. Mulder et al. perform several analyses on PLC hardware, firmware, and backplane activities to look for low-level information about PLC design and software that attackers can exploit, e.g., hardware properties and backplane traffic [17]. These efforts lead to the development of the WeaselBoard, a PLC backplane analyzer that captures backplane traffic and forwards it to an external system for intrusion analysis. The objective of this project was to perform a tabletop vulnerability assessment of WeaselBoard using a hypothetical ICS. The project consisted of the following tasks:

- Perform a threat analysis to create a threat profile for the target ICS;
- Perform a vulnerability analysis of the target ICS; and
- Develop potential attack scenarios in which persistent payloads are utilized to disrupt the operation of the target ICS without triggering an alarm from the WeaselBoard.

This project was the most challenging project to-date. Project tasks included searching the National Vulnerability Database for known vulnerabilities related to the platforms and software used in the target ICS.

6   Discussion

In this section we share a number of lessons learned related to delivering our project-based course about ICS security. We follow a learner-centric paradigm, resembling in many ways a flipped classroom where background and preparatory work occurs outside classroom contact hours and student-instructor interactions are reserved for interactive problem solving and planning. Over three years of delivering this capstone course, several modifications in course format and assessment have led to its current incarnation.

The first offering of the course was treated as a graduate-level advanced topics class in which students read papers to gain background knowledge. Direct instruction and a field trip (phase 1) were introduced in the next class, which significantly improved student understanding and reception. The second critical and biggest course improvement came after the introduction of simple introductory SCADA lab exercises, affirming that small, hands-on activities play a critical role in the learning process.

We found students were most actively engaged in research projects when elements of the assignment were familiar or if they had prior experience with the problem domain. For example, one student whose thesis project incorporated ArcSight was able to apply this knowledge in the context of the network security project (see Sect. 5.2). Projects with explicit hands-on experiments also increased student engagement, based on feedback and activity logs.

Student experience was highly variable cohort-to-cohort; although a few students had worked with shipboard ICS or had an undergraduate degree in computer science, most students lacked the technical background required by the projects designed by the SME. This mismatch made the formulation of appropriate project assignments difficult, as the collective experience of a cohort is not fully understood in phase 0, when project assignment areas are proposed.

The course structure had both advantages and disadvantages. It allowed frequent feedback from the SME which, in turn, provided opportunities for students to rise to new challenges. Many students, however, were only familiar with short class projects in which a strategy or approach, once selected, could be worked until completion. Our iterative research and design process was challenging to these students. Many viewed unanticipated problems as impediments, rather than opportunities for amelioration. When strategies required adjustment, students viewed this as time wasted on a poor strategy, rather than a process by which identification of a better strategy was itself a beneficial outcome.

We found that students had trouble in applying prior knowledge in new and unfamiliar contexts. For example, students learned about IPsec in other classes and had the skill to construct IPsec-based virtual channel networks, but they had difficulties researching ways to extend the core IPsec functionality to solve a more complex problem, e.g., using IPsec with multicast addressing. This trouble in horizontal transfer of knowledge led to improved scaffolding during phase 1, leveraging direct instruction in the project assignment domain. Students were similarly challenged in working with entirely new concepts, i.e., those not explicitly covered in prior courses, such as software development and revision control. This was worsened by the perception that these were not relevant to their course of study. More than direct instruction, interaction with SMEs who attested to the relevancy of these topics from a practical, cyber operations perspective was essential in overcoming this perception.

In summary, we found that students were able to demonstrate understanding of ICS security issues successfully, through interpreting and analyzing topics covered in class and in their research assignments. In particular, SME feedback indicated that final COA recommendations were sensible and, in some cases, targeted for adoption. This was, to us, one of the most essential indicator of student learning, demonstrated through individual presentations, group reports and SME reviews.

Recommendations. We found students felt overloaded when attempting knowledge transfer to the unfamiliar ICS domain; this worsened when the project assignment was itself foreign and in an unfamiliar context. The positive response to the addition of hands-on ICS laboratory exercises in phase 1 largely echoes prior successes reported by others with using hands-on modules for ICS education. A focused class on ICS security leveraging hands-on exercises would be an invaluable prerequisite to any course employing real-world ICS systems as case studies.

One of the most labor-intensive aspects of capstone development was travel logistics (associated with SME visits and field trips) and other phase 0 planning activities. As each course offering focused on disjoint topics, this topic refinement became time-consuming to both instructor and SME. Additionally, each project's learning curve was quite steep for the student teams. As a notable exception, when two capstone classes used identical case studies in different contexts (i.e., the list and ventilation control systems), the second class was able to leverage the prior class' reports very successfully. We believe following this pattern—where team assignments intentionally share context across cohorts—may be a highly successful strategy. In particular, it allows project outcomes from one cohort to inform the next, following an agile research process [3]; classes could review and re-evaluate past projects as case studies; and tech transfer is a recurring process in which team deliverables are transferred to stakeholders, to other teams and across cohorts. Projects may build on past deliverables, improving or reconsidering previous findings.

7   Conclusion

This paper presents an approach to teach ICS security as a capstone course using collaborative research projects designed by ICS experts. We described our course motivation, development efforts and instructor observations. We summarized lessons learned from running the course, based on three years of feedback.

Our observations largely echo those of other educators in reinforcing the importance of hands-on exercises for ICS education. We caution other educators attempting to use real-world ICS case studies, in absence of a prerequisite course on SCADA and ICS. Furthermore, having SME support, system owner's participation and field trips was imperative for reinforcing course content, especially for a practical domain like ICS, where nearly all practical experience is with large, complex legacy systems. We believe other ICS curriculum proposals have completely omitted these instructional aids. For an effective ICS capstone course, we recommend field trips to local industrial facilities, e.g., a waste water treatment plant or electrical substation, if possible.

Acknowledgements. The authors would like to thank David E. Reed (NSWCCD, Ship Systems Engineering Station), Mark Roman (NSWCCD) and John Mulder (Sandia) for collaboration during course projects, and Cynthia Irvine for guidance and course support under the Cyber Systems and Operations curriculum at the Naval Postgraduate School.

References

1. AlienVault OSSIM: The open source SIEM (2015). https://www.alienvault.com/products/ossim
2. Zabbix: the enterprise-class monitoring solution for everyone (2015). http://www.zabbix.com/
3. Dark, M., Bishop, M., Linger, R.C., Goldrich, L.: Realism in teaching cybersecurity research: The agile research process. In: Bishop, M., Miloslavskaya, N., Theocharidou, M. (eds.) WISE 9. IFIP AICT, vol. 453, pp. 3–14. Springer, Heidelberg (2015)
4. Department of Homeland Security (U.S.). Critical infrastructure and control systems security curriculum, March 2008
5. Digital Bond, Inc.: Quickdraw SCADA IDS (2014). http://www.digitalbond.com/tools/quickdraw/
6. Executive Order no. 13636. Improving Critical Infrastructure Cybersecurity, February 2013. http://www.gpo.gov/fdsys/pkg/FR-2013-02-19/pdf/2013-03915.pdf
7. Foo, E., Branagan, M., Morris, T.: A proposed australian industrial control system security curriculum. In: 2013 46th Hawaii International Conference on System Sciences (HICSS), pp. 1754–1762. IEEE (2013)
8. Foreman, J.C., Graham, J.H., Hieb, J.L., Ragade, R.K.: A curriculum model for industrial control systems cyber-security with sample modules. Technical Report 2012-14, Center for Education and Research, Purdue University (2012)
9. Francia III, G.A.: Critical infrastructure security curriculum modules. In: Proceedings of the 2011 Information Security Curriculum Development Conference (InfoSecCD 2011), pp. 54–58, Sept 2011
10. Francia III, G.A., Beckhouche, N.: Portable SCADA security toolkits. Int. J. Inf. Netw. Secur. (IJINS) **1**(4), 265–274 (2012)
11. Francia III, G.A., Snellen, J.: Embedded and control systems security projects. Inf. Secur. Educ. J. **1**(2), 77–84 (2014)
12. Irvine, C.: A cyberoperations program. IEEE Secur. Priv. Mag. **11**(5), 66–69 (2013)
13. Luallen, M.E., Labruyere, J.-P.: Developing a critical infrastructure and control systems cybersecurity curriculum. In: 46th Hawaii International Conference on System Sciences (HICSS), pp. 1782–1791. IEEE, January 2013
14. McGrew, R.W., Vaughn, R.B.: Discovering vulnerabilities in control system human-machine interface software. J. Syst. Softw. **82**(4), 583–589 (2009)
15. Mishra, S., Romanowski, C.J., Raj, R.K., Howles, T., Schneider, J.: A curricular framework for critical infrastructure protection education for engineering, technology and computing majors. In: 2013 IEEE Frontiers in Education Conference (FIE), pp. 1779–1781. IEEE, October 2013
16. Morris, T., Srivastava, A., Reaves, B., Gao, W., Pavurapu, K., Reddi, R.: A control system testbed to validate critical infrastructure protection concepts. Int. J. Crit. Infrastruct. Prot. **4**(2), 88–103 (2011)
17. Mulder, J., Schwartz, M., Berg, M., Van Houten, J.R., Mario, J.: WeaselBoard: zero-day exploit detection for programmable logic controllers. Technical report SAND2013-8274, October 2013

18. National Institute of Standards and Technology (U.S.): Framework for improving critical infrastructure cybersecurity, February 2014
19. National Security Agency (U.S.): Academic Requirements for Designation as a Center of Academic Excellence in Cyber Operations (2014). https://www.nsa.gov/academia/nat_cae_cyber_ops/nat_cae_co_requirements.shtml
20. The Snort Project. SNORT users manual (2014). http://manual.snort.org/snort_manual.htm
21. Tofino Security Inc.: Tofino SCADA security simulator (TSSS) user's guide, January 2013
22. Vaughn, R.B., Morris, T., Sitnikova, E.: Development & expansion of an industrial control system security laboratory, an international research collaboration. In: CSIIRW 2013: Proceedings of the Eighth Annual Cyber Security and Information Intelligence Research Workshop. ACM, January 2013
23. Weis, B., Gross, G., Ignjatic, D.: Multicast extensions to the security architecture for the internet protocol. RFC 5374, November 2008
24. Wightman, R.: S4x12: Project basecamp (2012). http://vimeopro.com/s42012/s4-2012/video/35783988

Trust Establishment in Cooperating Cyber-Physical Systems

Andre Rein[1], Roland Rieke[1,2]([✉]), Michael Jäger[3], Nicolai Kuntze[1],
and Luigi Coppolino[4]

[1] Fraunhofer Institute SIT, Darmstadt, Germany
[2] Philipps-Universität Marburg, Marburg, Germany
roland.rieke@sit.fraunhofer.de
[3] Technische Hochschule Mittelhessen, Giessen, Germany
[4] Universita Degli Studi di Napoli "Parthenope", Napoli, Italy

Abstract. Cooperating systems are systems of systems that collaborate for a common purpose. Cooperating cyber-physical systems often base important decisions on data gathered from external sensors and use external actuators to enforce safety critical actions. Using the example of a hydroelectric power plant control system, this paper analyzes security threats for networked cooperating systems, where sensors providing decision critical data are placed in non-protected areas and thus are exposed to various kinds of attacks. We propose a concept for trust establishment in cyber-physical cooperating systems. Using trusted event reporting for critical event sources, the authenticity of the security related events can be verified. Based on measurements obtained with a prototypical realisation, we evaluate and analyze the amount of overhead data transmission between event source and data verification system needed for trust establishment. We propose an efficient synchronisation scheme for system integrity data, reducing network traffic as well as verification effort.

Keywords: Trustworthy event management in cyber-physical systems · Security of cooperating systems · Trusted event reporting · Critical infrastructure protection

1 Introduction

Cooperating Cyber-Physical Systems (CPS) are systems of systems that collaborate for a common purpose. Systems in the physical world are linked to the cyber world by elements such as sensors, which capture data from the physical world and produce information that provides an abstraction of the state of the physical world for processing in the cyber world. Analysis of this information may lead to decisions in the cyber world. These, in turn, influence the physical world either directly, e.g., by actuator elements, or indirectly, e.g., by visualizing information for human actuators in the physical world. Prominent examples for novel cooperating CPS are future smart energy systems, vehicular ad hoc networks, air traffic management systems, and ecosystems for smart cities, which extend the cooperation of networked systems with cross-infrastructure interdependencies.

A. Bécue et al. (Eds.): CyberICS 2015/WOS-CPS 2015, LNCS 9588, pp. 31–47, 2016.
DOI: 10.1007/978-3-319-40385-4_3

Obviously, a certain level of trust in these emerging CPS is indispensible and, thus, adequate security concepts are utmost important for common acceptance of these systems. In smart energy systems, increased interconnection and integration introduces cyber vulnerabilities into the grid that do not yet exist in the current, rather fragmented grid infrastructure [10, 13, 38]. In the case of vehicular ad hoc networks, user safety is a major challenge with great impact on the security of these CPS [11]. Distributed air traffic management systems that collaborate for a common purpose, such as the smooth running of an airport, need continuous update and improvement to security [14]. New challenges with respect to smart city management comprise the provision of trustworthy shared information for cross-application use, the secure data exchange between devices and their users, and the protection of vulnerable devices [3].

As outlined above, sensors are important interfaces, connecting physical and cyber world. Thus, one important requirement common to all application domains of CPS is *the capability to prove that a measured value has been acquired at a certain time and within a specified "valid" operation environment.* Authenticity of such measures can only be assured together with authentication of the used device itself, it's configuration, and the software running at the time of the measurement. A similar requirement is necessary for cyber-controlled actuators in the physical world, namely, *the capability to prove that the actions triggered by decisions taken in the cyber world are executed at the scheduled time and within a specified "valid" operation environment.*

A specific problem in geographically dispersed infrastructures is that the interfaces connecting physical and cyber world are often placed in non-protected environments and attackers are able to access and manipulate this equipment with relative ease [43]. Therefore, when physical access to critical devices cannot be inhibited, *an effective security solution must address detection of manipulations.* Manipulated equipment can be used to cause misjudgement on the physical system's state and hide critical conditions, which in turn can lead to wrong decisions with severe impact on the overall CPS.

In this work, we analyze security threats for critical CPS by means of a representative example, namely, a hydroelectric power plant in a dam. We elicit adequate security requirements based on safety considerations and present a concept for trustworthy event reporting.

Digital signatures obviously can provide authenticity and integrity of recorded data [4]. However, a signature gives no information about the status of the measurement device at the time of measurement. Our solution, the *Trusted Information Agent* (TIA), is based on trusted computing technology [21] and integrates industry approaches to the attestation of event reporter states. We determine the overhead for trust establishment in the amount of transferred data and the calculation cost on the verifier and propose a scheme that efficiently handles the transmission and processing of the stored measurement log produced by the integrity measurement architecture.

The remainder of this paper is organized as follows: Sect. 2 introduces an exemplary application scenario, discusses security-related challenges for CPS and corresponding security requirements. Based on these requirements, we address a solution for our propositions and describe the concept of a TIA in Sect. 3. In Sect. 4, we analyze important scalability aspects of our approach based on a quantitative evaluation and propose a scheme for minimizing the overhead of trusted event reporting. Section 5 gives an overview of the related work and Sect. 6 concludes the paper and outlines directions for future research.

2   Application Scenario

Our security analysis is based on examples from a hydroelectric power plant in a dam, which is in many respects typical for a critical infrastructure. A dam is a layered CPS with intra- and cross-layer dependencies and with various other sources of complexity. Several distinct functionalities influence controlling and monitoring activities. Moreover, different components, mechanisms, and operative devices are involved, each one with different requirements in terms of produced data and computational loads. A huge number of parameters must be monitored in order to guarantee safety and security.

Among the most commonly used dam instrumentation sensors are water level sensors, thermometers, tiltmeters (measurement of wall or earth inclination), piezometers (water pressure), crackmeters (wall crack enlargement), pressure cells (concrete or embankment pressure), jointmeters (joint shrinkage), and turbidimeters (fluid turbidity). The heterogeneity of currently used devices is a relevant challenge in the dam process control: they range from old industrial control systems, designed and deployed over the last 20 years and requiring extensive manual intervention by human operators, to more recently developed systems, conceived for automatic operations (SCADA).

Indeed, the trend of development is toward increasingly automated dam control systems. While automation leads to more efficient systems and also prevents operating errors; on the downside, it poses a limit to human control in situations where an operator would possibly foresee and manually prevent incidents.

The remote management of such an infrastructure would require a hierarchical SCADA system (cf. Fig. 1(b)). The SCADA infrastructure gathers information from individual sensors manged by a Remote Terminal Unit (RTU). At regional level information is managed by a local Master Terminal Unit (MTU) and sent to a central MTU at the remote control center. Each MTU provides a Human Machine Interface useful to manage the controlled system.

As a severe disadvantage, increased automation and remote control raise a new class of security-induced safety issues, i.e., cyber attacks against the IT layer of the dam could ultimately result in damage to people and environment. Dam monitoring aims towards identifying anomalous behaviour related to the infrastructure. Table 1 summarizes a list of possible scenarios illustrating the necessity of monitoring specific parameters.

Figure 2 shows some of the functional dependencies between sensors, control station components, and actuators. Dam administrator decisions depend on the displayed measurements, whereas control display values are derived from the

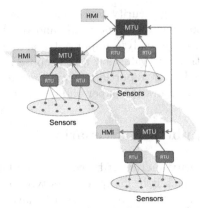

(a) Monte Cotugno dam: one of eight dams managed by EIPLI.

(b) Deployment of a SCADA system for monitoring the infrastructure.

Fig. 1. Water management infrastructure

Table 1. Security related scenarios and the respective monitoring

Event	Impact	Detection
Changes in the flow levels of the seepage channels	Seepage channels are monitored to evaluate the seepage intensity. A sudden change in flow levels could show that the structure is subject to internal erosion or to piping phenomena. This event can be the cause of dam cracks and failures	A weir with a known section is inserted into the channel. The water level behind the weir can be converted to a flow rate
Gates opening	Gates opening must be operated under controlled conditions since it may result in: (i) Flooding of the underlying areas; (ii) Increased rate of flow in the downstream and catastrophic flooding of down-river areas	A tiltmeter (angle position sensor) can be applied to the gate to measure its position angle
Vibration level changes	Increased vibrations of the infrastructure or the turbines can anticipate a failure. Possible reasons include: (i) earthquakes; (ii) unwanted solicitations to the turbines	Vibration sensors can be installed over structures or turbines to measure the stress level
Water levels above alert thresholds	Spillways are used to release water when the reservoir water level reaches alert thresholds. Otherwise, the water overtops the dam resulting in possible damage to the crest	Water level alarm helps detect unexpected discharge or other anomalous behaviour

sensor measurements. The overall function of the system requires authenticity of measurement values for several critical sensors.

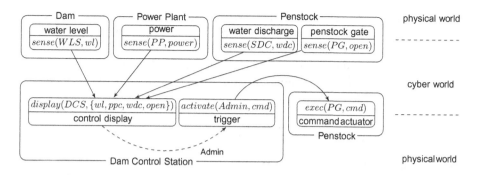

Fig. 2. Interfaces connecting physical and cyber world with functional dependencies

3   Trusted Information Agent

There is no point in monitoring large systems without having a certain level of confidence in the correctness of the monitoring data. To achieve this confidence, network security measures and provisions against technical faults are not enough. In order to address the serious problem of unrevealed manipulation of monitoring equipment, we now describe the concept of a *Trusted Information Agent* (TIA). According to [34], an *agent* is characterized by perceiving its environment through sensors and acting upon the environment through effectors. In this work, we address specific security aspects of these basic functionalities of an agent. The TIA concept is well-suited for a range of device types, in particular, for networked sensor and actuator devices, which are supposed to be critical for a cyber-physical system.

3.1   Trust Architecture

An approved technique to reveal software manipulation is software measurement: Each software component is considered as a byte sequence and thus can be measured by computing a hash value, which is subsequently compared to the component's reference value. The component is authentic, if and only if both values are identical. Obviously, such measurements make no sense if the measuring component or the reference values are manipulated themselves. A common solution is to establish a chain of trust: In a layered architecture, each layer is responsible for computing the checksums of the components in the next upper layer. At the very bottom of this chain a dedicated security hardware chip takes the role of the trust anchor.

Trusted Computing technology standards [21] provide a suitable trust architecture on top of a Trusted Platform Module (TPM). A TPM chip is equipped with several cryptographic capabilities like strong encryption, digital signatures, and some more advanced features. It is also hardened against physical attacks. TPMs have been proven to be much less susceptible to attacks than corresponding software-only solutions.

The key concept is the extension of trust from the TPM to further system components. This is used to ensure that a system is and remains in a predictable and trustworthy state and thus produces authentic results. Even very complex sensors and actuator devices are well-suited for this kind of integrity check concept. The proposed device architecture is presented in more detail now on the example of a trusted sensor device.

3.2   Trusted Sensor Data Aquisition

Figure 3 depicts an architecture for trusted sensor data aquisition consisting of a TIA and several infrastructure systems providing certification, verification and storage services. Those infrastructure components will typically be operated in protected environments, e.g., be all part of the same SCADA control center. The task of a TIA is to gather and report sensor data. Trusted data aquisition means revelation of any software manipulations of the device itself, authenticating the identity of the TIA, and protecting the sensor data against tampering attemps.

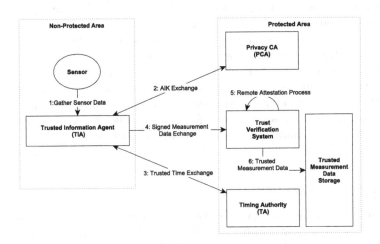

Fig. 3. TIA architecture

The TIA is expected to operate in unprotected environments with low physical protection and externally accessible interfaces such as wireless networks and USB access for maintenance. A necessary precondition to guarantee authenticity of the measures is a trustworthy state of the measurement device. To meet this requirement, the TIA is equipped with a TPM as trust anchor and implements a chain of trust [18]. Revelation of software manipulations is based on the comparison between the software checksums and the corresponding reference values by a remote verification system (remote attestation) [21].

In addition to the verification system, two infrastructure components are necessary to establish the authenticity of the gathered data. The TIA uses a

TPM-generated *attestation identity key* (AIK) as a digital signature key. A *privacy certificate authority* (PCA) issues a credential for this AIK. The certified AIK is, henceforth, used as an identity for the TIA. According to TCG standards, AIKs cannot only be used to attest origin and authenticity of a trust measurement, but also, to authenticate other keys and data generated by the TPM. However, the AIK functionality of a TPM is designed primarily to support remote attestation by signing the checksums of the TIA's software components, while signing arbitrary data is, in fact, not directly available as a TPM operation. We have shown elsewhere, how to circumvent this limitation [17]. Hence, we are able to use TPM-signatures for arbitrary data from the TIA's sensors.

Furthermore, a *time authority* (TA) is needed to approve the correctness of the measurement time stamps. Any TPM is equipped with an accurate timer. Each event signature includes the current timer value. However, the TPM timer is a relative counter, not associated to an absolute time. The TA issues a certificate about the correspondence between a TPM timestamp (tickstamp) and the absolute time. The combination of tickstamp and TA-certificate can be used as a trusted timestamp. Alternatively, another trusted time source, such as GPS, could have been used.

Putting it all together, a measurement record includes arbitrary sensor data, a TA-certified time stamp, and a hash value of the TIA's software components. The record itself is signed by the PCA-certified AIK.

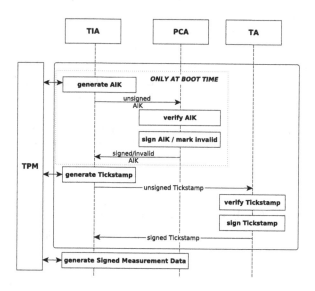

Fig. 4. Process model

Figure 4 shows the interactions between TIA and the trusted third party services PCA and TA, as well as the role of the TPM within the TIA. The more elaborate tasks of establishing trusted time and a trusted signature have to be accomplished only once during device initialization.

4   Scalability of Trust Establishment in Distributed SCADA Systems

The establishment of a trust concept for CPS requires the utilization of crypto-graphic techniques and, hence, the need to process data like hash values, time stamps, or digital signatures in addition to the sensor measurements. This may lead to a significant increase of the amount of data to be transmitted over the network and processed by the SCADA control station. Care must be taken that the security-related data overhead is kept within reasonable limits in order to guarantee uncompromised processing of the sensor data.

In this section, the essential scalability aspects of our trust concept are ana-lyzed. While the sensors used in our dam scenario are fairly simple devices, there is a growing use of highly complex sensoring devices, e.g., in automotive assistance systems [42]. Such systems are based on embedded versions of stan-dard operating systems [15], e.g., linux, or even on smartphone platforms, e.g., Android. Since the essence of our trust concept is the revelation of software manipulation, such complex sensors are in the focus of the scalability analysis. Whenever complex sensors are involved in a system, the existence of software flaws has to be taken into account. Reliable operation of such sensors typically requires occasional software updates, e.g., security patches. As a consequence, the sensor systems cannot be assumed to be static and a trust concept has to provide an adequate re-verification mechanism for the case of updates.

Based upon a more detailed description of the software attestation process the security-related data structures are investigated and quantified in Sect. 4.1. The computational costs of the proposed trust scheme have been evaluated using a prototypical implementation relying on the *Integrity Measurement Architecture (IMA)* [35] for system integrity measurement. The evaluation results are dis-cussed in Sect. 4.2. We then propose a scalable trust establishment concept and present corresponding algorithms for the generation and verification of trusted sensor data in Sect. 4.3.

4.1   Quantitative Analysis of Security-Related Data

According to [25,29], two principal data structures are needed for trusted data acquisition:

TPM Quote. A Quote is the result of a special TPM "quote" operation gen-erating an approved sensor value. It contains (1) a time stamp approved by the trusted Time Authority, (2) hash values for the verification of the system integrity measurement results, and (3) the sensor data. The Quote is signed with the TPM's PCA-approved AIK. The hash values (aka *PCR values*) for checking the system integrity measurement results are stored in the TPM's manipulation-protected *Platform Configuration Registers (PCRs)*.

Stored Measurement Log (SML). The SML is a log file including all values necessary to verify the current system state. It is generated by the Integrity Measurement Architecture. The SML contains all values necessary to reconstruct the PCRs included in the generated Quote and can be obtained directly from the system through a system kernel interface.

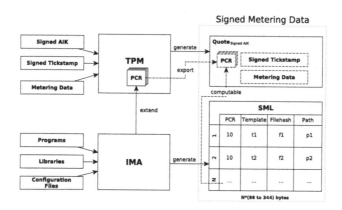

Fig. 5. Quote and SML generation process

Figure 5 shows the generation of signed sensor data as introduced in Fig. 3 based on Quotes, SML and PCR values. Within the scope of system integrity measurement, the IMA measures each software component by computing a hash value, recording the result as a new SML entry, and performing a TPM "extend" operation extending a hash chain with a hash of the new SML entry. The last hash value of this chain is always stored in a manipulation-protected PCR.

The size of a Quote is the size of the sensor data plus some fixed overhead for the other Quote components. The SML is a rather large list growing continuously during system runtime. Each intermediate system state creates a new SML entry containing hash values and the file system path of the hashed software component. Depending on the length of the path, the size of an SML entry varies from 88 to 344 Bytes. In practice, the SML size varies from a couple of KB, right after system start-up, up to certain MB depending on (i) runtime, (ii) type, and (iii) measured intermediate states of the system. On our evaluation system the size for 10.000 SML entries was approximately 1.4 MB. However, for sensors, running a limited amount of software with infrequent updates, but rather long system runtime, we expect the SML to contain 300–1000 entries.

In order to verify sensor data, the verification system needs the Quotes and the SML from the TIA. Considering the size of the SML and the large amount of sensor values processed in a SCADA system, it is quite obvious that efficiency with respect to communication bandwidth and computational effort are crucial for a practicable solution.

4.2 Computational Costs

To determine the trustworthiness of the data acquisition system, the SML must always be verified comprehensively. The hash chain approach described above uses one hash value – the last one in the chain - as a checksum for the integrity of the whole TIA system. A drawback of this approach is that the necessary verification steps cannot be parallelized, as each element of the hash chain c_{i+1} depends on the predecessor value c_i. The length of the chain is the number of entries of the SML.

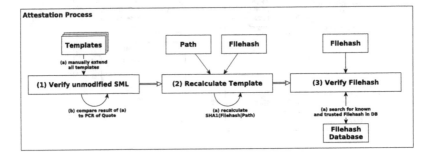

Fig. 6. Attestation process

Specifically, this means that even if a preceding verified trusted state was ascertained, the entire attestation process must be repeated entirely before a new sensor measurement can be accepted. To get a better understanding for the attestation process and the computational costs the process induces, we examined a common attestation scheme shown in Fig. 6, which illustrates the verification of each intermediate system state. Furthermore, we provide time-based measurement results for SMLs of different dimensions in Table 2. In particular, we analyzed the verification time for SMLs with 100, 500, 1000, 5000 and 10000 entries. The attestation process was executed on a 64-Bit Intel Core I5 760 CPU@ 2.800 GHz. The measurements of (1), (2), and (3) were obtained using a python script. As shown in Table 2, file size and verification time grow linearly with the number of SML entries. Analysis of the time-based measurement results

Table 2. SML measurements

SML Entries	100	500	1000	5000	10000
File Size	12 KB	60 KB	127 KB	676 KB	1.4 MB
(1) PCR Verification	0.31 ms	1.60 ms	3.42 ms	16.07 ms	33.17 ms
(2) Template Verification	6.42 ms	35.43 ms	70.8 ms	342.99 ms	680.63 ms
(3) Hash Verification	0.262 s	1.356 s	2.741 s	13.308 s	26.778 s
Complete Verification	0.296 s	1.671 s	3.402 s	15.229 s	30.717 s

shows that hash verification (3) is the critical step with respect to computational effort. Whereas (1) PCR verification steps must be performed strictly sequential, (2) template verification, and (3) hash verification can be parallelized. While we expect a parallelized computation of (2) and (3) to be notably faster than our sequential approach, it would not reduce the amount of data exchanged between TIA and verifier.

4.3   Scalable Data Generation and Verification

In the following, we propose a scalable attestation algorithm composed of the TIA part in Algorithm 1 and the verifier part in Algorithm 2.

Algorithm 1. TIA: Signed Measurement Data Generation Scheme

Require: $i = 0, c_i = 0$

  function *generate_sensor_measurement*( )

    $q_i = get\_quote()$

    $sml_i = get\_sml()$

    $store\_sml\_count(c_i)$

    if $i == 0$ **then**

      $send\_sensor\_measurement(q_i, sml_i)$

    else

      $\delta_{sml_{i-1}:sml_i} = truncate\_sml\_until(c_{i-1})$

      $send\_sensor\_measurement(q_i, \delta_{sml_{i-1}:sml_i})$

    end if

    $increment(i)$

  end function

Algorithm 2. Verifier: Signed Measurement Data Verification Scheme

---

Require: $h_{aik}, quote_i, sml_i, AIK_{pub}$

  function *verify_sensor_measurement*$(quote_i, sml_i)$

    if $verify\_quote(quote, AIK_{pub})$ **then**

      if $verify\_sml(sml_i, h_{aik})$ **then**

        $h_{aik} = extract\_hash(quote_i)$

        return "*TRUSTED*"

      else

        $h_{aik} = ""$ ▷ Reset h_{aik}

        return "*UNTRUSTED*"

      end if

    end if

    return "*UNTRUSTED*"

  end function

The central idea is that the TIA transmits the entire SML only with the first Quote. On any subsequent execution, the SML sml_i is truncated until the last known line c_i. This generates our subsequent SML-delta $\delta_{sml_{i-1}:sml_i} = truncate\_sml\_until(c_{i-1})$, which replaces the complete SML that is transmitted to the verifier, reducing the amount of transferred data to a minimum. Consequently, the verifier only needs to recalculate the templates of the changed SML entries $\delta_{sml_{i-1}:sml_i}$, which significantly reduces computations. However, we expect additional SML entries to appear on very rare occasions, basically only after designated software updates or in case an attack happened. Hence, in most subsequent attestation processes, $\delta_{sml_{i-1}:sml_i}$ can be omitted entirely, or will only comprise a couple of new entries, which renders the computational effort negligible.

In order to make this scheme work, the verifier stores the last known trusted hash value in a tuple $\{AIK \rightarrow h_{aik}\}$ for the least known state of the TIA. Then, $\delta(sml_{i-1} : sml_i)$ is sufficient to synchronize the verifier's SML with the changed TIA's SML and to verify the current system state without recalculation of the entire SML sml_i, necessary without the modifications made.

5   Background and Related Work

Dam monitoring applications with Automated Data Acquisition System (ADAS) are discussed in [22,26]. Usually, an ADAS is organized as a SCADA system with a hierarchical organisation (cf. Fig. 1(b)). Details on SCADA systems organisation can be found in [5,6]. In the majority of cases, SCADA systems have very little protection against the escalating cyber threats. Compared to traditional IT systems, securing CPS poses unique challenges. In order to understand those challenges and the potential danger, [43] provides a taxonomy of possible cyber attacks including cyber-induced cyber-physical attacks with respect to SCADA systems. Specific SCADA related security problems are discussed in [8]. An overview of the challenges and the current state-of-the-art in modeling CPS in general is given in [9].

Besides identification of security requirements, the further security engineering process has to address issues such as how to mitigate risks resulting from connectivity and how to integrate security into a target architecture [2]. In [16], some of the open issues in future energy networks are discussed and a vision of a security infrastructure for such networks built on hardware security anchors is described. In [1], a framework for the protection of energy control systems is introduced that integrates different state-of-the-art technologies in order to improve status management, anomaly prevention, and security. In [13], security, trust and quality of service requirements in next-generation control and communication for large power systems are examined and the GridStat middleware addressing these requirements is introduced. In [39], a suite of security protocols to provide authenticated channels optimized for SCADA systems is proposed.

Specific mechanisms for enforcement of authenticity requirements that have been derived by the method proposed in this article are based on integration of TC concepts into CPS systems. The key concept of TC [21] is the extension of trust from a root of trust (such as the TPM) to further system components [37]. This concept ensures that a system is and remains in a predictable and trustworthy state and thus produces authentic results. An approach for the generation of secure evidence records was presented in [29]. This approach, which was the basis for our proof-of-concept implementation in [7], makes use of established hardware-based security mechanisms for special data recording devices. Our work presented here, additionally analysed scalability properties of the approach by measurements of overhead for trust establishment and suggest efficient schemes for evidence generation and evidence verification. For secure evidence generation, those parts of the TPM that identify the device, bind data to the identity of the device, and provide authentic reports on the current state of the device are essential [29]. Evidence collectors can add semantic information to the evidence record and make it available for distribution and storage [27,28]. The cumulative attestation proposed by LeMay and Gunter [19] provides additional records and attests to the history of the boot process. In the context of digital cameras, the feasibility of the use of TPMs for the protection of digital images has already been proposed [29] and demonstrated [40]. In [36], advanced schemes allowing for scalable attestation have been proposed. In CPS it can also be necessary to establish a peer-to-peer structure without any central node. In order to ensure that all events can be ordered by time, the synchronisation of time ticks can be combined with other existing security mechanisms [20]. General properties of time synchronisation protocols and algorithms have been analysed in [12].

Security information and event management (SIEM) systems [24] are generic consumers of sensor events. From the architectural perspective of a SIEM system, the TIA implements a specific software appliance residing in edge payload nodes. Based on the requirements of CPS for novel SIEM architectures [30], in the European project MASSIF [31] we developed the TIA that implements a MASSIF compliant remote smart sensor, which provides authenticated component event reporting [23]. The trustworthiness of the information from the TIA is indispensable, when process control in critical infrastructures is dependent on this information. We have shown this in applications reported in [32,33] on misuse case scenarios from the hydroelectric power plant introduced in Sect. 2. In addition to integrity and authenticity provided by the TIA, it is important to enforce a resilient communication among the edge devices and core nodes of a SIEM infrastructure. In the MASSIF architecture, a resilient event bus [23] provides several mechanisms and routing strategies to deliver messages in a secure and timely way. We assume that in addition to the use in generic SIEM systems, the TIA scalability concept proposed in this work can also be applied in specific agent-based architectures, such as the autonomic agent trust model proposed in [41].

6 Conclusion and Future Work

With the emerging CPS demanding new security challenges arise at the interface between the cyber and physical world. In particular, the geographically dispersed placement of sensors and actuators in non-protected environments makes them vulnerable for various attacks with possibly disastrous impact on critical infrastructures and their human users.

Protection of CPS against those attacks is a multifaceted complex task. In this paper, we addressed three important aspects related to this task based on a model of a typical cyber-physical application scenario, a hydro-electric powerplant.

Firstly, the elicitation of critical security requirements has been investigated. We used a model-based approach to systematically identify security requirements in CPS. The action-oriented approach considers control flow and information flow between interdependent actions, in particular, the boundary actions, which represent the interaction of the physical with the cyber world. Secondly, we developed the TIA, a holistic protection concept for critical event sources, particularly addressing the problem of unrevealed software manipulation. Finally, we analysed scalability properties of the TIA approach and presented scalable trust establishment algorithms.

We envision to extend the TIA approach to other types of devices, which are known to be critical for trusted monitoring within CPS. Particularly, we think of network devices, which often also operate in unprotected environments. The software complexity of such devices is comparable to the smart sensors and Trusted Computing concepts should be applicable for their protection.

Acknowledgements. Roland Rieke, Nicolai Kuntze, and Luigi Coppolino developed the work presented here in the context of the project MASSIF (ID 257475) being co-funded by the European Commission within FP7.

References

1. Alcaraz, C., Lopez, J., Zhou, J., Roman, R.: Secure SCADA framework for the protection of energy control systems. Concur. Comput. Pract. Exp. **23**(12), 1431–1442 (2011)
2. Bodeau, D.J.: System-of-systems security engineering. In: Proceedings of the 10th Annual Computer Security Applications Conference, Orlando, Florida, pp. 228–235. IEEE Computer Society (1994)
3. Bohli, J.M., Langendörfer, P., Skarmeta, A.F.: Security and privacy challenge in data aggregation for the IoT in smart cities. In: Internet of Things: Converging Technologies for Smart Environments and Integrated Ecosystems, pp. 225–244. River Publishers (2013)
4. Choi, J., Shin, I., Seo, J., Lee, C.: An efficient message authentication for non-repudiation of the smart metering service. In: ACIS/JNU International Conference on Computers, Networks, Systems and Industrial Engineering, pp. 331–333 (2011)
5. Coppolino, L., D'Antonio, S., Romano, L., Spagnuolo, G.: An intrusion detection system for critical information infrastructures using wireless sensor network technologies. In: 2010 5th International Conference on Critical Infrastructure (CRIS), pp. 1–8 (sept 2010)
6. Coppolino, L., D'Antonio, S., Romano, L.: Dependability and resilience of computer networks (SCADA cybersecurity). In: Critical Infrastructure Security: Assessment, Prevention, Detection, Response. WIT press (in press)

7. Coppolino, L., Jäger, M., Kuntze, N., Rieke, R.: A trusted information agent for security information and event management. In: ICONS 2012, The Seventh International Conference on Systems, February 29 - March 5, 2012, Reunion Island, pp. 6–12. IARIA (2012)
8. Dan, G., Sandberg, H., Ekstedt, M., Björkman, G.: Challenges in power system information security. IEEE Secur. Priv. **10**(4), 62–70 (2012)
9. Derler, P., Lee, E.A., Sangiovanni-Vincentelli, A.: Modeling cyber-physical systems. Proc. IEEE (Spec. Issue CPS) **100**(1), 13–28 (2012)
10. Gao, J., Xiao, Y., Liu, J., Liang, W., Chen, C.L.P.: A survey of communication/networking in smart grids. Future Gener. Comp. Syst. **28**(2), 391–404 (2012)
11. Gerlach, M.: Trusted network on wheels. ERCIM News, pp. 32–33, October 2005
12. Gladyshev, P., Patel, A.: Formalising event time bounding in digital investigations. Int. J. Digital Evid. **4**, 1–14 (2005)
13. Hauser, C.H., Bakken, D.E., Dionysiou, I., Gjermundrød, K.H., Irava, V.S., Helkey, J., Bose, A.: Security, trust, and qos in next-generation control and communication for large power systems. IJCIS **4**(1/2), 3–16 (2008)
14. Hawley, M., Howard, P., Koelle, R., Saxton, P.: Collaborative security management: Developing ideas in security management for air traffic control. In: Proceedings of 2013 International Conference on Availability, Reliability and Security, ARES 2013, pp. 808–806. IEEE Computer Society (2013)
15. IBM: A strategic approach to protecting scada and process control systems. Technical report, IBM Corporation (2007). http://www.iss.net/documents/whitepapers/SCADA.pdf. Accessed13 May 2015
16. Kuntze, N., Rudolph, C., Cupelli, M., Liu, J., Monti, A.: Trust infrastructures for future energy networks. In: Power and Energy Society General Meeting - Power Systems Engineering in Challenging Times (2010)
17. Kuntze, N., Mähler, D., Schmidt, A.U.: Employing Trusted Computing for the forward pricing of pseudonyms in reputation systems. In: Axmedis 2006, Proceedings of the 2nd International Conference on Automated Production of Cross Media Content for Multi-Channel Distribution, Volume for Workshops, Industrial, and Application Sessions (2006)
18. Kuntze, N., Rudolph, C.: Secure digital chains of evidence. In: Sixth International Workshop on Systematic Approaches to Digital Forensic Engeneering (2011)
19. LeMay, M., Gunter, C.A.: Cumulative attestation kernels for embedded systems. In: Backes, M., Ning, P. (eds.) ESORICS 2009. LNCS, vol. 5789, pp. 655–670. Springer, Heidelberg (2009)
20. Liu, J., Yu, F., Lung, C.-H., Tang, H.: Optimal combined intrusion detection and biometric-based continuous authentication in high security mobile Ad Hoc networks. IEEE Trans. Wirel. Commun. **8**(2), 806–815 (2009)
21. Mitchell, C.: Trusted Computing. Institution of Electrical Engineers (2005)
22. Myers, B.K., Dutson, G.C., Sherman, T.: Utilizing automated monitoring for the franzen reservoir dam safety program. In: 25th USSD Annual Meeting and Conference Proceedings (2005)
23. Neves, N., Kuntze, N., Sarno, C.D., Vianello, V., et al.: Resilient SIEM framework architecture, services and protocols. Deliverable D5.1.4, FP7-257475 MASSIF European project, September 2013
24. Nicolett, M., Kavanagh, K.M.: Magic Quadrant for Security Information and Event Management. Gartner Reasearch, May 2010

25. Oberle, A., Rein, A., Kuntze, N., Rudolph, C., Paatero, J., Lunn, A., Racz, P.: Integrating trust establishment into routing protocols of today's MANETs. In: Wireless Communications and Networking Conference (WCNC), 2013 IEEE, pp. 2369–2374. IEEE (2013)
26. Parekh, M., Stone, K., Delborne, J.: Coordinating intelligent and continuous performance monitoring with dam and levee safety management policy. In: Association of State Dam Safety Officials, Proceedings of Dam Safety Conference 2010 (2010)
27. Pollitt, M.: Report on digital evidence. In: 13th INTERPOL Forensic Science Symposium. Citeseer (2001)
28. Reith, M., Carr, C., Gunsch, G.: An examination of digital forensic models. Int. J. Digital Evid. 1(3), 1–12 (2002)
29. Richter, J., Kuntze, N., Rudolph, C.: Security digital evidence. In: 2010 Fifth International Workshop on Systematic Approaches to Digital Forensic Engineering, pp. 119–130. IEEE (2010)
30. Rieke, R., Coppolino, L., Hutchison, A., Prieto, E., Gaber, C.: Security and reliability requirements for advanced security event management. In: Kotenko, I., Skormin, V. (eds.) MMM-ACNS 2012. LNCS, vol. 7531, pp. 171–180. Springer, Heidelberg (2012)
31. Rieke, R., Prieto, E., Diaz, R., Debar, H., Hutchison, A.: Challenges for advanced security monitoring – The MASSIF project. In: Fischer-Hübner, S., Katsikas, S., Quirchmayr, G. (eds.) TrustBus 2012. LNCS, vol. 7449, pp. 222–223. Springer, Heidelberg (2012)
32. Rieke, R., Repp, J., Zhdanova, M., Eichler, J.: Monitoring security compliance of critical processes. In: 2014 22th Euromicro International Conference on Parallel, Distributed and Network-Based Processing (PDP), pp. 525–560. IEEE Computer Society, February 2014
33. Rieke, R., Zhdanova, M., Repp, J.: Security compliance tracking of processes in networked cooperating systems. J. Wirel. Mob. Netw. Ubiquit. Comput. Dependable Appl. (JoWUA) 6(2), 21–40 (2015)
34. Russell, S.J., Norvig, P.: Artificial Intelligence: A Modern Approach, 2nd edn. Pearson Education, Paris (2003)
35. Sailer, R., Zhang, X., Jaeger, T., Van Doorn, L.: Design and implementation of a tcg-based integrity measurement architecture. In: USENIX Security Symposium, vol. 13, pp. 223–238 (2004)
36. Stumpf, F., Fuchs, A., Katzenbeisser, S., Eckert, C.: Improving the scalability of platform attestation. In: Proceedings of the Third ACM Workshop on Scalable Trusted Computing (ACM STC 2008), pp. 1–10. ACM Press, Fairfax, 31 October 2008
37. Trusted Computing Group TPM Working Group: TCG Specification Architecture Overview. (2007). http://www.trustedcomputinggroup.org/resources/
38. Wang, W., Xu, Y., Khanna, M.: A survey on the communication architectures in smart grid. Comput. Netw. 55(15), 3604–3629 (2011)
39. Wang, Y.: sscada: Securing SCADA infrastructure communications. CoRR abs/1207.5434 (2012). http://arxiv.org/abs/1207.5434
40. Winkler, T., Rinner, B.: TrustCAM: security and privacy-protection for an embedded smart camera based on trusted computing. In: Proceedings of the Conference on Advanced Video and Signal-Based Surveillance (2010)

41. Xu, X., Bessis, N., Cao, J.: An autonomic agent trust model for iot systems. Procedia Comput. Sci. **21**, 107–113 (2013). the 4th International Conference on Emerging Ubiquitous Systems and Pervasive Networks (EUSPN-2013) and the 3rd International Conference on Current and Future Trends of Information and Communication Technologies in Healthcare (ICTH)

42. Zaldivar, J., Calafate, C.T., Cano, J.C., Manzoni, P.: Providing accident detection in vehicular networks through obd-ii devices and android-based smartphones. In: 2011 IEEE 36th Conference on Local Computer Networks (LCN), pp. 813–819. IEEE (2011)

43. Zhu, B., Joseph, A., Sastry, S.: A taxonomy of cyber attacks on scada systems. In: Proceedings of the 2011 International Conference on Internet of Things and 4th International Conference on Cyber, Physical and Social Computing, ITHINGSCP-SCOM 2011, pp. 380–388. IEEE Computer Society, Washington, DC (2011)

Security Monitoring for Industrial Control Systems

Alessio Coletta[1,2,3]([✉]) and Alessandro Armando[2,4]

[1] GCSEC – Poste Italiane, Rome, Italy
alessio.coletta@gcsec.org, {acoletta,armando}@fbk.eu,
alessio.coletta@unitn.it
[2] Fondazione Bruno Kessler, Trento, Italy
[3] DISI, University of Trento, Trento, Italy
[4] DIBRIS, University of Genova, Genova, Italy
alessandro.armando@unige.it

Abstract. An Industrial Control System (ICS) is a system of physical entities whose functioning heavily relies on information and communication technology components and infrastructures. ICS are ubiquitous and can be found in a number of safety-critical areas including energy, chemical processes, health-care, aerospace, manufacturing, and transportation. While originally isolated and inherently secure, ICS are recently becoming more and more exposed to cyber attacks (e.g. Stuxnet).

Many existing ICS do not feature cyber security protection, with liability issues and high costs in case of incidents. Since existing ICS are normally based on components and protocols that cannot be modified nor updated, redesign is usually not feasible. In this paper we propose a monitoring framework for the run-time verification of ICS. The framework is based on a formal language that supports the precise specification of high-level safety requirements as well as of the relevant threat model, and on a passive monitoring technique that detects and notifies if the system state is close to a critical state.

Keywords: Cyber security · Industrial control systems · Intrusion detection systems · Run-time security monitoring · Optimization · SMT

1 Introduction

Industrial Control Systems (ICS) are composed by Information and Communication Technology (ICT) devices that interact and communicate to control physical entities. Originally ICS used to be isolated systems based on proprietary protocols. Standard ICT technology has been increasingly used since it offers higher flexibility and reducing costs. At the same time, ICS have become distributed and interconnected networked systems to allow remote control and management. Unfortunately this trend is exposing ICS to typical vulnerabilities and threats of the ICT world.

© Springer International Publishing Switzerland 2016
A. Bécue et al. (Eds.): CyberICS 2015/WOS-CPS 2015, LNCS 9588, pp. 48–62, 2016.
DOI: 10.1007/978-3-319-40385-4_4

ICS present many differences from ICT systems [17]. The order of importance of security requirements in terms of confidentiality, integrity, and availability is reversed. The lifespan of ICS devices is much longer than that of standard ICT devices and may even be measured in decades, and shutdowns or changes are not acceptable in most cases. Thus, legacy software and hardware is usually present in many existing ICS installations. Change management and software updates are usually very difficult, and often just impossible, due to cost or liability issues. For these reasons information security solutions designed for general ICT systems seldom apply to ICS and *passive* security solutions, e.g. monitoring, that do not affect the·system are usually preferred.

In this work we propose a *security monitoring framework for the run-time verification of industrial control systems*. The framework is able to detect anomalous behaviours of the system that may result from cyber attacks. The framework provides a *formal specification language* that allows for the unambiguous specification of the set of critical states, i.e. the ones that must be considered anomalous. The definition of anomalies mainly derives from the a-priori knowledge of the system gained during the design phase.

Since the anomaly detection must be *predictive* (i.e. it must detect a criticality *before* the system reaches it), a notion of proximity to criticalities, expressing "how close" the system is to any critical state, must be defined. The monitoring framework is passive, i.e. it does not interfere with the operations of the system. If the proximity to criticalities is lower than a threshold, an alarm must be raised.

Relevant works concerning cyber security for ICS are presented in Sect. 2. The proposed framework is presented in Sect. 3. Final remarks are presented in Sect. 4.

2   Related Work

Cyber security of industrial control systems gained importance in recent years. Governamental bodies, standard organizations like ISO and IEC, and international agencies like NIST, NERC, and ENISA developed general standards and guidelines for securing SCADA systems [10,17] and more specific ones for Smart Grids [7,16], gas pipeline [1], and so on. Usually these standards and guidelines describe high level security requirements and only contain high level security controls that rarely address real vulnerabilities without further implementation of specific countermeasures, but are a valuable starting point for identifying the security issues of most ICS.

One of the main source of vulnerability for ICS is the lack of security mechanisms in communication protocols, like authentication, authorisation, and confidentiality. For this reason several efforts developed hardened communication solutions among industrial system components. However, these security approaches relies on the actual capability to redesign and replace at least some parts of the system. This requires to shutdown the ICS (at least partially), but most critical ICS cannot afford any downtime. Moreover, many existing ICS presents legacy components and redesign is not an option due to the high costs and risks related to any possible change. For this reason it is crucial to develop passive security measures.

Intrusion detection systems have been widely used in all kind of ICT systems with good results. For general IT system signature-based IDS, like Snort [5,15], are abled to express *bad* IP packet that can be detected. Since cyber attacks are combination of different actions and communications, signature-based IDS usually fall short in detecting complex attacks. The IT industry employs *Security information and event management* (SIEM) software to perform real-time analysis of data collected from different sources and sensors deployed in corporate networks [11]. Typical SIEM systems feature log data aggregation and event correlation, providing useful support to forensic analysis of cyber incidents and to attack prevention through real-time alerting.

Literature contains a similar approach called *anomaly-based* network intrusion detection systems [3,8,9]. Anomaly-based is a general term to express any technique that distinguish normal and licit behaviours from the anomalous ones. [8] classifies network IDS in three main categories:

1. *statistical-based* techniques, which analyse the network traffic in order to create a stochastic behaviour profile that is later compared with the traffic at runtime. The comparison gives a score indicating the degree of anomaly.
2. *machine learning-based* techniques, which establish a model of licit and anomalous behavioural patterns. Such techniques require labelled training data sets.
3. *knowledge-based techniques*, for which a human ICS expert defines a behavioural model of what is legitimate and what is anomalous.

Setting up a proper statistical analysis capturing the intended notion of anomalous behaviour may be tricky. Moreover, statistical-based techniques typically suffer from high false positive rates. Machine learning approaches usually require big amount of labelled data that are often not available. It is possible to use a learning time window, during which every observed behaviour is considered legitimate, but this is risky if a cyber attack or any kind of misuse occurs during that time. For these reasons this work focuses on the third approach.

The main advantage of the knowledge-based approach is that false positive rates are extremely low or zero when enough knowledge of the system is available. The main drawback is the difficulty of defining appropriate models in terms of accuracy and computational feasibility. While this is a major obstacle with general IT systems due to their variability, each industrial control system typically shows predictable and repeatable behaviours over time. Moreover the design phase of a critical infrastructure is detailed and documented, providing valuable knowledge to be modelled. Hence, knowledge-based techniques seem to be a good approach for developing security monitors for ICS.

Several works present anomaly-based intrusion detection systems specific for industrial control system with a knowledge-based approach. [20] proposes an intrusion detection for smart utility in the power sector that uses timing analysis of host-based auditing data. [6] presents an IDS that transforms protocol, communication pattern, and service availability specifications into a format compatible with EMERALD and Snort, using Modbus [13,18] packet inspection. [12] proposes a behaviour-rule specification-based technique for intrusion detection of medical devices, where a state machine is derived from human-constructed behaviour rules and several notion of distances are considered. [19] presents a non-intrusive solution for smart utility (water) that combines a workflow that collects auditing data from the hosts with a simulation manager that predicts how the attack can propagate.

Nai et al. [4,14] developed an Intrusion Detection and Prevention System methodology specific for SCADA systems. The methodology combines some knowledge about the physical process, gained from the process design phase, with the cyber behaviour to monitor, in a model-based fashion as described above. The assumptions is that cyber attacks can be performed by a sequence of licit commands, impossible to spot with signature-based IDS, that leads the system to some unwanted states. The key idea of the approach is to keep track of the current state of the ICS and to compute on-the-fly its distance from the nearest critical (i.e. bad) state. As soon as the system reaches a state whose distance is smaller than a given threshold an alarm is raised. A key feature of the approach is that it allows for the activation of corrective measures *before a critical state is reached*. Since the approach monitors the system evolution and not the (possibly unknown) evolution of an attack, it is equally effective—unlike traditional filtering techniques—in detecting known attacks as well as zero-day attacks. The language presented in [4,14] is very simple, in order to keep the corresponding computational complexity low. However, that language is not expressive enough for real-case scenarios. Our monitoring framework extends that methodology and targets these limitations.

3   The Monitoring Framework

Our run-time monitoring extends [4,14]. It is based on a formal language for defining the states of the systems that are considered *critical*, denoted by the predicate $\phi(\vec{x})$, and a formal notion of distance between the current state $\vec{s}$ and a critical state $\vec{x}$, denoted by $d(\vec{s}, \vec{x})$. At the core of the approach two techniques are possible:

1. using a set of *thresholds* $k_1 < k_2 < \ldots < k_h$ expressing different levels of alarms, and determining whether there is a critical state $\vec{x}$ which is closer to the current state $\vec{s}$ than a threshold k_i. Precisely, whether there exists a state $\vec{x}$ such that

$$\phi(\vec{x}) \quad \wedge \quad k_i \leqslant d(\vec{s}, \vec{x}) < k_{i+1} \tag{1}$$

   for some k_i where $\vec{s}$ is the current state of the system. If (1) is satisfied, an alert of level i is raised.
2. calculating the distance from critical states, i.e. solving the problem of the form

$$\begin{cases} \text{minimize } d(\vec{s}, \vec{x}) \\ \quad \vec{x} \\ \text{subject to } \phi(\vec{x}) \end{cases} \tag{2}$$

where $\vec{x}$ is a n-uple of variables representing an arbitrary system state, $\vec{s}$ is the (known) current state, $d(\vec{s}, \vec{x})$ is an expression denoting the distance from $\vec{s}$ to $\vec{x}$ according to some given metrics, and $\phi(\vec{x})$ is a formula representing the set of critical states.

Approach (1) does not require the actual computation of the distance $d(\vec{s}, \vec{x})$, but only to determine whether it is less than a given threshold. As we will see in the following sections, this is a big difference in terms of computational complexity and of feasible reasoning engines that can be used at the core of the monitor. However approach (2) allows to monitor how the distance $d(\vec{s}, \vec{x})$ changes in time. In particular, observing the first derivative in time of this quantity it is possible to understand if the system is "getting closer" to some critical state. Since the second approach is more precise but also computationally more complex than the first one, it seems appropriate to consider both.

In [14] it is assumed that *(i)* $d(\vec{s}, \vec{x})$ is either the Manhattan distance or a Hamming distance and *(ii)* $\phi(\vec{x})$ is a disjunction of conditions of the form

$$x_1 \leqslant c_1 \wedge \cdots \wedge x_n \leqslant c_n$$

where x_i and c_i are state variables and numeric constants respectively, for $i = 1, \ldots, n$. The assumption on the form of $\phi(\vec{x})$ plays a crucial role for the efficiency of the approach, but it also severely limits its applicability. First of all, complex relationships among the state variables cannot be expressed. For instance, the set of critical states of a system where the sum of the temperature of two thermometers is above a given threshold cannot be expressed. Secondly, overly long specifications may be necessary to specify sets of critical states that can otherwise be succinctly represented. For instance, the specification of a set of critical states where at most k out of n valves can be open at the same time requires $\sum_{i=1}^{k} \binom{n}{i} = 2^k - 1$ disjuncts.

Our first results show that the approach can be considerably improved by letting $\phi(\vec{x})$ be an arbitrary Boolean combination of linear constraints, i.e. atomic formulae of the form

$$a_1 x_1 + \cdots + a_n x_n \leqslant b$$

and by using a state-of-the-art linear optimisation tools and Satisfiability Modulo Theory (SMT) solvers to tackle problems of the form (1) and (2). We assume that the measurement of component values x_i is reliable, i.e. that measurement errors are negligible. In this work we do not use the Hamming distance but only the Manhattan distance.

3.1   A Motivating Example

Consider an industrial system made by a boiler, a heater of the boiler, three thermometers for the temperature of the boiler, and two fans that cool down the boiler. The system can:

1. check if the thermometers are available, i.e. if the PLC controlling the thermometer is functioning and the communication link is working properly. The unavailability of the three thermometers is represented by the Boolean variables $Temp_i.NA$, $i \in \{1, 2, 3\}$.

2. measure the temperature of the boiler through the three thermometers represented by the integer-valued variables $Temp_i.T$;
3. detect the on/off status of the heater and whether the boiler is empty, represented by the Boolean variables $Heater.On$ and $Boiler.Empty$;
4. control (i.e. read and write) the rotational speed of both fans, represented by the integer-valued variables $Fan_1.S$ and $Fan_2.S$.

To define the set of critical states of the system we consider (the complement of) the functional requirements of the physical process to control and the ICT infrastructure, i.e. the logical negation of the formulae expressing normal behaviours.

Requirement #1. The first requirement is about the behaviour of the physical process. The temperature of the boiler should not exceed 225° C. The complement of this requirement can be readily expresses by the following linear constraint:

$$\frac{1}{3} Temp_1.T + \frac{1}{3} Temp_2.T + \frac{1}{3} Temp_3.T \geqslant 225 \qquad (3)$$

Requirement #2. The second requirement is slightly more complex: the two fans must have a rotational speed that is enough to cool the boiler down when the temperature is greater than 50° C. We do not require a threshold of the speed of each fan, but only on the average speed of the two. Moreover, the threshold is not a constant, but a value proportional to the average temperature as measured by the three thermometers. This formally captures the fact that the fans must have higher speeds for higher temperatures. Assuming that the proportional constant is 20, the critical states representing the states that do not satisfy these requirements can be represented by the conjunction of the following two linear constraints:

$$\frac{1}{3}(Temp_1.T + Temp_2.T + Temp_3.T) \geqslant 50 \qquad (4)$$

$$\frac{1}{2} Fan_1.S + \frac{1}{2} Fan_2.S \leqslant \frac{20}{3}(Temp_1.T + Temp_2.T + Temp_3.T) \qquad (5)$$

Requirement #3. The third requirement is a set of Boolean conditions related to the state of the ICT components and the state of the physical process, namely:

1. the heater is on and the two fans are off,
2. the boiler is empty and the heater is on, and
3. there are more than one thermometers that are not available.

It is worth noting that neither Requirement #1 nor Requirement #2 can be expressed in the framework proposed in [14].

In this simple example the monitoring framework will detect any cyber attack leading to critical states that do not satisfy requirements #1, #2, and #3, without requiring to specify any peculiarity of such attacks. In this way the operator does not need to know ICT security technicalities in order to be able to detect cyber incidents. This is an important feature of our framework, which is also crucial for detecting 0-days attacks.

3.2 Critical States Specification Language

We model the state of the industrial control system as the collection of the states of its components. A system component can be:

1. a boolean register of a PLC, called *coil*;
2. a numerical register of a PLC (integer or rational), simply called *register* in this work;

Let $\mathbf{C}$ and $\mathbf{R}$ be the (disjoint) sets of coils and numerical registers in the PLCs of the system. A state σ is an assignment of boolean and numerical values to the coils and numerical registers respectively, i.e. $\sigma = \sigma_c \cup \sigma_r$, where $\sigma_c : \mathbf{C} \to \mathbb{B}$, $\sigma_r : \mathbf{R} \to \mathbb{B}^{16} \cup \mathbb{B}^{32} \cup \mathbb{F}$, and $\mathbb{B}^{16}, \mathbb{B}^{32}$ and $\mathbb{F}$ are 16 bit integers, 32 bit integers, and floating point numbers respectively.

The set of critical states of the system can be specified by a set of rules whose syntax is defined by the following grammar:

$$
\begin{array}{llr}
Rule & ::= PC \to \mathbf{Alert} & \text{(Rule)} \\
PC & ::= A \,|\, A \wedge PC & \text{(Precondition)} \\
A & ::= B \,|\, LE \leqslant n & \text{(Atomic Formula)} \\
LE & ::= n * r \,|\, n * r + LE & \text{(Linear Expression)} \\
B & ::= L \,|\, \mathtt{AtMost}_k(L_1, \ldots, L_n) \,|\, \mathtt{AtLeast}_k(L_1, \ldots, L_n) & \text{(Boolean Constraint)} \\
L & ::= c \,|\, \neg c & \text{(Literal)}
\end{array}
$$

where $r \in \mathbf{R}$, $c \in \mathbf{C}$, and $n \in \mathbb{Q}$ denotes a numeral (i.e. a numeric constant).

The value of a linear expression LE in σ, in symbols $[LE]_\sigma$, is recursively defined as follows:

$$[n * r]_\sigma = n \cdot \sigma(r)$$
$$[n * r + LE]_\sigma = n \cdot \sigma(r) + [LE]_\sigma$$

With a little abuse of notation, in the following we use common mathematical notations for linear constraints, with mixed use of $\leqslant$ and $\geqslant$, to indicate the equivalent linear expression in the form $LE \leqslant n$.

We say that a precondition of a rule PC holds in state σ, in symbols $\sigma \models PC$ iff

$$
\begin{array}{lll}
\sigma \models c & \text{iff} & \sigma(c) = 1 \\
\sigma \models \neg c & \text{iff} & \sigma(c) = 0 \\
\sigma \models \mathtt{AtMost}_k(L_1, \ldots, L_n) & \text{iff} & \displaystyle\sum_{i=1}^{n} \sigma(L_i) \leq k \\
\sigma \models \mathtt{AtLeast}_k(L_1, \ldots, L_n) & \text{iff} & \displaystyle\sum_{i=1}^{n} \sigma(L_i) \geq k \\
\sigma \models LE \leq N & \text{iff} & [LE]_\sigma \leq N \\
\sigma \models A \wedge PC & \text{iff} & \sigma \models A \text{ and } \sigma \models PC
\end{array}
$$

Given a set of rules $\mathcal{R}$, the set of critical states $\mathbf{CS}(\mathcal{R})$ is formally defined as

$$\mathbf{CS}(PC) = \{\sigma | \sigma \models PC\} \tag{6}$$

$$\mathbf{CS}(\mathcal{R}) = \{\sigma | \sigma \models PC \text{ for some } (PC \rightarrow \mathbf{Alert}) \in \mathcal{R}\} \tag{7}$$

Notice that for any precondition PC, the set $\mathbf{CS}(PC)$ is a *closed polyhedron*. Given a set of rules

$$\mathcal{R} = \{PC_1 \rightarrow \mathbf{Alert}, \dots, PC_h \rightarrow \mathbf{Alert}\}$$

we use $\phi = PC_1 \vee \cdots \vee PC_h$ to denote the logical disjunction of the preconditions of the critical rules. Notice that, since every precondition PC_i is a logical conjunction of atomic formulae, the formula ϕ is in *disjunctive normal form* (DNF).

$$\left(\frac{1}{3} Temp_1.T + \frac{1}{3} Temp_2.T + \frac{1}{3} Temp_2.T \geqslant 225\right) \rightarrow \mathbf{Alert} \tag{8}$$

$$\left(\begin{array}{c} \frac{1}{3}(Temp_1.T + Temp_2.T + Temp_3.T) \geqslant 50 \quad \wedge \\ \frac{1}{2} Fan_1.S + \frac{1}{2} Fan_2.S \leqslant \frac{20}{3}(Temp_1.T + Temp_2.T + Temp_3.T) \end{array}\right) \rightarrow \mathbf{Alert} \tag{9}$$

$$Heater.On \wedge \neg Fan_1.On \wedge \neg Fan_2.On \rightarrow \mathbf{Alert} \tag{10}$$

$$Boiler.Empty \wedge Heater.On \rightarrow \mathbf{Alert} \tag{11}$$

$$AtLeast_2(Temp_1.NA, Temp_2.NA, Temp_3.NA) \rightarrow \mathbf{Alert} \tag{12}$$

Fig. 1. Critical states definition example.

Figure 1 shows the critical states rules that define the critical state described in Subsect. 3.1.

Given a set $\mathcal{R}$ of critical state rules, our monitoring system is able to detect if the current system state σ is critical. However, our approach is aimed not only at detecting if the system is in a critical state, but also to check if the system is close or getting closer to a critical state. To this aim we use the *notion of distance from critical states*.

Since the domains of values of system components $\mathbb{B}^{16}$, $\mathbb{B}^{32}$, and $\mathbb{F}$ are subset of the set of real numbers $\mathbb{R}$, then the space of system states can be seen as subset of $\mathbb{R}^n$, where n is the number of system components. Thus, a system state can be represented by a vector $\vec{s} \in \mathbb{R}^n$, and any metrics on $\mathbb{R}^n$ can be used to express the notion of distance from critical states.

Definition 1. *Given a distance d on $\mathbb{R}^n$, the distance of a point $\vec{s} \in \mathbb{R}^n$ from a subset $\mathbf{S} \subseteq \mathbb{R}^n$ is defined as*

$$d(\vec{s}, \mathbf{S}) = \inf_{\vec{t} \in \mathbf{S}} d(\vec{s}, \vec{t}) \tag{13}$$

The notion of distance of the current system state, represented by $\vec{s}$, from the critical states defined by the set $\mathcal{R}$ or critical rules is:

$$d(\vec{s}, \mathbf{CS}(\mathcal{R})) \tag{14}$$

According to Eqs. (6) and (7), since the critical formula ϕ corresponding to rules $\mathcal{R}$ is in disjunctive normal form, the following equation holds:

$$d(\vec{s}, \mathbf{CS}(\mathcal{R})) = \min_{i=1\cdots h} d(\vec{s}, \mathbf{CS}(PC_i)) \tag{15}$$

$$= \min_{i=1\cdots h} \min_{\vec{t} \in \mathbf{CS}(PC_i)} d(\vec{s}, \vec{t}) \tag{16}$$

where min safely replaces inf of Eq. (13) because the sets of critical states are closed.

The previous definitions are parametric with respect to the actual metric d on $\mathbb{R}^n$. In this work we consider the L_1 metric on $\mathbb{R}^n$, also known as the *Manhattan* distance, defined as

$$d(\vec{x}, \vec{y}) = \sum_{i=1}^{n} |x_i - y_i| \tag{17}$$

Then, the critical states distance is

$$d(\vec{s}, \mathbf{CS}(\mathcal{R})) = \min_{i=1\cdots h} \min_{\vec{t} \in \mathbf{CS}(PC_i)} \sum_{k} |s_k - t_k| \tag{18}$$

3.3 Distance Thresholds Approach

In this section we show how to solve problem (1). This boils down to determining whether there exists a state $\vec{x}$ such that

$$\phi(\vec{x}) \wedge d(\vec{s}, \vec{x}) \leqslant k_i \tag{19}$$

for $i \in \{1, \ldots, h\}$.

To ease the following sections we introduce a new notation. Given a positive constant k and a boolean combination ψ of linear atomic formulae, we use the notation $\psi^{\leqslant k}$ to denote the logic formula defined as

$$\psi^{\leqslant k}(\vec{y}) \quad \text{iff} \quad d(\vec{y}, \mathbf{CS}(\psi)) \leqslant k \tag{20}$$

Notice that $\mathbf{CS}(\psi) \subseteq \mathbf{CS}(\psi^{\leqslant k})$

The problem (19) can be reformulated as checking if the current state $\vec{s}$ satisfies $\phi^{\leqslant k}$. We hereafter describe two approaches: an approximated and a precise one.

Approximated Linear Approach. This approach constructs an easy upper approximation of $\phi^{\leqslant k}$, given a DNF critical formula ϕ corresponding to a set of critical rules $\mathcal{R}$ and a threshold k.

Since the critical formula ϕ is a DNF form of closed linear atomic inequalities, the set $\mathbf{CS}(\mathcal{R})$ of critical states is the union of a number of closed polyhedra in $\mathbb{R}^n$. Indeed, each polyhedron corresponds to one precondition PC of $\mathcal{R}$ and is the intersection of half spaces that correspond to the linear constraints in PC.

From a half space H it is possible to obtain the set $H^{\leqslant k}$ thought a simple translation in $\mathbb{R}^n$. Formally, given a threshold k, for each atomic formula $H = \sum_i a_i x_i \leqslant b$ it is possible to prove that

$$H^{\leqslant k} = \sum_i a_i x_i \leqslant (b + k \max_i |a_i|) \tag{21}$$

However, replacing each linear constraint H occurring in a polyhedron PC with the corresponding $H^{\leqslant k}$ does not yield the set $PC^{\leqslant k}$ but an higher approximation. Formally, given a conjunctive clause $PC = H_1 \wedge \ldots \wedge H_m$ corresponding to the precondition of a critical rule, the following holds:

$$PC^{\leqslant k} \subseteq H_1^{\leqslant k} \wedge \ldots \wedge H_m^{\leqslant k} \tag{22}$$

Hence, $PC' = H_1^{\leqslant k} \wedge \ldots \wedge H_m^{\leqslant k}$ is an over approximation of $PC^{\leqslant k}$ and in the general case PC' is a strict subset of $PC^{\leqslant k}$. The formal proof is omitted, but Fig. 2 geometrically represents an example of the conjunction of three linear atomic formula H_j corresponding to half planes in $\mathbb{R}^2$: the red area represents the critical states represented by $PC = H_1 \wedge H_2 \wedge H_3$, the union of the red and light-blue areas corresponds to $PC^{\leqslant k}$, and the dark-blue areas correspond to the error of approximation, i.e. to the the states of PC' that do not belong to $PC^{\leqslant k}$.

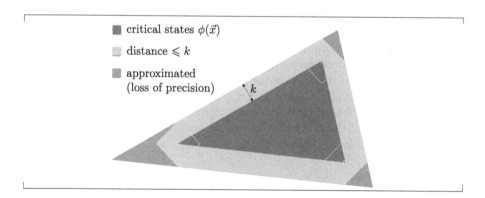

■ critical states $\phi(\vec{x})$

▨ distance $\leqslant k$

■ approximated (loss of precision)

Fig. 2. Polyhedron upper approximation with L_1 norm.(Color figure online)

Consequently, replacing each atomic formula H occurring in ϕ with $H^{\leqslant k}$ gives a formula ϕ' that is an over approximation of $\phi^{\leqslant k}$.

Precise Linear Approach. Figure 2 also shows the precise set satisfying $\phi^{\leq k}$, represented by the union of light-blue area and the red one (the critical state represented by ϕ). It can be noted how that area can be represented by the convex hull of the yellow squares centred in the vertex of the critical state area. The yellow squares depict the closed *metric balls* of radius k using the L_1 norm. Formally, a closed metric ball is defined as $B[\vec{c}, k] = \{\vec{x} \mid d(\vec{x}, \vec{c}) \leq k\}$.

In general, the formula $\phi^{\leq k}$ can be calculated as follow: for each PC_j occurring in ϕ, $PC_j^{\leq k}$ is the convex hull of the metric balls $B[\vec{v}_i, k]$ for each vertex $\vec{v}_i$ of the polyhedron corresponding to PC_j. It is possible to use existing software libraries to manipulate sets of linear constraints and calculating convex hulls. We developed a test prototype using the the Parma Polyhedra Library [2], which is able to determine the vertices v_i and the convex hull of such balls. Moreover, the library returns the convex hull in form of the set of linear constraints corresponding $PC_j^{\leq k}$. The intended result of this approach, i.e. the formula $\phi^{\leq k}$, is the disjunction of formulae $PC_j^{\leq k}$. Once this formula is calculated as described, it is easy to verify whether it is satisfied by the current state of the system using any tool for linear constraint verification, e.g. libraries like the PPL or SMT solvers with linear arithmetic, as in the previous case.

3.4   Calculating the Distance

In this section we show preliminary results for the approach following (2), i.e. how to actually compute the distance from critical states.

Pure Linear Programming Approach. Computing the expression

$$d(\vec{s}, PC_i) = \min_{\vec{t} \in \mathbf{CS}(PC_i)} \sum_k |s_k - t_k|$$

require to minimise a non-linear function on a set of linear constraint, thus is not purely a linear programming problem. However, it is possible to convert it to a linear programming problem with a proper variable substitution. For any real number w, its absolute value $|w|$ is the minimum non-negative real u such that $-u \leq w \leq u$ (this already implies that $u \geq 0$). Thus, in the original problem, we can add a vector $\vec{u} \in \mathbb{R}^n$ with the constraints $-\vec{u} \leq \vec{s} - \vec{x} \leq \vec{u}$. Notice that, in this formulation of the problem, the current system state $\vec{s}$ is a constant.

The original problem is translated in computing

$$d(\vec{s}, PC_i) = \min \sum_{i=1}^n u_i \qquad \text{s.t.:} \begin{cases} \vec{x} \vDash PC_i \\ \vec{x} - \vec{u} \leq \vec{s} \\ -\vec{x} - \vec{u} \leq -\vec{s} \end{cases}$$

which is a pure linear programming problem solvable with the simplex algorithm and any LP program or library.

SMT: Linear Arithmetic with Quantifiers. Given the current system state vector $\vec{s}$, the notion of distance of $\vec{s}$ from critical states $d(\vec{s}, \mathbf{CS})$, defined in (15), can be rephrased as finding the minimum value $d(\vec{s}, \vec{x})$ such that $\vec{x}$ is critical, while $\vec{s}$ is a constant of the problem. In other terms, it is equivalent to finding if there exists a vector $\vec{x}$ satisfying the following condition

$$\texttt{critical}(\vec{x}) \wedge \left(\forall \vec{y}.\texttt{critical}(\vec{y}) \rightarrow d(\vec{s}, \vec{x}) \leqslant d(\vec{s}, \vec{y}) \right) \tag{23}$$

If there exists such $\vec{x}$, then distance of $\vec{s}$ from critical states is $d(\vec{s}, \vec{x})$.

It is possible to define such problem using SMT solvers that support linear integer arithmetic with quantifiers. In this case, it is sufficient to define the criticality predicate $\texttt{critical}(\vec{x})$ that represents $\vec{x} \in \mathbf{CS}$ and to present the problem to the solver exactly as it is define in (23).

Notice that this formulation of the problem enable to relax the condition that the critical formula ϕ must be a DNF formula.

SMT: Quantifier-Free Linear Arithmetic. Another solution is shown in Fig. 3. The method solves the previous problem without quantifiers. It is based on searching if there exists a critical system state. If it is not found, the set of critical states is empty, thus this case is not interesting for our purpose. Instead if there is at least a critical state $\vec{x}$, then the algorithm searches for another critical state which is closer to the current state $\vec{s}$ than $\vec{x}$. This is done iteratively until there is no closer critical state. This means that the last critical state found is the closest to the current state $\vec{s}$, and that distance is the result of the computation.

---

function DISTANCE(rules $\mathcal{R}$, current state $\vec{s}$)
    define $\texttt{critical}(x_1, ..., x_n)$ as a boolean combination of atomic linear integer arithmetic formulae A (normal form not required).
    $\vec{x} \leftarrow SMT\_Solve(\texttt{critical}(\vec{x}))$
    if $\vec{x}$ is not found **then**
        return null (there is no critical state)
    else
        repeat
            $\vec{p} \leftarrow \vec{x}$
            $d \leftarrow d(\vec{s}, \vec{p})$
            $\vec{x} \leftarrow SMT\_Solve(\texttt{critical}(\vec{x}) \wedge d(\vec{s}, \vec{x}) < d)$
        until $\vec{x}$ is not found
        return $d(\vec{s}, \vec{p})$

Fig. 3. SMT Pseudo-code: Quantifier free linear arithmetic.

4   Final Remarks

In this work we presented a promising approach to express effective critical states of industrial control systems and a framework for the run-time monitoring of the system against such criticalities. The framework not only detects if the current state of the system is critical, but is also predictive: it monitors the proximity of the system to some criticality before reaching it. The notion of proximity from criticalities is based on a formal definition of distance on the state space of the system.

The basic methodology and notions are an extension of the seminal work in [4,14], where the language for defining critical state is particularly simple in order to keep the computational complexity of the distance low. The drawback of those works is that the language is not expressive enough for real cases. Our work improves this limitation while keeping the complexity to feasible levels, in order to make the general methodology practical for real scenarios.

The critical state definition language is enriched with linear constraints among the values of system components. Such constraints cannot be expressed in [4,14]. In industrial control systems, where the process is controlled by different devices, linear constraints can be a natural way to express certain critical states, as shown in the motivating example of Sect. 3.1.

Adding linear constraints to the definition language makes the sets of critical states more complex. As a consequence, the computational complexity of the distance from critical states becomes higher. In our work several approaches to handle the increased complexity are developed and presented.

The first approach is to detect if the proximity to critical states reaches alerting thresholds. This approach does not require to actually compute the distance, but only to manipulate sets of linear constraints in a proper way. An approximated and a precise method are presented.

Another approach is to actually compute the distance from the critical states, which presents a higher computational complexity than detecting alerting thresholds. However, while thresholds can be sufficient in simpler scenarios, computing the critical distance during the evolution of the system, and tracking how this values changes in time, provide information about the *direction* of the system, i.e. whether and how quickly the system is getting closer to critical states. For this reason several computing methods are developed and presented.

The first method is based on standard linear programming (LP) techniques. The advantage of LP is that literature provides a good knowledge base and efficient tools. The other methods are based on *Satisfiability Modulo Theory* (SMT) solvers. It is worth noticing that the comparison between LP and SMT techniques is not limited to performance issues, but also concerns expressiveness. Indeed, while linear programming and the polyhedra libraries permit to define only mixed integer and rational linear constraints, SMT-based techniques enable a wider set of constraints, depending on the underneath theory selected. Another important difference to notice is that SMT solvers do not need *disjunctive normal form* formulae. Transforming any logical formula into an equivalent DNF formula is not trivial, being a NP-complete problem.

For each approach and method presented in this work, a working prototype has been developed as a preliminary evidence of general feasibility. However, a complete set of experiments is currently under development. The expected output is supposed to characterise and to compare the approaches in terms of performance and computational feasibility. The development of relevant experiments and the analysis of the results is the objective of our next future work.

References

1. American Gas Association: Aga-12: cryptographic protection of scada communications (2006)
2. Bagnara, R., Hill, P.M., Zaffanella, E.: The parma polyhedra library: toward a complete set of numerical abstractions for the analysis and verification of hardware and software systems. Sci. Comput. Programm. **72**(1–2), 3–21 (2008)
3. Bolzoni, D., Zambon, E., Etalle, S., Hartel, P.: Poseidon: a 2-tier anomaly-based network intrusion detection system. In: Proceedings of the Fourth IEEE International Workshop on Information Assurance, IWIA 2006, pp. 144–156. IEEE Computer Society, Los Alamitos. http://doc.utwente.nl/64935/
4. Carcano, A., Coletta, A., Guglielmi, M., Masera, M., Fovino, I.N., Trombetta, A.: A multidimensional critical state analysis for detecting intrusions in scada systems. IEEE Trans. Ind. Inform. **7**(2), 179–186 (2011)
5. Caswell, B., Beale, J.: Snort 2.1 Intrusion Detection. Syngress, Rockland (2004)
6. Cheung, S., Dutertre, B., Fong, M., Lindqvist, U., Skinner, K., Valdes, A.: Using model-based intrusion detection for scada networks. In: Proceedings of the SCADA Security Scientific Symposium, 46, pp. 1–12 (2007)
7. European Union Agency for Network and Information Security (ENISA): Smart grid security - recommendations for europe and member states, July 2012
8. Garcia-Teodoro, P., Diaz-Verdejo, J., Maciá-Fernández, G., Vázquez, E.: Anomaly-based network intrusion detection: techniques, systems and challenges. Comput. Secur. **28**(1), 18–28 (2009)
9. Guralnik, V., Heimerdinger, W., VanRiper, R.: Anomaly-based intrusion detection, uS Patent App. 11/189,446, 26 July 2005
10. Leszczyna, R., Egozcue, E., Tarrafeta, L., Villar, V.F., Estremera, R., Alonso, J.: Protecting industrial control systems - recommendations for europe and member states. Technical report, European Union Agency for Network and Information Security (ENISA) (2011)
11. Miller, D., Harris, S., Harper, A., VanDyke, S., Blask, C.: Security Information and Event Management (SIEM) Implementation. McGraw Hill Professional, New York (2010)
12. Mitchell, R., Chen, I.R.: Behavior rule specification-based intrusion detection for safety critical medical cyber physical systems. IEEE Trans. Dependable Secur. Comput. **5971**, 1 (2014). http://ieeexplore.ieee.org/lpdocs/epic03/wrapper.htm?arnumber=6774867
13. Modbus, I.D.A.: Modbus application protocol specification v1. 1a. North Grafton, Massachusetts (2004). www.modbus.org/specs.php
14. Fovino, I.N., Coletta, A., Carcano, A., Masera, M.: Critical state-based filtering system for securing SCADA network protocols. IEEE Trans. Ind. Electron. **59**(10), 3943–3950 (2012). http://ieeexplore.ieee.org/lpdocs/epic03/wrapper.htm?arnumber=6111289

15. Roesch, M., et al.: Snort: lightweight intrusion detection for networks. LISA **99**, 229–238 (1999)
16. Smart Grid Interoperability Panel Cyber Security Working Group and others: Nistir 7628-guidelines for smart grid cyber security, vol. 1–3 (2010)
17. Stouffer, K., Falco, J., Scarfone, K.: Guide to Industrial Control Systems (ICS) Security: Supervisory Control and Data Acquisition (SCADA) Systems, Distributed Control Systems (DCS), and Other Control System Configurations such as Programmable Logic Controllers (PLC). Technical report, National Institute of Standards and Technology, Gaithersburg, MD. http://nvlpubs.nist.gov/nistpubs/SpecialPublications/NIST.SP.800-82r1.pdf
18. Swales, A.: Open Modbus/TCP specification. Schneider Electr. 26, 29 March 1999
19. Xiao, K., Chen, N., Ren, S., Shen, L., Sun, X., Kwiat, K., Macalik, M.: A workflow-based non-intrusive approach for enhancing the survivability of critical infrastructures in cyber environment. In: Third International Workshop on Software Engineering for Secure System, SESS 2007, ICSE Workshop, p. 4 (2007). http://ieeexplore.ieee.org/lpdocs/epic03/wrapper.htm?arnumber=4273330
20. Zimmer, C., Bhat, B., Mueller, F., Mohan, S.: Time-based intrusion detection in cyber-physical systems. In: Proceedings of the 1st ACM/IEEE International Conference on Cyber-Physical Systems, pp. 109–118. ACM (2010)

WirelessHART NetSIM: A WirelessHART SCADA-Based Wireless Sensor Networks Simulator

Lyes Bayou[1][✉], David Espes[2], Nora Cuppens-Boulahia[1],
and Frédéric Cuppens[1]

[1] LabSTICC, Télécom Bretagne, 2 Rue de la Châtaigneraie, Césson Sévigné, France
lyes.bayou@telecom-bretagne.eu
[2] LabSTICC, University of Western Brittany, Brest, France

Abstract. The security of SCADA systems is a major concern. Indeed, these systems are used to manage important infrastructures. However, conducting security analyzes on these systems is almost impossible. Therefore, using simulators is the best way to do that. In this paper, we describe our simulator for WirelessHART SCADA-based systems. It implements the whole protocol stack and both field devices and the Network Manager including routing and scheduling algorithms. The simulator is specially tailored to assess WirelessHART security mechanisms and to test attacks and countermeasures. It includes scenarios for testing several kinds of attacks such as sybil and denial of service (DoS) attacks. Also, new scenarios can easily be added to test other kinds of attacks.

1 Introduction

Supervisory Control and Data Acquisition (SCADA) systems are automated systems for controlling and monitoring industrial and critical infrastructure systems such as water supply, energy grid, pipeline, etc. When deployed in a large area, these systems are called Industrial Control Systems (ICS). Typically, SCADA systems rely on data collected from a set of remote sensors. Due to the role these systems play in the economic sector they are considered as vital infrastructures. Therefore, the security of SCADA systems is a major States and industrials concern.

However, it is difficult to conduct any security analysis on a working SCADA system. Indeed, they are expected to work without any interruption for several years. Thus, conducting studies in real facilities is practically impossible. Consequently and in the absence of real test-bed specially deployed for research needs, using simulation is the best way to analyze SCADA systems.

This is more true for security analyzes. Indeed, a simulator allows conducting deep tests and having an accurate assessment of existing security mechanisms. It also allows testing several attack scenarios and counter-measures which can be evaluated and validated easily. Another advantage is that we can evaluate the impact of the proposed security mechanisms on the system's operations,

© Springer International Publishing Switzerland 2016
A. Bécue et al. (Eds.): CyberICS 2015/WOS-CPS 2015, LNCS 9588, pp. 63–78, 2016.
DOI: 10.1007/978-3-319-40385-4_5

for instance in terms of availability and real-time requirement. Such simulator must be enough flexible to permit the elaboration of different scenarios in an easy way.

In this paper, we present a simulator for WirelessHART SCADA-based systems. WirelessHART is the first international approved standard for industrial process automation. It is the leading standard of all wireless industrial communication protocols, installed in more than 30 million devices worldwide [1]. The proposed simulator fully implements the WirelessHART stack and both field devices and the Network Manager including routing and scheduling algorithms. It is based on OMNet++ [2], a discrete event simulator based on C++ language. Our simulator includes scenarios for testing several kinds of attacks such as sybil and denial of service (DOS) attacks. It can be easily extended in order to test other kinds of attacks.

The rest of the paper is organized as follows. Section 2 gives an overview of available WirelessHART simulators. In Sect. 3 we present the protocol WirelessHART. Section 4 describes implementation details. We focus in Sect. 5 on WirelessHART security. We present in Sect. 6 results of our tests. Section 7 describes a security case study. Finally, we conclude with some insights and relative perspectives, in Sect. 8.

2   Related Works

In literature, there are two categories of available WirelessHART simulators, partial [3–5] and full [6] protocol stack implementation.

Partial implementations are mostly developed to study WirelessHART performances and its ability to be used in industrial environment. Therefore, only the Data Link Layer and basic Network layer are generally implemented.

De Biasi et al. developed in [3] a WirelessHART simulator to address the problem of clock drift in a WirelessHART network. This problem occurs when no synchronization exists between two devices which causes packet losses. The proposed simulator uses TrueTime (a Matlab/Simulink-based environment) and implements only some features particularly in the MAC layer.

In [4], De Diminicis and al. investigate coexistence issues when a WirelessHART network and another Wireless Network (WirlessHART, WIFI or IEEE 802.15.4) are in the same radio coverage area. They implement their simulator on OMNet++, an open source simulation environment. As this study focused on interferences and aim to determine optimal network setup parameters for each kind of network, the simulator only implements the physical and the MAC layer.

Nobre et al. in [5] develop a module for the NS-3 simulator. They focus on the implementation of the Physical layer in order to use it as the basis for the development of the other layers such as MAC and Application.

We find that there is only one full implementation. Indeed, Zand et al. propose in [6] an implementation of the Network Manager as well as the whole WirelessHART stack. The simulator is developed on NS-2 and validated using sniffed traffic from a real testbed. However, this implementation does not focus on security aspects of WirelessHART as it is developed to assess performances and to test several routage and scheduling algorithms.

We chose to develop our own simulator, primarily for getting a complete implementation (including network devices and the Network Manager) and also to have an adapted environment to conduct studies on WirelessHART security mechanisms. It also permits to built basic and complex attack scenarios. Therefore, we use OMNet++ which is more flexible and easy handling than other simulation frameworks.

3   WirelessHART Standard Overview

3.1   Topology of a WirelessHART Network

A typical WirelessHART network, illustrated in Fig. 1, is composed of the following devices:

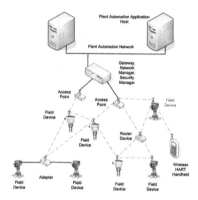

Fig. 1. Example of a WirelessHART network [7]

- a Gateway that connects the wireless network to the plant automation network, allowing data to flow between the two networks. It can be also used to convert data and commands from one protocol to another one;
- a Network Manager that is responsible for the overall management, scheduling, and optimization of the wireless network. It generates and maintains all of the routing information and also allocates communication resources;
- a Security Manager that is responsible for the generation, storage, and management of cryptographic keys;
- Access Points that connect the Gateway to the wireless network (a wired connection);
- Field devices deployed in the plant field and which can be sensors or actuators;
- Routers used for forwarding packets from one network device to another;
- Handheld devices that are portable equipments operated by the plant personnel used in the installation and maintenance of network devices.

3.2 WirelessHART Stack

WirelessHART [1] is based in its physical layer upon the IEEE 802.15.4 standard [8] and shares the same application layer with the wired HART protocol (with the add of wireless commands). It defines its own network layer and data link layer. A brief description of WirelessHART protocol stack is given below:

- The Physical Layer (PhL): it is based on IEEE 802.15.4-2006 standard and operates in the 2.4 GHz. It is responsible for wireless transmission and reception. It implements Time Division Multiple Access (TDMA), channel hopping and channel blacklisting.
- The Data Link Layer (DLL): it is responsible for preparing packets for transmission, managing time slots and updating different tables. It provides hop-by-hop authentication.
- The Network Layer (NL): it ensures end-to-end integrity and confidentiality. It provides routing features and receives packets from the Data Link Layer. It checks if they have to be transmitted to the Application Layer or have to be resent to the Data Link Layer in order to be forwarded to the next device.
- The Transport Layer (TL): it provides mechanisms to ensure data delivery without losses, duplication or misordering to its final destination. It supports acknowledged and unacknowledged transactions.
- The Application Layer (AL): it is a command based layer. It is used to send sensing data from field devices to Network Manager, and to send commands from the Network Manager to field devices. Additionally to WirelessHART commands, it also supports common HART commands (inherited from wired version).

4 WirelessHART Implementation

In this section we present an overview of each WirelessHART protocol layer and details of their implementation:

4.1 Physical Layer Implementation

The OMNet++ extension InetManet [9] provides the implementation of several wireless protocols, including the full stack of the IEEE 802.15.4 protocol [8]. Therefore and as WirelessHART physical layer is based on the IEEE 802.15.4 one, we use the implementation provided by InetManet as an implementation of the Physical Layer of our simulator.

4.2 Data Link Layer Overview

Time Division Medium Access (TDMA): WirelessHART uses Time Division Medium Access (TDMA) to control access to the medium. It provides collision free and deterministic communication between two wireless devices.

Each communication between two devices occurs in one slot of 10 ms. Superframes are collection of slots repeated continuously with a fixed repetition rate. Typically, two devices are assigned to one time slot (i.e., one as the sender and the second as the receiver). Only one packet is transmitted in one slot from the sender to the receiver which has to reply with an acknowledgment packet in the same slot. In the case of a broadcast message, there is one sender and multiple receivers and the message is not acknowledged.

Channel Hopping and Blacklisting: To enhance reliability, channel hopping is combined with TDMA to provide frequency diversity and avoid interferences. Each slot is used on multiple channels at the same time by different nodes. The 2.4 GHz band is divided into 16 channels numbered from 11 to 26 (channel 26 is not used) which provides up to 15 communications in the same slot. So, each slot is identified by a number called Absolute Slot Number (ASN) and a channel offset. The ASN represents the count of elapsed slots since the start of the network and the communication channel is retrieved from the *ActiveChannelArray*.

WirelessHART also allows channel blacklisting. The Administrator can restrict the channel hopping by the devices to selected channels. This can be done for example in order to avoid interferences on some channels caused by another wireless network. Thus, the *ActiveChannelArray* represents the active channel used in the network.

Data Link Protocol Data Unit (DLPDU): In WirelessHART there are five (05) DLPDU types:

1. Data DLPDU: it encapsulates packet from the network layer in transit to their final destination device. The source and the destination for Data DLPDUs is the Network Layer;
2. Ack DLPDU: it is the immediate link level response that is received by the source after transmitting an unicast DLPDU;
3. Keep-alive DLPDU: it is used for maintaining connections between neighboring devices;
4. Advertise DLPDU: it is used for providing information to neighboring devices trying to join the network;
5. Disconnect DLPDU: it is used to inform neighboring devices that the device is leaving the network.

We should note that Ack, Advertise, Keep-Alive and Disconnect DLPDUs are generated and consumed in Data Link Layer and are not propagated to the Network Layer or forwarded through the network.

4.3   Data Link Layer Implementation

We modify the implementation of the MAC layer of the IEEE 802.15.4 protocol provided in InetManet to support TDMA, channel hopping, slot communication, and modify Data frame format. We also add communication tables used in DLL and their relationship as neighbor table, link table, graph table, and superframe table.

We use a *timer* to simulate the start of a slot. Thus, each 10ms the node wakes up and identifies the current slot. On the base of information in Link Table, an indication is sent to the Physical layer to put the transceiver in reception or transmission mode. In transmission mode, the appropriate DLPDU is selected from the buffer based on the destination address.

4.4 Network Layer Implementation

In the Network layer, we implement graph routing support and session mechanism to ensure end-to-end reliability as retry. We merge it with the Transport layer to ensure end-to-end acknowledgment and assembly/fragmentation. We also add routing table and correspondent table (Table making relation between an end-receiver and a route to it).

The Network Layer is responsible for routing the packet sent by the Application Layer. The address of the next hop is recovered from the routing table using the final destination address.

When a packet is received from the DLL, the Network Layer checks the destination address field. The packet is either passed to the Application Layer or sent again to the Data link Layer to be forwarded to the next hop.

4.5 Transport Layer Implementation

In our implementation, we choose to merge the Transport Layer into the Network Layer. We implement only acknowledgment and retry mechanisms.

4.6 Application Layer Overview

The Application Layer of WirelessHART is a command based layer. They are used by the Network Manager to configure nodes with routing and scheduling information.

Routing Strategy: In WirelessHART, communications rely on graph and source routing. Graph routing is used for commands and data transmission while source routing is used for maintenance purpose. The construction of routing table is an important feature of the Network Manager. It is based on information transmitted to the Network Manager by wireless devices through health reports.

A basic routing strategy is summarized below.

1. If there is a one hop path to the gateway it should be used.
2. The maximum number of hops to be considered when constructing the initial graph is 4.
3. Minimize the ratio of signal strength on number of hops.

Scheduling Strategy: The Network Manager executes the scheduling algorithm to allocate slots to wireless devices. To do that, it needs to have a good knowledge about the network topology and connections quality between devices. The scheduling algorithm is executed each time a new device joins the network and when significant changes are reported.

WirelessHART do not provide a scheduling algorithm but proposes the strategy summarized below:

1. **Data superframes:**
   (a) Slots are allocated starting with the fastest to the slowest scan rate.
   (b) Starting from the device furthest from the gateway, one link for each en-route network device to the gateway is allocated. A 2nd dedicated slot for retry is also allocated.
   (c) Each transmission is also scheduled with a retry on another path, if one is available.
   (d) One network device can only be scheduled to receive once in a slot.
   (e) Event notification shares data slots.
2. **Management superframe:**
   (a) Management superframe has priority over data superframes.
   (b) The graph should be traversed by breathfirst search, starting from the gateway.
   (c) It includes Advertisement slots and command request/response slots.

4.7   Application Layer Implementation

We implement only necessary commands which can be classified into several categories: managing routing and graphs, managing superframes and links, and network health report commands.

We choose to implement the Network Manager, the Gateway and the Security Manager as the same entity. The Network Manager is based on the implementation of WirelessHART device. We add at its Application Layer several management algorithms for routing and communication scheduling. Each time a new device joins the network, these algorithms are executed to:

- provision the joining device with necessary credential (nickname and keys),
- create a downlink graph from the Network Manager to the joining device,
- allocate communication scheduling,
- and to update parent's tables with routing and scheduling information.

In the Network Manager's Application layer, we implement routing and scheduling algorithms. The routing algorithm creates for each node two graphs (an uplink graph from the node to the Network Manager and a downlink graph from the Network Manager to the node). Based on these graphs, the Network Manager builds routing tables using the Dijkstra algorithm. The link weight on these graphs is function of the Received Signal Strength Indication (RSSI) between both vertices of the link.

The scheduling algorithm allocates a sending slot (and another one for retry) from each node to the Network Manager following the uplink graph in order to transmit the sensing data. It also allocates a sending slot from the Network Manager to each node following the downlink graph for command request and another one following the uplink for command response.

4.8 WirelessHART Procedures Implementation

After implementing the WirelessHART stack, the Network Manager and the field devices, we implemented some WirelessHART procedures. These procedures include joining process, advertisement, neighbor discovery and disconnect. A procedure is a set of actions leading to execute an exchange sequence. Some of them such as joining are executed at different layers.

An advertisement is an invitation sent by a device which is already part of the wireless network to new devices wanting to join the network. It contains needed information as current ASN, Join links which are slots in which a new device can send a join request.

The joining process, illustrated in Fig. 2, is an exchange sequence between a device wanting to join the wireless network and the Network Manager. It also includes a proxy device which is a device acting as the parent of the new device during this procedure. During this process, the new device, previously configured with a Join Key (used as a session key), sends a join request to the Network Manager through the proxy device. The Network Manager after checking the request responds to the device by sending a nickname and session keys. The Network Manager will also create a downstream to the new device and configure all devices belonging to it. Finally, communication schedule will be allocated and transmitted to the new device and its parents. At the end of this procedure, the new device is entirely integrated in the network and starts to send sensing data to the Network Manager.

5   WirelessHART Security

5.1   WirelessHART Security Overview

WirelessHART implements several mechanisms to ensure data confidentiality, authenticity and integrity in hop-by-hop and end-to-end transmissions.

The hop-by-hop transmission security is provided by the Data Link Layer (DLL) using a cryptographic key called "Network Key" shared by all devices part of the wireless network. It defends against attackers who are outside the network and do not share its secret (Outside attacker). The end-to-end security is provided by the Network Layer (NL) using a cryptographic key called "Session Key" known only by the two communicant devices. It defends against attackers who may be on the network path between the source and the destination (Inside attacker).

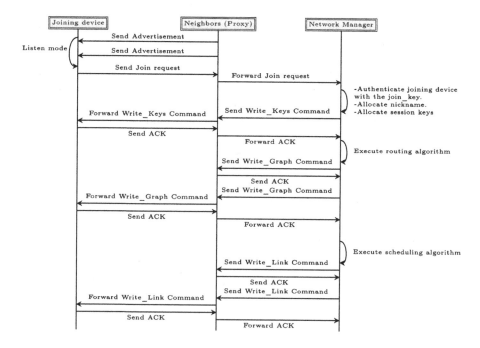

Fig. 2. Joining message exchange sequence

Security at Data Link Layer: To ensure hop-by-hop security a keyed Message Integrity Code (MIC) is implemented in Data Link Layer. In WirelessHART, each DLPDU is authenticated by the sending device using a cryptographic key shared by all devices part of the network. Therefore, before processing any received DLPDU, a device must check the MIC to verify the identity of the sending device. We must note that the DLPDU itself is not enciphered but authenticated by a four-byte MIC generated with CCM* mode (Combined Counter with CBC-MAC (corrected)) using the AES-128 block cipher. Each device is configured with two kinds of cryptographic keys:

- The well-known key which is used in the Advertisement and joining process. It is identical for all devices and has a built in value set to *7777 772E 6861 7274 636F 6D6D 2E6F 7267* hexadecimal,
- and The network key which is used for all other DLPDUs. It is supplied by the Network Manager to a device when it joins the network.

Security at Network Layer: The network layer also uses a keyed Message Integrity Code (MIC) for the authentication of the Network Protocol Data Unit (NPDU). Additionally, it is used to encrypt and decrypt the NPDU payload. The end-to-end security is session oriented i.e., it provides a private and secure communication between a pair of network devices. Each session is defined by a dedicated

128-bits cryptographic key and a message counter which defends against replay attacks. It is also used to form the nounce used to generate the MIC.

Four sessions are set up as soon as any device joins the network. They allow the transmission of sensing data from a device to the Network Manager, and the transmission of commands from the Network Manager to a field device. Though, TDMA supports multicast communications, WirelessHART only supports unicast and broadcast communications. Indeed, each communication can be done in an unicast or a broadcast mode.

In addition, each device has a join session which cannot be deleted. The Join_key is the only key that is written once connecting to the device's maintenance port. It can also be updated by the Network Manager once the device is successfully connected. All other keys are distributed by the Network Manager.

5.2   WirelessHART Security Implementation

We implement all WirelessHART security mechanisms for hop-by-hop and end-to-end transmission and also cryptographic key management. Our simulator also allows to define different attack scenarios such as jamming, denial of service, wormhole and blackhole. A brief description of these attacks is given below.

- Jamming attack: in this kind of attacks, a malicious node emits periodically or continuously on one or more frequencies. This will create interferences which will disturb transmissions of nearby nodes.
- Denial of Service (DoS) attack: it can be executed by flooding a node. A malicious node sends a great amount of packets to a node. The targeted node will be overwhelmed and will not be able to receive legitimate packets.
- Wormhole and blackhole attacks: in this kind of attack a malicious node misleads routing algorithm by transmitting false information to the Network Manager. As result a part of the traffic will be redirected to the malicious node which can drop partially (wormhole) or totally (blackhole) packets.

5.3   Disconnect Sybil Attack Description

Additionally to simple attacks previously described, we can also conduct complex attacks such as sybil attacks [10]. Sybil attacks was first described by Douceur in [11]. He shows that in the absence of a central identification authority that checks correspondence between entity and identity, a malicious entity can present multiple identities. This kind of attack can be used to target several types of protocols in WSN such as distributed storage, routing, data aggregation, voting, fair resources allocation and misbehavior detection algorithms [12]. A disconnect attack is a sybil attack in which an attacker spoof the identity of a legitimate device by forging fake Disconnect DLPDU and setting the source address to the targeted device's address. As a result, the targeted device will be disconnected from the network since its device neighbors will remove it from their tables.

When a Disconnect DLPDU is received by a device, it removes the sending device from its neighbor list, and deletes all links connecting to the sending device. Also, the neighbors indirectly inform the network manager with health reports (i.e., periodic statistics transmitted to the Network Manager by each device about its neighbors) about the device disconnection. The Network Manager updates device's routing table to forward packets through other routes and reallocates disconnected device's resources (Ex.: slots). By that, the disconnected device has not anymore any allocated resources and shall go through a complete rejoin sequence. The overall message exchange is summarized in Fig. 3.

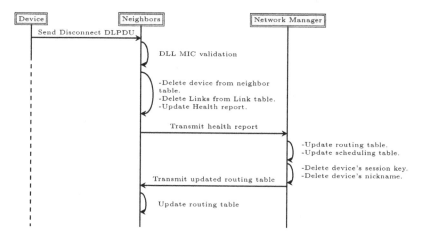

Fig. 3. Disconnect message exchange sequence

To perform a Disconnect Sybil Attack, an attackers only needs to know the Network Key. After a short listening period, it can gather all the required information before launching the attack [10].

5.4 Disconnect Sybil Attack Implementation

We implement an entirely automated attack in which a legitimate device usurps the identity of another device by forging a fake Disconnect DLPDU and setting the nickname (short address) of the target device as the source address of the forged DLPDU.

The implementation of the malicious device is based on the implementation of a WirelessHART device. Initially, the malicious device acts as a normal device. When triggered, it enters a search mode in which it waits for getting an Advertisement from the parent of the targeted device. When done, it will use the join link of the parent device to send to it the forged Disconnect DLPDU. At the reception of this DLPDU, the parent device validates it with the Network Key and processes it by removing the sending device from its neighbors table and also all links related to this device. By so, the targeted device is automatically disconnected from the network since it has not anymore any connection with its parent and has to go through the entire join procedure. The attack is summarized in Fig. 4.

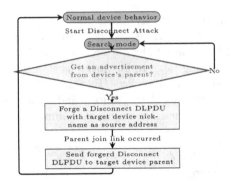

Fig. 4. Sybil disconnect attack

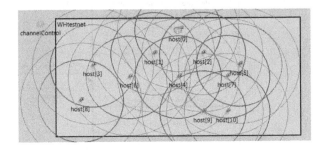

Fig. 5. Simulation network topology

6 Simulation Results

To test our simulator, we build a wireless network composed of one Network Manager and ten wireless devices as shown in Fig. 5. We start the simulation by initiating the network: the Network Manager begins to send Advertisement DLPDU and wireless devices enter joining procedure. Each time a new device joins the network, it will start to send sensing data at a periodic time of 4 s and advertisement DLPDU.

6.1 The Joining Process

Figure 6 illustrates the global topology of the wireless network as seen by the Network Manager after that all devices joined the network.

6.2 Data Sending

For simulating sensing data sending, each device, after the success of the joining procedure, starts to send sensing data at a periodic time of 4 s. As illustrated in Fig. 7, data reception frequency by the Network Manager is exactly 4 s, which indicates that our implementation fulfills realtime transmission requirements.

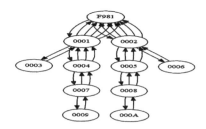

Fig. 6. Simulation network topology

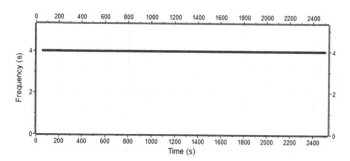

Fig. 7. Device 0x0004 Data sending frequency

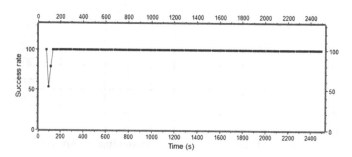

Fig. 8. Device 0x0004 Data sending success rate

We also analyze the sending success rate for each device which indicates the number of acknowledged packets by the total number of sent packets. Figure 8 shows that the sending success rate is 100 %.

7   Case Study: A Sybil Attack on WirelessHART SCADA-Based Systems

7.1   Disconnect Sybil Attack Results

To test the attack, we restart the simulation and we launch the Disconnect Sybil Attack at T = 800 s. The device with nickname 0x0003 is configured to be the

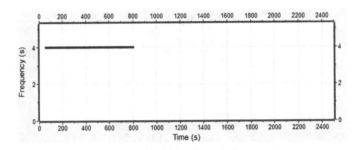

Fig. 9. Device 0x0004 Data sending frequency with attack

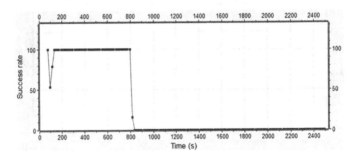

Fig. 10. Device 0x0004 Data sending success rate with attack

"malicious" device and the device with nickname 0x0004 will be the "target" device. The "parent" device will be the device with nickname 0x0001.

According to Fig. 9, we can see that in the beginning the Network Manager receives sensing data from target device at a fixed frequency of 4 s. When the attack is launched at T = 800 s the Network Manager stops to receive data from the target node. Figure 10 shows that the data send success rate for the target node falls quickly from 100 % to 0 % immediately after that the attack was conducted.

Comparatively to Fig. 8, in Fig. 10 we can see clearly that the target device is completely disconnected from the network and even if it continues to try to send its own packets or to forward packets received from its children devices, the success rate is 0 %. So by disconnecting a device we disconnect also its children (devices 0x0007 and 0x0009 in this case).

In Fig. 11 we variate the position of the target device to show the impact of the Disconnect Attack on the network charge. We can see that the decrease of the network load is directly correlated with the number of hops to reach the Network Manager and the number of its children. Consequently, an attack on a device situated at two hops (see Fig. 11(b)) decreases the network load by almost 37 %, an attack against a device situated at three hops (see Fig. 11(c)) decreases the network charge by 29 % and an attack against a device at four hops decrease it by 16 % (see Fig. 11(d)).

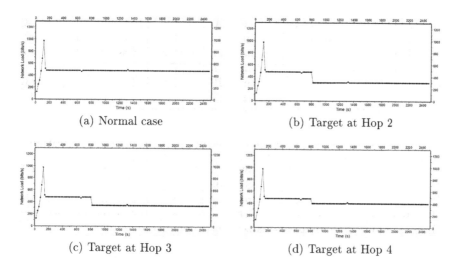

(a) Normal case   (b) Target at Hop 2

(c) Target at Hop 3   (d) Target at Hop 4

Fig. 11. Network load in byte "before and after attack"

8 Conclusion and Future Works

We describe in this paper a simulator for security analyzes of WirelessHART SCADA-based systems. This simulator implements the whole protocol stack and particularly its security mechanisms. We implemented several kinds of attacks to assess its robustness. The simulator allows us to test a complex attack in which a malicious node usurps the identity of a legitimate one. The simulation of this scenario demonstrates the feasibility of this attack and its harmful impact on the network. Moreover, the presented simulator can be used by researchers to test new attacks and disclose unknown vulnerabilities.

As future work, we aim to add multipath included in WirelessHART. This mechanism allow to a node to switch automatically from a path to another path if the first one used is unreachable. In another hand, as WirelessHART uses the same application layer that the wired protocol HART, we can study attack scenario against an infrastructure that mixes wired and wireless connections. So we can propose a complete security solution that cover all threats targeting industrial infrastructures.

References

1. HART Communication Foundation: WirelessHART. http://www.hartcom.org
2. OMNeT++. http://www.omnetpp.org/
3. De Biasi, M., Snickars, C., Landern, K., Isaksson, A.: Simulation of process control with wirelesshart networks subject to clock drift. In: 2014 IEEE 38th Annual Computer Software and Applications Conference, pp. 1355–1360 (2008)

4. De Dominicis, C., Ferrari, P., Flammini, A., Sisinni, E., Bertocco, M., Giorgi, G., Narduzzi, C., Tramarin, F.: Investigating wirelesshart coexistence issues through a specifically designed simulator. In: Instrumentation and Measurement Technology Conference, I2MTC 2009, pp. 1085–1090. IEEE, May 2009
5. Nobre, M., Silva, I., Guedes, L., Portugal, P.: Towards a wirelesshart module for the ns-3 simulator. In: 2010 IEEE Conference on Emerging Technologies and Factory Automation (ETFA), pp. 1–4, September 2010
6. Zand, P., Mathews, E., Havinga, P., Stojanovski, S., Sisinni, E., Ferrari, P.: Implementation of wirelesshart in the ns-2 simulator and validation of its correctness. Sensors **14**(5), 8633–8668 (2014)
7. Deji, C., Mark, N., Aloysius, M.: WirelessHART: Real-Time Mesh Network for Industrial Automation. Springer, US (2010)
8. IEEE 802.15.4-2006,: Standard for Local and metropolitan area networks-Part 15.4: Low-Rate Wireless Personal Area Networks (LR-WPANs). http://www.ieee.org
9. InetManet. https://github.com/aarizaq/inetmanet-2.0
10. Bayou, L., Espes, D., Cuppens-Boulahia, N., Cuppens, F.: Security issue of WirelessHART based SCADA systems. In: Lambrinoudakis, C., et al. (eds.) CRiSIS 2015. LNCS, vol. 9572, pp. 225–241. Springer, Heidelberg (2016). doi:10.1007/978-3-319-31811-0_14
11. Douceur, J.R.: The sybil attack. In: Druschel, P., Kaashoek, M.F., Rowstron, A. (eds.) IPTPS 2002. LNCS, vol. 2429, pp. 251–260. Springer, Heidelberg (2002)
12. Newsome, J., Shi, E., Song, D.X., Perrig, A.: The sybil attack in sensor networks: analysis & defenses. In: Ramchandran, K., Sztipanovits, J., Hou, J.C., Pappas, T.N. (eds.) Proceedings of the Third International Symposium on Information Processing in Sensor Networks, IPSN 2004, Berkeley, California, USA, 26–27 April, 2004, pp. 259–268. ACM (2004)

Remote Attestation for Embedded Systems

Markku Kylänpää[✉] and Aarne Rantala

VTT Technical Research Centre of Finland, Espoo, Finland
{markku.kylanpaa, aarne.rantala}@vtt.fi

Abstract. Large distributed systems, like Industrial Control Systems, should be able to verify that devices that are connected to trusted entities are real authorized network nodes running unmodified firmware. Remote attestation is a mechanism that can provide limited confidence of device identity and integrity. Remote attestation allows a remote verifier, e.g. a service provider, to verify integrity of the connecting system before providing a service. The current standard practice in remote attestation, defined by the Trusted Computing Group (TCG), is based on integrity measurements whose results are stored into an isolated trusted component called Trusted Platform Module (TPM) inside the system to be attested. The proof-of-concept scenario implementing similar functionality using an ARM processor secure environment is discussed. The implementation is done using ARM processor emulator which includes emulation for ARM TrustZone Trusted Execution Environment (TEE) providing isolated trusted component functionality. Challenges and security issues of the chosen approach are discussed.

Keywords: Embedded systems · Industrial control systems · Internet of things · Cyber-physical systems · Security · Attestation · Trusted execution environment

1 Introduction

1.1 Background

Nowadays many embedded devices also include network connectivity. The connection allows the devices to be configured and controlled remotely via network connection. The devices can also be a part of larger system like Industrial Control System (ICS). Industrial Internet, Cyber-Physical Systems (CPS), and Internet of Things (IoT) concepts also implicitly include connectivity. These systems can form large networks of sensor, actuator, and computing nodes that may cover large geographical area and multiple physical premises. From security point of view this also means that it is not easy to guarantee physical security of all network nodes. Important question is who is able to control this network. Embedded systems have often been designed as security as afterthought attitude and obscurity has protected these systems. Stuxnet incident [1] showed that also Industrial Control Systems can be a target for attacks.

In order to mitigate attack threats, security of network nodes should be improved. One way is to start to use secure hardware that provides secure boot and integrity protection for connected network nodes. However, this is often seen as too expensive

© Springer International Publishing Switzerland 2016
A. Bécue et al. (Eds.): CyberICS 2015/WOS-CPS 2015, LNCS 9588, pp. 79–92, 2016.
DOI: 10.1007/978-3-319-40385-4_6

and too complex for low-end devices like sensors. Low-end microcontrollers do not have any secure hardware elements. However, we can assume that things will improve during time, as security will become more important requirement. In future, availability of secure hardware even for low-end microcontrollers will be more wide spread.

In network communications it is crucial that identity and integrity of network nodes can be verified. Tamper resistant hardware and secure boot can be used to mitigate physical attack threats but it is still possible that attackers are able to utilize network connectivity and vulnerabilities in order to install modified firmware containing unauthorized software. Remote attestation provides a mechanism for service provider nodes to verify that the connecting device has only executed authorized software after boot and that the device has known identity.

1.2   Attestation Model

Trusted Computing Group (TCG) has created a series of specifications [2] that specify functionality of a co-processor chip called Trusted Platform Module (TPM) and also guidelines how it can be used for integrity measurements. A TPM chip includes a set of predefined functions and an array of integrity protected registers called Platform Configuration Registers (PCRs). There is also storage for RSA keys and the public key part can be certified. Integrity measurements are usually conducted in kernel for all userspace executables by calculating cryptographic hash of the executables during loading, using the measurement as one input in the *TPM_extend* function calculation, and storing the result into one of PCRs whose previous value was also used as the second input for the function. Measurement information is also appended to a measurement log that is typically maintained in kernel. Each component is measured only once unless the component is modified. An example of Linux-based integrity measurement implementation is described in [3]. Attestation scenario including intermediate steps is presented in Fig. 1.

Remote verifier can request state of a network node by sending an attestation request containing a nonce value (step 2 in Fig. 1.). The network node can then use the *TPM_quote* function to create a signed blob containing the received nonce and PCR values (step 3). The network node then sends the blob and the message log to the remote verifier who verifies the signature of the signed blob and also checks that the

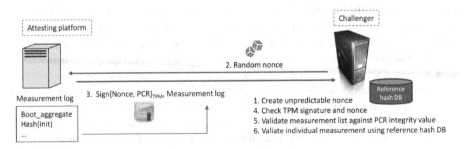

Fig. 1. Remote attestation basic scenario

nonce value is the same as in the request message (step 4). The verifier is expected to have reference integrity metrics so that the verifier can replay the message log verifying that the final PCR register value matches to the measurement log (step 5) and also that all measured components are part of authorized software image (step 6).

1.3 Challenges

The basic TCG attestation scenario presented in Fig. 1 is relatively simple but attestation systems have many challenges including the following:

1. TPM chip is common only in ×86 devices and is typically not available in embedded systems.
2. Attestation is based on measurements that are taken from executables during loading. If there are vulnerabilities, like buffer overflows, it is still possible that attackers are able to execute their malicious code in a way that is hidden from measurement mechanism.
3. Kernel-based measurement mechanism is by default able to measure native code program executables, shared libraries and also scripts that are started as commands. However, if scripts include other scripts files or if bytecode is loaded to virtual machine then these are not measured by default.
4. The verifier must store a large amount of software versions and reference integrity values in order to be able to verify the reply message. Maintaining configurations is difficult as software versions are regularly updated and heterogeneous systems multiply this effort.
5. Key management, certification, and identity management is a challenge in large distributed systems.

This study mainly deals with the first problem by utilizing ARM TrustZone in low-cost systems without a separate TPM chip. As such our approach resembles Trusted Computing Group's Mobile Reference Architecture [4], although our simplified implementation is better suited to low-cost systems with resource-starved Trusted Execution Environments (TEEs). In Sect. 2 related work is presented and various attestation ideas are described. Section 3 presents our attestation architecture utilizing ARM TrustZone [5] based TEE and system components of our proof of concept prototype. In Sect. 4 addressing above-mentioned challenges, comparison to existing approaches, and implementation aspects of our architecture are discussed. Conclusions and potential future work are described in Sect. 5.

2 Related Work

2.1 Introduction

Several approaches have been proposed to solve some of challenges described in the previous section. Various approaches are analyzed in [6]. Also a survey article of mobile trusted computing [7] describes many of these approaches.

2.2 Software-Based Attestation

An approach, called software-based attestation, is trying to support remote attestation without security hardware element, like TPM. Early example is the Genuinity system [8] that was based on side-effects of the system that attackers cannot easily simulate. Another example SWATT [9] is used to calculate checksum of memory area in such a way that any modification to data affects to externally observable running time of the operation. Other examples of software-based attestation systems are Pioneer [10] and Conqueror [11]. However, software-based attestation schemes are considered to be impractical and unlikely to succeed without trusted hardware [12]. Shortcomings of software-based attestation are also analyzed in [13].

2.3 Property-Based Attestation

A concept called property-based attestation is trying to tackle complexity of multiple software configurations (challenge 4). Instead of relying on low-level cryptographic hash integrity measurements, higher-level properties could be used [14]. This approach would partially solve problems with multiple software configurations. However, this typically leads to addition of a new trusted actor to the system that is responsible of mapping low-level measurements to high-level properties. Although many property-based attestation schemes are proposed [15–17], technology is not widely deployed, partly due to lack of concrete use cases, difficulties on defining high-level properties, and lack of trusted mapping actor [18].

2.4 Hypervisor-Based Attestation

Utilizing hypervisor to do measurements from guest Virtual Machines (VMs) is proposed. HIMA [19] has moved integrity measurements to hypervisor level and is also using a separate management guest VM to store measurement lists of other guest VMs. Hypervisor provides isolation between the measurement target and the measurement agent. Hypervisor-based approaches need also mechanism to handle Time of Check to Time of Use (TOCTOU) based attacks. Attackers may find ways to modify executable code inside guest VM after it has been measured. Therefore HIMA is actively monitoring critical guest VM events and includes also memory protection so that guest VMs cannot modify measured executable code without awareness of HIMA. SIMA [20] is using a different approach by including special sensor agents, implemented as kernel modules, to secured guest VMs. The sensor agents communicate using mapped shared memory segments that are called blackboards. Both HIMA and SIMA are local solutions whereas the system described by Pardo-Castello and Lang [21] also includes a mechanism to communicate integrity measurements to a remote verifier.

2.5 Extending Microcontrollers

Low-end microcontrollers do not contain secure hardware like TPM chip or ARM TrustZone. There are attempts to systematically analyze architecture in order to detect what components are really needed to develop attestation architecture and to provide minimalist security framework [22, 23] and to provide extensions to microcontroller designs in a way that also supports remote attestation scenarios. SMART [24] and Sancus [25] both extend microcontroller designs e.g. 16-bit TI MSP430 [26] that is freely available in OpenCores [27]. TrustLite [28] and TyTAN [29] introduce a concept called Execution-Aware Memory Protection Unit (EA-MPU) and implement their design using Intel Siskiyou Peak 32-bit research platform.

2.6   TPM Mobile

Implementing TPM functionality utilizing a TEE, available in many processors used in embedded systems, is discussed in [30] and [4]. TPM Mobile abstracts TPM chip functionality to be a higher-level more abstract concept, called Protected Environment. Protected Environment is based on system components providing required isolation. TPM Mobile Reference Architecture [4] covers multiple ways of implementing isolated Protected Environment. This will ensure that TCG specifications are still usable with increasing diversity of secure hardware solutions like utilizing hardware isolation techniques (e.g. ARM TrustZone), hypervisor-based virtualization or dedicated core for the Protected Environment in multicore Application Specific Integrated Circuit (ASIC). GlobalPlatform compliant TEE is mentioned as one implementation option. The specification [4] also gives guidelines for implementation. TPM Mobile compliant implementation is recommended to use capabilities of the Protected Environment, should implement one or more of the application interfaces defined by TCG, and must implement at least one TCG-defined profile.

2.7   Measuring Non-native Code

Typical policy for integrity measurement mechanism like [3] only measures native executables, scripts started as programs, and data files read by the root user. This means that quite a lot executable content is not measured e.g. libraries for script interpreters, Java applications and libraries. Platforms like Android, where significant portion of functionality is implemented in Java bytecode, require measurement mechanisms that can also cover bytecode. Extending integrity measurement mechanism to Android Dalvik VM bytecode is described in [31].

2.8   Attestation Protocol

Attestation protocol to communicate attestation request and reply messages between the challenger and the verifier is described in high-level in Fig. 1. TCG Platform Trust Services contain more detailed specifications like utilizing attestation protocol bindings [32] with Trusted Network Connect (TNC) [33]. There are also other protocols that can be used to transfer attestation request and reply messages. Object Management Group (OMG) Data Distribution Service (DDS) based approach is described in [21].

3 Attestation Architecture for Embedded Devices

3.1 Introduction

Integrity of networked systems requires that integrity of network endpoints can be verified. Future Industrial Control Systems will be target of attacks and one target of attackers is to install modified software to the system. Remote attestation can provide limited integrity guarantees making systems more robust and protecting against attacks.

3.2 Utilizing ARM TrustZone as a Platform for Attestation

Many embedded devices are using ARM-based ASICs. Low-end ARM Cortex-M microcontroller family has only limited security functionality. High-end ARM Cortex-A family includes ARM TrustZone security architecture, which has long been used in mobile phones. We can assume that high-end design is in future affordable also for low-end targets although there will always be low-end applications that will use just the simplest available solution. One obstacle for adoption has been complex provisioning of ARM TrustZone security features as chipset manufacturers were mainly serving their high-volume customers. Nowadays some ARM TrustZone ASICs are field programmable (e.g. Freescale [34]) making it easier also for small system vendor to utilize this technology. ARM TrustZone provides security element functionality, which is more flexible than TPM as ARM TrustZone isolated execution environment is able to execute signed programs called Trusted Applications (TAs).

3.3 Attestation System Components

Instead of developing new attestation architecture we decided to emulate TCG TPM-based attestation architecture using ARM TrustZone and Trusted Execution Environment. As measurement and reporting parts of the architecture are very much dependent on the availability of a TPM chip, we decided to implement special TPM driver for Linux kernel that communicates with ARM TrustZone and Trusted Execution Environment (TEE) running our TA code. TPM register storage and extend function calculation are implemented using this ARM TrustZone based security element utilizing TPM-like interface. TPM should also contain RSA keypair that can be used to sign the current values of the protected registers and random nonce included in the attestation request. Also this is implemented utilizing TEE functionality. Using the signed message, measurement list, and reference values of authorized software, the challenger can verify integrity of the device by recalculating the measurement list. Main system components of the attestation architecture are described in Fig. 2.

Measurements are carried out using the Integrity Measurement Architecture (IMA) [35] Linux kernel component and the results are stored into the TPM. The presented architecture implements small subset of TPM functionality in software, as a Trusted Application (TA) protected by the ARM TrustZone Trusted Execution Environment (TEE) [36]. The TA generates an RSA keypair used to sign the attestation response, stores the keypair in Secure Storage and publishes the public key, maintains

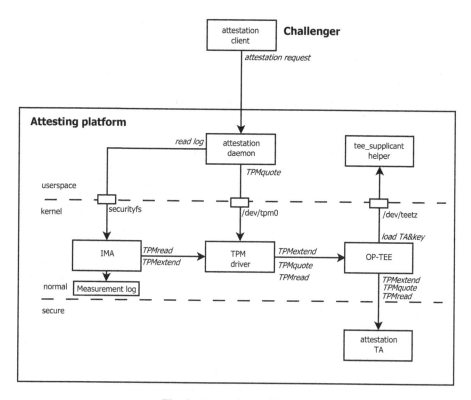

Fig. 2. Attestation architecture

Platform Configuration Registers (PCRs) in secure memory and implements their *TPM_extend*, *TPM_readPCR*, and *TPM_quote* operations. *TPM_extend* operation updates PCR contents with a new measurement and *TPM_quote* operation produces an appropriately signed attestation response from a given nonce and current values of chosen PCRs.

The demonstrator is an attestation scenario containing a challenger node sending an attestation request with a nonce value to the attesting platform that is running in a simulator. The challenger node includes a nonce to the attestation request as replay attack prevention. The challenger expects that the response message contains the same nonce and that the response message is signed by a private key known to belong exclusively to the responding trusted component. The kernel of the attesting platform includes a measurement component. A Trusted Application running in simulated TrustZone maintains PCR values and on request signs a set of PCR values and the nonce included in the request. Also measurement log is returned as part of the attestation reply message as seen in Fig. 1. The challenger is assumed to have access to a database that contains reference hash values for all firmware executables. The demonstrator is a software-only implementation running under Linux. The following system components are used:

- **Bootloader** – As a bootloader the system is using UEFI bootloader [37] with ARM Trusted Firmware components [38]. UEFI has been configured to use customized initramfs and then mount OpenEmbedded Linux root filesystem image. IMA kernel command line parameters have been added to UEFI configuration in order to support IMA specific kernel options.
- **Trusted Execution Environment** – Linaro OP-TEE [39] is used as Trusted Execution Environment (TEE).
- **Attestation TA** – Trusted Application (TA) has been developed to implement limited TPM functionality and to store PCR values.
- **Kernel** – Linux kernel with IMA functionality enabled is used. TPM driver has been developed as without TPM IMA does not try to extend PCR register value with new measurement and it cannot be used for attestation. TPM driver is implemented as a static kernel module. Also OP-TEE Linux kernel driver was configured as a static kernel module. TPM driver implements a set of commands using OP-TEE and attestation TA.
- **Initramfs** – Custom initramfs contains OP-TEE userspace helper application tee_supplicant, developed Trusted Applications, and secure storage to store device key. The helper application tee_supplicant is started from initramfs. IMA has been configured not to measure initramfs files which are already verified as initramfs is part of kernel image that is verified in secure boot.
- **Userspace** – Linux distribution OpenEmbedded [40] was used in the demonstrator. An attestation daemon is added to the filesystem image and is configured to start from init scripts after boot. The daemon is listening incoming attestation requests.
- **Attestation components and protocols** – Simple custom attestation protocol is used in the demonstrator. The system includes an attestation daemon that is listening incoming attestation requests and sends *TPM_quote* requests to TPM.

Linux kernel IMA component has been configured to measure loaded executables. As TPM interface is found the measurements are stored into PCRs of TPM by using *TPM_extend* operation. Attestation reply contains PCR values with random data nonce signed using the private key of the TPM. In the demonstrator architecture shown in Fig. 2 measurements are stored by pseudo TPM driver. The driver implements PCR registers using OP-TEE attestation TA. Userspace component, the attestation daemon, can receive attestation requests and sends *TPM_quote* calls to the TPM. IMA is generating measurements that are pushed into TPM. The TPM is utilizing OP-TEE kernel API to access TEE and extend PCR values that are implemented in the attestation TA only and can only be modified using *TPM_extend* as in real TPM chip. Userspace component, the attestation daemon, is communicating only with TPM interface and OP-TEE userspace client API is not used.

Instead of using real hardware e.g. ARM development board a free ARM simulator called Fixed Virtual Platform (FVP) [41] is used to simulate ARM processor architecture. FVP simulates also ARM TrustZone so it is possible to implement components to ARM Secure Environment.

4 Discussion

4.1 Addressing Attestation Challenges

In Sect. 1.3 we listed couple of challenges related to remote attestation. Our system effectively solves the first challenge, lack of TPM chip in embedded devices, by implementing required TPM functionality using ARM TrustZone-based TEE. The second challenge is common to all attestation mechanisms, as measured code may still contain vulnerabilities like buffer overflows. However, as our approach is not based on hypervisor-based measurements, we do not need complex TOCTOU consistency checking mechanisms to ensure that guest VM does not modify executables measured by the hypervisor. On the other hand we must trust in kernel and secure boot. Lack of non-native code measurements (challenge 3) may not be such a big issue in Industrial Control System context if majority of software is native code software. Also system configurations in Industrial Control Systems are more fixed than in general purpose computers making challenge 4 (need to store lots of configuration information) more tolerable. Challenge 5 (key management) requires establishing PKI system. Field programmable ASICs are required.

4.2 Comparison to Other Attestation Approaches

In Sect. 2 several attestation approaches are described. Software-based attestation mechanisms should only be considered if there is no secure hardware as basing attestation only in side-effects is not considered sufficient [12]. Our approach is utilizing secure hardware and measures executable code. Property-based attestation requires that each system to be attested includes a trusted mapping actor and that there is a mapping from low-level measurements to high-level properties. According to [18] it has been difficult to agree on what these high-level properties are. Adoption of property-based attestation mechanisms has been slow. In Industrial Control System context the local mapping agent could just verify the firmware version and report the version information as a property for the verifier who has a catalogue of trusted software versions. However, even this adds lots of information to the attested system that needs to be integrity protected. In comparison our system requires just an implementation of measurement mechanism that would be also needed in property-based attestation scenarios.

Hypervisor-based attestation solutions provide isolation of measurement agent. However, hypervisor layer also adds complexity and is unnecessary if there is just one guest VM. Hypervisor-based attestation examples also contain TPM chip that is just only accessed via hypervisor layer. So this approach is either not suitable for systems that do not have TPM chip or TPM functionality must be simulated as in our system. Hypervisor-based systems also need additional mechanism to prevent TOCTOU based attacks in guest VM. Our approach assumes that in future ARM TrustZone enabled microcontrollers will be used in safety critical systems whereas other designs are trying to modify low-end microcontrollers so that those can be used to support remote attestation.

Our approach resembles one of TPM Mobile TEE-based implementation option. TPM Mobile is generic specification allowing Protected Environment to be implemented in many different ways including TEE-based implementation. TEE Mobile does not set strict requirements to use of GlobalPlatform TEE features. However, implementation of at least one TCG profile is mandatory. In our system only attestation specific TPM functions are implemented as there is no need to support additional TCG functionality e.g. sealing. Smaller functionality set would make it possible to implement our solution also in resource constrained TEE environments.

Non-native code measurement requires modifications to script interpreters and bytecode VMs but basically also our system can be modified to support these measurements for example in similar way as in [30]. Currently our system is using custom attestation protocol but could be adapted to utilize other alternatives.

4.3   Implementation Challenges

TPM functionality is implemented using an OP-TEE Trusted Application (TA) utilizing Global Platform Internal API [42] for cryptographic and secure storage operations. The PCRs are stored in TrustZone secure RAM memory area. The asymmetric key pair needed in signing responses to *TPM_quote* requests belongs solely to the attestation TA. Therefore, even if some malware were able to completely penetrate the public side OS, it could neither change PCR values nor sign bogus *TPM_quote* responses with the recognized key pair. The attestation TA implements operations for initializing the signing key pair and PCRs, displaying and extending PCR values and producing *TPM_quote* response. The TA was implemented using the supplied example [3] as a starting point.

There are problems with utilization of attestation TA to perform TPM-like operations to support IMA. IMA starts to make measurements in early boot and by calculating so called boot_aggregate (SHA1 hash over registers PCR0-PCR7). IMA code is reading the PCR values and is then using *TPM_extend* operation to update the PCR10 value. However, attestation TA is loaded from initramfs and the volume is not yet even mounted when IMA initialization is run. Another problem is that by default IMA is also trying to measure initramfs executables, which could cause a deadlock when measuring tee_supplicant executable as attestation TA that is supposed to handle measurements is loaded from initramfs and is not available early enough. Another problem is that because also secure storage is in initramfs updates to secure storage are lost. This is not a problem in attestation use case although it adds complexity for device labelling phase.

There are ways to solve this problem:

- **Delayed invocation** – Store *TPM_extend* request values in kernel during early boot and extend attestation TA PCRs only after tee_supplicant userspace process has started from initramfs and the attestation TA has been loaded. IMA generates eight *TPM_readPCR* and one *TPM_extend* operations during early boot. These events correspond to the first measurement called boot_aggregate, which measures current values of PCR register. The TPM driver should display zero value for read operations and should delay the first *TPM_extend* operation.

- **Disable initramfs IMA measurements** – An attempt to measure tee_supplicant executable when it is starting from initramfs would cause a deadlock. IMA should be configured to disable initramfs measurements. If we are assuming secure boot this should be safe as initramfs is part of kernel image and if there is some kind of secure boot then initramfs is verified when the kernel has been verified. All initramfs programs are implicitly verified during secure boot as secure boot should fail if integrity check fails.
- **Self-loading** – Instead of relying on userspace component tee_supplicant to load trusted applications, the kernel itself could load trusted applications. The loading should happen before the first measurement is done but after the filesystem has been mounted. There could be a special partition for TAs or alternatively TA binary could be embedded into kernel image.
- **Secure storage area** – Currently the secure storage area is part of initramfs. There should be separate non-rootfs filesystem to store secure storage to prevent loss of updates and to ease labelling phase.
- **Bootloader loading** – TrustZone can be initialized also in bootloader phase and also attestation TA could be loaded by bootloader. This may actually be needed to fully support trusted/secure boot as all components have to be verified.

The current implementation is using delayed invocation approach and all IMA measurements for initramfs have been disabled. As initramfs is part of the kernel image and loading kernel image is part of the Secure Boot phase [4] trust chain integrity is preserved.

The current implementation also largely ignores issues related to trustworthiness of the attestation response signing key. The only support function in this area is displaying the public signing key (i.e. the modulus of the RSA keypair – it is assumed that the public exponent 0x10001 is always used) when the signing keypair is generated. However, that public key is currently neither certified nor sent to the challenger.

5 Conclusions and Future Work

An overview of the building blocks to develop ARM TrustZone aware remote attestation system is given and demonstration implementation and implementation related challenges are discussed. Attestation TA to implement TPM-like functionality to support attestation use case has been developed. Attestation TA is called from kernel-based software TPM implementation that is used by kernel IMA component. Main challenges have been synchronizing initialization of components in early boot. Use of processor simulator instead of ARM-based development board is a cost effective way to develop low-level software. However, performance evaluation cannot be done.

Remote attestation can be used to verify integrity of connected devices. However, as attestation measurements are only taken during startup and loaded executable files are verified, it is always possible that attackers are able to utilize existing vulnerabilities (e.g. buffer overflows) to load their code for execution. Another weakness is that only native executables and scripts started as commands are verified by default. Script files that are included to other scripts and bytecode executables for virtual machines are not measured by default.

Future work could consist of updating the demonstrator to utilize ARM TrustZone aware open source qemu emulator instead of using FVP emulator. Qemu provides better system emulation allowing simulated system to also use graphical user interfaces. One platform option is also to use real ARM TrustZone-based hardware. Another future work item is to move TEE initialization and TA loading to bootloader phase and to use separate partition as secure storage area. IMA-based measurement mechanism also has limitations. The default IMA policy only measures native executables, scripts started as commands, and files read by the root user. For example Java applications are libraries are data files from IMA point of view. The measurement mechanism should be extended to various script and bytecode interpreters.

In order to ensure the trustworthiness of attestation response signing keys, the next phase should be either storing the public key in a database of trusted public keys or certifying it and utilizing Public Key Infrastructure (PKI) [43]. In the latter approach the resulting attestation certificate can be stored in the device, in the challenger or anywhere else deemed appropriate, and it can be revoked when it is no more trustworthy. Therefore, utilizing PKI is the preferred option because of its flexibility and existing software support.

Acknowledgements. The work presented here has been carried out in two research projects launched by the Finnish Strategic Centre for Science, Technology and Innovation Digile Ltd.: the IoT Program (2012–2015) and CyberTrust (2015).

References

1. Kushner, D.: The real story of stuxnet. Spectr. IEEE **50**(3), 48–53 (2013). doi:10.1109/MSPEC.2013.6471059
2. Trusted Computing Group: Trusted Platform Module (TPM) Specifications. http://www.trustedcomputinggroup.org/resources/tpm_main_specification
3. Sailer, R., Zhang, X., Jaeger, T., van Doorn, L.: Design and implementation of TCG-based integrity measurement architecture. In: Proceedings of the 13th USENIX Security Symposium, San Diego, CA, USA, August 2004
4. Trusted Computing Group: TPM 2.0 Mobile Reference Architecture Specification. http://www.trustedcomputinggroup.org/resources/tpm_20_mobile_reference_architecture_specification
5. ARM Ltd: TrustZone. www.arm.com/products/processors/technologies/trustzone/index.php
6. Coker, G., Guttman, J., Loscocco, P., Herzog, A., Millen, J., O'Hanlon, B., Ramsdell, J., Segall, A., Sheehy, J., Brian Sniffen, B.: Principles of remote attestation. Int. J. Inf. Secur. **10**(2), 63–81 (2011). doi:10.1007/s10207-011-0124-7
7. Asokan, N., Ekberg, J.-E., Kostiainen, K., Rajan, A., Rozas, C., Sadeghi, A.-R., Schulz, S., Wachsmann, C.: Mobile trusted computing. Proc. IEEE **102**(8), 1189–1206 (2014)
8. Kennell, R., Jamieson, L.H.: Establishing the genuinity of remote computer systems. In: Proceedings of the 12th USENIX Security Symposium, Washington D.C., USA, August 2003

9. Seshadri, A., Perrig, A., van Doorn, L., Khosla, P.: SWATT: softWare-based attestation for embedded devices. In: 2004 IEEE Symposium on Security and Privacy, Proceedings, pp. 272–282, 9–12 May 2004. doi:10.1109/SECPRI.2004.1301329

10. Seshadri, A., Luk, M., Shi, E., Perrig, A., van Doorn, L., Khosla, P.: Pioneer: verifying integrity and guaranteeing execution of code on legacy platforms. In: Proceedings of ACM Symposium on Operating Systems Principles (SOSP) (2005)

11. Martignoni, L., Paleari, R., Bruschi, D.: Conqueror: tamper-proof code execution on legacy systems. In: Kreibich, C., Jahnke, M. (eds.) DIMVA 2010. LNCS, vol. 6201, pp. 21–40. Springer, Heidelberg (2010)

12. Shankar, U., Chew, M., Tygar, J.D.: Side effects are not sufficient to authenticate software. In: Proceedings of the 13th Conference on USENIX Security Symposium, San Diego, CA, USA, August 2004

13. Castelluccia, C., Francillon, A., Perito, D., Soriente, C.: On the difficulty of software-based attestation of embedded devices. In: Proceedings of the 16th ACM Conference on Computer and Communications Security (CCS 2009), pp. 400–409. ACM, New York, NY, USA (2009). doi:10.1145/1653662.165371

14. Sadeghi, A.-R., Stüble, C: Property-based attestation for computing platforms: caring about properties, not mechanisms. In: Proceedings of the 2004 Workshop on New Security Paradigms (NSPW 2004), pp. 67–77. ACM, New York, NY, USA (2004). doi:10.1145/1065907.1066038

15. Kühn, U., Selhorst, M., Stüble, C.: Realizing property-based attestation and sealing with commonly available hard- and software. In: Proceedings of the STC 2007, ACM Workshop on Scalable Trusted Computing (2007)

16. Nagarajan, A., Varadharajan, V., Hitchens, M., Gallery, E.: Property based attestation and trusted computing: analysis and challenges. In: Proceedings of the NSS 2009, Network and System Security (2009)

17. Chen, L., Löhr, H., Manulis, M., Sadeghi, A.-R.: Property-based attestation without a trusted third party. In: Wu, T.-C., Lei, C.-L., Rijmen, V., Lee, D.-T. (eds.) ISC 2008. LNCS, vol. 5222, pp. 31–46. Springer, Heidelberg (2008)

18. Kostiainen, K., Asokan, N., Ekberg, J.-E.: Practical property-based attestation on mobile devices. In: McCune, J.M., Balacheff, B., Perrig, A., Sadeghi, A.-R., Sasse, A., Beres, Y. (eds.) Trust 2011. LNCS, vol. 6740, pp. 78–92. Springer, Heidelberg (2011)

19. Azab, A.M., Ning, P., Sezer, E.C., Zhang, X.: HIMA: a hypervisor-based integrity measurement agent. In: Proceedings of the 25th Annual Computer Security Applications Conference (ACSAC 2009), Honolulu, Hawaii, USA, December 2009

20. Stelte, B., Kock, R., Ullman, M.: Towards integrity measurement in virtualized environments – a hypervisor based sensory integrity measurement architecture (SIMA). In: Proceedings of the 2007 IEEE Conference on Technologies for Homeland Security, Woburn, MA, USA (2007)

21. Pardo-Castellote, G., Lang, U.: Trusted remote attestation for secure embedded systems, 04 March 2013, Embedded.com

22. Francillon, A., Nguyen, Q., Rasmussen, K.B., Tsudik, G.: A minimalist approach to remote attestation. In: Proceedings of the Conference on Design, Automation and Test in Europe (DATE 2014), Article 244, 6 p. European Design and Automation Association, 3001 Leuven, Belgium (2014)

23. Francilloin, A., Nguyen, Q., Rasmussen, K.B., Tsudik, G.: Systematic treatment of remote attestation. IACR Cryptology ePrint Arch. Article no. 2012, p. 713 (2012)

24. Eldefrawy, K., Tsudik, G., Francillon, A.: SMART: secure and minimal architecture for (establishing dynamic) root of trust. In: NDSS (2012)

25. Noorman, J., Agten, P., Daniels, W., Strackx, R., van Herrewege, A., Huygens, C., Preneel, B., Verbauwhede, I., Piessens, F.: Sancus: low-cost trustworthy extensible networked device

with a zero-software trusted computing base. In: Proceeding SEC 2013 Proceedings of the 22nd USENIX Conference on Security, pp. 479–494. USENIX Association Berkeley, CA, USA (2013)

26. MSP Low-Power Microcontrollers, Texas Instruments. http://www.ti.com/lit/sg/slab034ab/slab034ab.pdf

27. The OpenCores Project. http://opencores.org/

28. Koeberl, P., Schulz, S., Sadeghi, A.-R., Varadharajan, V.: TrustLite: a security architecture for tiny embedded devices. In: Proceeding EuroSys 2014 Proceedings of the Ninth European Conference on Computer Systems (2014)

29. Brasser, F., Koebert, P., El Mahjoub, B., Sadeghi, A.-R., Wachsmann, C.: TyTAN: tiny trust anchor for tiny devices. In: 52nd Design Automation Conference (DAC) 2015, June 2015

30. Trusted Computing Group: TPM MOBILE with Trusted Execution Environment for Comprehensive Mobile Device Security, White paper, June 2012. http://www. trustedcomputinggroup.org/files/static_page_files/5999C3C1-1A4B-B294-D0BC20183757815E/TPM%20MOBILE%20with%20Trusted%20Execution%20Environment%20for%20Comprehensive%20Mobile%20Device%20Security.pdf

31. Nauman, M., Khan, S., Zhang, X., Seifert, J.-P.: Beyond kernel-level integrity measurement: enabling remote attestation for the android platform. In: Acquisti, A., Smith, S.W., Sadeghi, A.-R. (eds.) TRUST 2010. LNCS, vol. 6101, pp. 1–15. Springer, Heidelberg (2010)

32. Trusted Computing Group: TCG Attestation PTS Protocol: Binding TNC IF-M, Specification Version 1.0, Revision 28, 24 August 2011

33. Trusted Computing Group: TNC Architecture for Interoperability, v1.3 (2008)

34. Freescale: Security Reference Manual for i.MX 6Dual, 6Quad, 6Solo, and 6DualLite Families of Application Processors, Document Number: IMX6DQ6SDLSRM, Rev. 0, March 2013

35. Safford, D., Kasatkin, D., Zohar, M., Sailer, R., Hallyn, S.: Integrity Measurement Architecture (IMA). http://sourceforge.net/p/linux-ima/wiki/Home/

36. Bech, J.: LCU14-103: How to create and run Trusted Applications on OP-TEE, Linaro, September 2014. http://www.slideshare.net/linaroorg/lcu14103-how-to-create-and-run-trusted-applications-on-optee

37. Unified Extensible Firmware Interface Forum: Home page. http://www.uefi.org

38. ARM: ARM Trusted Firmware, source code. https://github.com/ARM-software/arm-trusted-firmware

39. Linaro: OP-TEE, web page. https://wiki.linaro.org/WorkingGroups/Security/OP-TEE

40. OpenEmbedded: OpenEmbedded Linux distribution home page, web page. http://www.openembedded.org/wiki/Main_Page

41. ARM: ARM®v8 Foundation Model User Guide, Version: 1.0 (2013). http://infocenter.arm.com/help/index.jsp?topic=/com.arm.doc.dui0677b/index.html

42. Global Platform: Global Platform Specifications, web page. http://www.globalplatform.org/specificationsdevice.asp

43. Guttman, P.: Everything you Never Wanted to Know about PKI but were Forced to Find Out, University of Auckland. https://www.cs.auckland.ac.nz/~pgut001/pubs/pkitutorial.pdf

WOS-CPS 2015 Papers

LiMon - Lightweight Authentication for Tire Pressure Monitoring Sensors

Cristina Solomon and Bogdan Groza(✉)

Faculty of Automatics and Computers, Politehnica University of Timisoara,
Timisoara, Romania
cristina_solomon@ymail.com, bogdan.groza@aut.upt.ro

Abstract. Modern vehicles offer a raw territory for designing security solutions as the over-increasing design complexity demanded massive advances in electronics in the absence of a crisp vision over the adversary model. The vehicle Tire Pressure Monitoring System (TPMS) is a sub-system that recently triggered some attention in the light of several reported attacks. In this work we start from analyzing existing proposals and reckon some shortcomings, e.g., academic proposals are not yet tested on real-world components while a patented security solution from the industry (likely deployed in practice) is completely insecure. Motivated by these, we design a new solution and deploy it on real-world components that are used in the automotive industry. Designing security for this subsystem proves to be especially relevant as the computational resources for TPM systems are somewhat at the minimum to be found in automotive embedded devices. Our solution is deployed on Infineon SP37 sensors and takes advantage of some recently proposed light-weight cryptographic designs, e.g., SPECK and PRESENT.

Keywords: Authentication · Wireless sensors · Vehicles

1 Intoduction

Contemporary vehicles are a powerful example of a cyber-physical system with advanced functionalities, complex electronics, numerous communication interfaces and yet only sparse security layers. The urgent demand for adding security is proved by many of the recently reported attacks [5,14] to which so far there was little response from the industry.

The standard functionality for tire sensors is to monitor the pressure inside the tire which further impacts on at least three directions. First, it reduces tire wear and fuel consumption, resulting in cost efficiency on the driver's side. Second, it reduces $CO2$ emissions comforting the environment. Third, it improves the breaking distance and the control of the vehicle, thus having a positive effect on the safety of drivers and passengers. However, it is worth mentioning that a recent study showed the benefits of TPMS in reducing $CO2$ emissions to be only marginal [17]. Still, for safety and comfort the advantages of the system

© Springer International Publishing Switzerland 2016
A. Bécue et al. (Eds.): CyberICS 2015/WOS-CPS 2015, LNCS 9588, pp. 95–111, 2016.
DOI: 10.1007/978-3-319-40385-4_7

are undisputed. Besides pressure monitoring, the system usually monitors the temperature and acceleration. Future functionalities may include monitoring for tire wear and adapting driving characteristics to the tire specifications (e.g., winter vs. summer tire). The TPMS system became mandatory in the US since 2008 and in the EU since 2014.

Generally, there are two distinct kind of implementations: (i) direct systems (the common choice and the subject of this work) in which a sensor is located inside the tire and (ii) indirect systems which rely on information from the ABS (improperly inflated tires lead to detectable differences when breaking, but such systems are inaccurate and not commonly used). While some TPMS deployments were initially based on four receivers, one nearby each wheel, the current trend is to have a single receiver that gathers the frames from each wheel sensor. This lowers the production cost, but has the additional disadvantage that the system has to learn or be set to recognize the exact wheel from which the data originates. This association is done either by active learning, e.g., by correlating the acceleration reported by the sensor with the acceleration independently reported by the ABS system on each wheel, or it is set in an off-line manner with a diagnosis tool based on the ID of each sensor.

SECURITY ISSUES. The TPMS is considered part of the safety system of the car since improperly inflated tires can lead to accidents with catastrophic consequences. Still, security mechanisms are completely absent from such systems and recent research works [12] were quick in determining several attacks on such platforms: eavesdropping can be easily performed at a range of 10m (and with improved instrumentation at up to 40 m), vehicles can be tracked by using the ID that is broadcast by the sensors, packets can be injected in the system, triggering false alarms on the display (beside the obvious discomfort, these may determine the driver to stop the car for inspection which could cause further incidents), battery drainage is possible if there are packets that could trigger an immediate response from the sensors. The attacks presented in [12] require just an average adversary that is in possession of some easy to find radio equipments. Further capabilities of the adversary such as side-channel attacks can be mentioned, but these do not appear to be a serious concern yet.

While so far the information from the TPMS system has only a passive (informative) role, the recent patent application for TPMS security from Continental [16] proves that the industry is aware and concerned by such attacks. The patent suggests that the main concern is on the fact that the driver can be determined to stop the car in case that an adversary injects data claiming that the tires are under-inflated [16] (a similar scenario is also outlined in the work that initially showed these attacks [12]). Clearly, threats can become much more serious in the near future if information from the TPMS sensors will be also actively used by breaking or stability controls inside the car. As a consequence to these, opening road for research in this direction is clearly necessary.

2   Analysis of Previous Proposals

To the best of our knowledge there are only two previous proposals for assuring security in TPMS sensor systems. The first is a proposal from the academic research community [18] and the second is the patent application from Continental [16] which may be already deployed on the market.

We discuss both these proposals in what follows but let us note from the beginning that, probably not surprising, the proposals are situated on two extremes. The patent [16] tries to build an inexpensive solution by garnering what already exists on the sensors but fails to result in a secure protocol. Xu et al. [18] provide a rigorous security design but the experimental results are obtained on an Arduino platform which makes it unclear if the solution can be readily deployed on real world TPM systems.

CONTINENTAL'S PATENT EP2719551 [16]. On the positive side, this appears to be the first attempt from the industry to address these security issues. At the very least the patent shows that the industry is aware of the problem and the solution can be viewed as an improvement to the no-security option. On the negative side, the solution completely fails in assuring security as the proposed mechanism can be trivially broken, moreover, the brief security analysis provided in the patent application is wrong (as we discuss next). The solution works as follows: two PRNGs are used (both implemented around a CRC polynomial) one for the wheel unit, the other for the receiver. Since there are four wheels, each wheel has its own PRNG built on the same CRC code but initialized with a distinct seed, while the receiver keeps 4 instances, one for each of them. A seed, generated from data that is exchanged between the wheel units and the receiver at vehicle start-up, is used as input to the PRNG and the output (referred as authentication marker) is XORed with the CRC of each message in order to assure authentication. We now enumerate the problems in this proposal starting with the more severe ones:

1. CRCs (Cyclic Redundancy Checks) are used to build an *authentication marker*. It is commonly known that while CRCs can assure integrity checks (against unintentional errors) they fail in assuring authenticity (even if one embeds a secret key in the construction) because they are linear transformations. Each packet sent from the wheel unit has its CRC XORed with an authentication marker that is generated by another CRC over a secret seed, i.e., $data||CRC(data)\oplus CRC(seed)$. Obviously, this protection is useless, since CRCs are linear transformations one can simply XOR the genuine data with a distinct value and do the same for the CRC and the packet will be valid, i.e., $data \oplus data'||CRC(data) \oplus CRC(seed) \oplus CRC(data')$. Thus breaking the scheme is effortless and does not require to find the secret key at all.

2. The secret seed can be easily found. The patent is not really clear on the size of the underlying CRC code, however under paragraph [0034] it claims that it can be very light, 8 bits being sufficient since for an emission period of 60 seconds since to observe the full period of 256 rounds one would need 4.25 hours. This claim actually misses the fact that the CRC, being a LFSR,

can be broken just after witnessing a sequence equal to its size, in this case 8 packets. This makes the time required to gather enough information for recovering the seed at around 8 min instead of 4.25 hours.

3. The key-sharing procedure for exchanging the seed between the wheel units and the central receiver has no protection at all. Since there is no cryptography implemented on the nodes, the seed value is exchanged unencrypted when the system starts. This makes it easy to mount an attack if the adversary witnesses the communication right from the beginning. But in the light of the previous attacks, this would be a minor issue.

4. A final problem are the ambiguities in the patent. For example the patent claims that "at least a part of each data packet is encoded with an authentication marker" but fails to make it clear which part. Since such information can be easily revealed by a simple analysis of the packet we believe that such ambiguities were not demanded by technical concerns (i.e., making the mechanism more secure, since in fact it isn't at all secure) but rather by legal issues (i.e., making the patent cover a larger area of applications). The same ambiguities are in describing the exact security level that is expected, i.e., the size of the secret seed, the CRC polynomial, etc. While avoiding such details may help in extending the legal range of the patent, this solution is insecure and it is highly unlikely for it to have any practical benefits.

XU ET AL. [18]. The protocol is well designed, particularly targeting spoofing and tracking attacks. The core of the protocol is built around the 32-bit symmetric encryption algorithm KATAN and uses CBC-MAC to assure message authentication. Additionally, a LFSR is used to generated sequential numbers that look pseudo-random in order to prevent replay-attacks (the use of a simple counter is avoided in order to prevent tracking of the device, as sequence numbers are predictable). To ensure privacy, as vehicles can be tracked by the use of the sensor's ID, a pseudo-ID is randomly generated before the generation of each session key. A proof-of-concept implementation is provided on an Arduino based platform. The shortcoming that we see for this proposal is that it is deployed on a platform that does not matches the real-world deployments, our experimental analysis showed that KATAN is too intensive for real-world TPMS sensors. We give more details on the real-world system specification in the following section.

3   Experimental Setup

The devices used in our experiments are two dedicated TPMS development kits from Infineon. The first is the SP37T development kit [9], used for programming the TPMS sensors. This is a real-world TPMS sensor used by leading car manufacturers. It is based on a standard 8051 low performance microcontroller. Beside the microcontroller and the TPMS specific sensors, the development kit includes a LF receiver, a RF transmitter unit and an ADC converter for signal conditioning. Because power consumption is an essential aspect for a TPMS sensor, the SP37 sensor has a low power design and several low power operating modes. The power consumption peak lies in the RF transmission, which means that the shorter the sent telegrams are, the longer the battery lifetime will be. The SP37 sensor can be programmed to transmit the data frames in a cyclic fashion or based on requests.

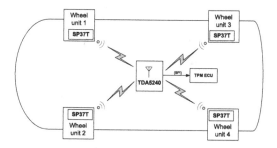

Fig. 1. TPM system with Infineon SP37 sensors and TDA5240 receivers

The second development kit represents the receiver kit for TPMS messages, which is a SmartLewisRx TDA5240 [11] receiver kit. The TDA5240 chip is an enhanced Sensitivity Multi-Channel Quad - Configuration Receiver with Digital Baseband Processing, meaning that it can listen to up to 4 parallel sources, in our case, the TPM sensors. It has an autonomous receive mode, which reduces the noise of the host processor, improves the sensitivity and also reduces the power consumption of the system. The TDA5240 integrated circuit does not rely on a microcontroller, so it must be attached to an external one in order to evaluate and compute the received information from the sensors. This receiver is specifically designed for TPM systems.

The boards of the development kits (one with the SP37 sensor and the other one with the TDA5240 receiver chip) are connected through System Interface Boards (SIB) via USB to standard notebooks for development purposes. In case of the TDA5240, the controller from the SIB board represents the aforementioned external microcontroller. Figure 1 presents a TPMS deployment based on a central receiver that also corresponds to the setup addressed in our work. The technical specifications of the SP37 sensor are presented in Table 1 and compared with the Arduinno platform from [18].

The SP37 TPMS sensor is able to transmit the data frames at the 315 MHz or 433 MHz bands (UHF) and to employ ASK (Amplitude Shift Keying) or FSK (Frequency Shift Keying) modulation. The same configuration is supported also by the receiver TDA5240. In our test environment we use 433 MHz and FSK. Regarding the message encoding format, we use Manchester encoding.

The rough format of the data frames from the sensor is depicted in Fig. 2. The frame contains 32 bits for the specific sensorID, and 16 bits for the temperature, acceleration, pressure measurements and battery status. The status data of the sensor is comprised by the unique sensorID and the internal battery status.

Table 1. Characteristics of ATmega328p vs. Infineon SP37 8051 sensors

Characteristic	ATmega328P	Infineon's SP37 (8051 based)
Operating Voltage	5V	3.3V
Supply voltage range	1.8 - 5.5V	1.9 - 3.6V
Digital I/O Pins	14	19
Analog Input Pins	6	8
DC Current per I/O Pin	40 mA	10 mA
Flash Memory	32 KB	**6 KB**
RAM	2 KB (SRAM)	**256 Bytes**
EEPROM	1 KB	**31 byte emulated EEPROM**
		(+ 12 KB ROM)
Clock Speed	16 MHz	12 MHz
Temperature range	-40°C to 85°C	-40°C to 125°C

32 bit	16 bit	16 bit	16 bit	16 bit
ID	Temperature	Pressure	Acceleration	Battery status

Fig. 2. TPMS data frame format with 16-bit data and 32-bit ID

The reported wheel parameters are: acceleration, temperature and pressure (all measured within the sensor specific ranges [8]).

For the TPMS sensor configuration and measurement, as well as for establishing the RF communication between the sensor and the receiver, we used the available SP37T ROM Library configuration and measurement functions provided with the SP37T development kit. These functions are described in the SP37T ROM library guide for which the reader is referred to [10].

4   Protocol Design

Before getting to the protocol description, let us briefly caps on some of our design goals:

- *Lightweight cryptography.* We make use of some of the lightest symmetric primitives to assure real-time security. Ideally, we should rely on hardware implementations of current standards, e.g., AES. But since such an implementation is missing from the sensors, we make use of some of the lightest designs published so far SPECK and PRESENT. In the results section we provide quantitative measurements on the performance of software implementations for these primitives.
- *Optional confidentiality and privacy.* Keeping the information private from eavesdroppers at the cost of additional encryption operations does not appear

to be the default option since privacy does not appear to be the main concern (it is energy consumption and authenticity that are more critical). We keep frame encryption, which implies hiding the ID as a second option in our protocol.

- *ISO based key-exchange.* While establishing a master key between each sensor and the receiver leads to a more surreptitious discussion, a fresh session key needs to be established regularly. Coming with a per-paper key-exchange protocol is not a desired option, especially when we address an area standardized by the industry. For this reason, we rely on well established ISO based key-exchange protocol.
- *Energy efficiency.* This is an obvious design goal, also expressed by the first two objectives, in addition to these it is clear that our protocol can rely only on symmetric cryptography. In the results section, we provide a crisp image on energy consumption.

4.1   Master and Session Key Establishment

Before designing the authentication protocol between the wheel sensors and receiver, a shared key between the two needs to be established. This proves to be a difficult issue because we cannot rely on public-key infrastructure due to the computational constraints at the sensor level. We first review the alternatives as they are proposed in related work.

Xu et al. [18] propose for the initialization of the secret master key to be triggered only by the sensor and only at events that are less likely to happen, e.g., when the tire is inflated for the first time. The procedure is also assumed to happen in some authorized garage, ensuring a safe environment for the key-exchange. The procedure is correct but it also bears a drawback. It seldom happens that drivers need to change the wheel on their own as the car is located hundreds of kilometres away from any authorized garage, or the driver may simply want to avoid the strains of finding an authorized garage. In this case the aforementioned procedure does not offer enough support. In Continental's patent [16], the key is exchanged in clear-text each time the vehicles starts. This procedure is easy to implement but also easier to eavesdrop, nullifying the security of the protocol that follows.

To bring a crisper image, we proceed further by classifying the key sharing alternatives in two categories:

1. *The resurrecting duckling.* The seminal work of Stajano [15] introduces the idea of imprinting by relating to a metaphor inspired from biology: a duckling emerging from its egg recognizes as its mother the first moving object it sees that makes a sound, a phenomenon called imprinting. The same idea is extended in [15] to devices: they are to be paired with the first entity that sends them the key. While the procedures in the Continental's patent [16] and the ones from the work of Xu et al. [18] may seem of distinct nature, they are in fact both particular cases of the *imprinting* phenomenon. Trying to refine all the procedures from [16,18], we can distinguish between three options.

- *Rare event imprinting* is the case when the key is imprinted when a rare event takes place, e.g., wheels stopped rapidly at high speed (or oscillating clockwise and counter clockwise at a very low speed). Such events can happen only when the car (or wheel) is in special circumstances, e.g., on an elevator.
- *External tool imprinting* is the case when the key is imprinted by the use of an external tool via a secure communication medium. This tool can be an OBD (On-Board Diagnosis) device that is paired with the driver's phone via a secure Bluetooth connection allowing easy configuration from the driver's side.
- *Safe environment imprinting* requires the key to be imprinted in a secure environment, e.g., at an authorized garage. In this case the key can be simply sent in plaintext, for example when the wheel is used for the first time. Sending the key in plaintext each time the car starts, similar to the solution of the patent, cannot be considered a safe environment imprinting since there are no security guarantees for such a scenario.

In all situations we assume that imprinting pairs the sensor with the first device that sends it a key. As noted in the work of Stajano [15] a reset procedure is also needed (this is in fact referred as *escrowed seppuku* meaning that the device can be killed in order to resurrect it for a new key). We believe that this procedure could also call either for a rare event, or for a master reset-key that is dedicated to this purpose. Likely, this master-reset key can be also imprinted by the manufacturer and delivered to the owner in a closed envelope. This is indeed similar to the PIN vs. PUK code in mobile telephony. That is, the PIN is usually a short code chosen by the user, if the user loses the PIN then this can be reset by the longer PUK code that was imprinted by the manufacturer.

2. *Environmental data.* We should not forget a relevant aspect, all these sensors are located in the same environment which can provide a reach common entropy that is hard to be guessed by outsiders. First, accelerometer data is available both to the internal ABS unit as well to the wheel sensor. This data was previously used to learn the wheel on which a tire is connected, but can be as well used to generate a shared key. Generally, vibrations from the environment can be easily captured and they should be similar for devices located on the same vehicle. There is extensive literature on using accelerometer data to generate a shared key. Since this key will not provide an exact match on the sender and receiver side, fuzzy cryptography [6] can be applied to correctly extract a key.

To conclude on the master-key sharing procedure, we believe that choosing from one of the above depends mostly on the manufacturer and a more comprehensive analysis of the advantages and disadvantages is out of reach for our current work.

A fresh session key needs to be established each time the protocol starts or whenever the session counter reaches the maximum value, e.g., 0xFFFF in case of 16 bit counters. Given the industry driven nature of the application area, it is best to stay to current standards in order to make such solutions viable for adoption by manufacturers. The ISO/IEC 9798 provides a well known family of authentication protocols based on both symmetric and asymmetric primitives. Recently, this standard was subject to rigorous formal analysis which lead to several improvements and fixes [1]. Once the master-key is shared between the sensor and receiver, the session key-establishment can be done with any mutual authentication protocol. For example, the ISO 9798-2-4 three-pass mutual authentication scheme. In Fig. 3 we depict the structure of this key-exchange protocol. The notations are the expected ones: $\mathbb{K}_{ms}$ denotes the master key shared between the sensor and the receiver, N is the regular notation for cryptographic nonces, i.e., random values, while $\mathsf{Sens_{ID}}$ and $\mathsf{Receiver}$ are the identities of the sending sensor and of the central receiver. The session key $\mathbb{K}_{ses}$ can be simply derived from the exchanged values $N_{\mathsf{Sens_{ID}}}$, N_{Receiver} and the master key $\mathbb{K}_{ms}$ with the help of some key derivation process. This incurs only a small computational cost in the order of an additional encryption and can be straight-forwardly built upon the primitives that we deploy for the rest of the protocol.

Handshake for session-key establishment

---

1. $\mathsf{Sens_{ID}} \rightarrow \mathsf{Receiver}$: $\mathsf{Sens_{ID}}, N_{\mathsf{Sens_{ID}}}$
2. $\mathsf{Receiver} \rightarrow \mathsf{Sens_{ID}}$: $\{N_{\mathsf{Sens_{ID}}}, N_{\mathsf{Receiver}}, \mathsf{Receiver}\}_{\mathbb{K}_{ms}}$
3. $\mathsf{Sens_{ID}} \rightarrow \mathsf{Receiver}$: $\{N_{\mathsf{Receiver}}, N_{\mathsf{Sens_{ID}}}\}_{\mathbb{K}_{ms}}$

Fig. 3. Example of session key establishment based on ISO 9798-2-4 three-pass mutual authentication based on symmetric primitives

4.2 Frame Authentication and Encryption

Having fixed the the session key $\mathbb{K}_{ses}$ we again derive by some standard key derivation technique the authentication key $\mathbb{K}_{aut}$ and the encryption key $\mathbb{K}_{conf}$.

Frame authentication is done with the standard CBC-MAC based on SPECK as outlined in Fig. 4 (i). This construction is secure as the data field has a fixed size of 64 bits in our example (the length of the full frame is 96 bits since 32 bits are added for the authentication tag). The 8-bit data fields suggested in Fig. 4 serve us only as a baseline, giving the minimum expected size for such frames. We decided to scale down the 16 bits data fields to 8 bits since this resolution should be enough for most applications and will significantly improve energy consumption. If larger data is collected, then the fields can be extended to 16-bits without impacting the authentication tag which stays at 32 bits, however this will require to switch to a larger block size for SPECK as well.

Frame encryption is added only as an option but not as part of the default protocol description as outlined in Fig. 4 (ii). The reason behind this is that the benefit of encrypting the frames seem to be somewhat marginal. The main

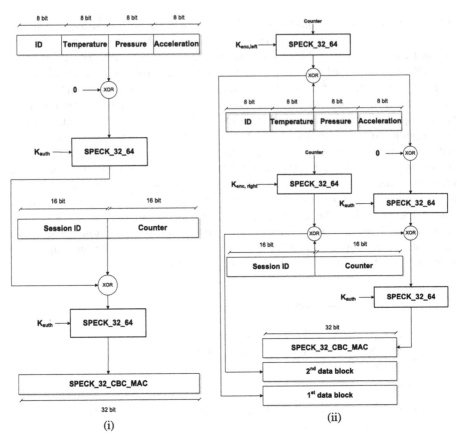

Fig. 4. A 96 bit frame: (i) authenticated with CBC-MAC and (ii) with authenticated encryption (encrypt-then-MAC) based on SPECK CBC-MAC

intention is to assure privacy for the user, e.g., the ID of the sensors is hidden and thus it cannot be tracked (this is the motivation from [18]). However, it is unclear if privacy should really be a concern since there are countless way to track a car besides recording the ID of the TPMS sensors, e.g., the myriad surveillance cameras dispatched on the roads. Besides tracking the user, exposing information related to tire condition to outsiders seems to have no security implication (finally, the condition of tire, in extreme cases, e.g., deflated tire, can be recognized by outsiders from visual inspection). However, if assuring confidentiality of the frame is a desired security objective, then we can enable the encryption option.

The steps perfomed by the sender sensor are summarized in Algorithm 1. The check for authenticity is depicted in Algorithm 2 and proceeds from verifying the session counter and id up to checking the tag which is the more demanding operation (note that verification is performed only by receivers). Finally, Algorithm 3 outlines the steps of the receiver. Here in order to avoid an anonymization of the sensor ID or sending it in cleartext in order to select the particular key, we opted out for trying to decrypt with each key and check its authenticity. This procedure does not add significant additional costs since decryption requires only XOR-ing with a key stream that already exists (and will be used when the frame encrypted with the corresponding key arrives). Moreover, frame verification in case when the selected key is not that of the sender will likely fail at verifying the session id so it does not incur additional costs, e.g., checking for authenticity. To obtain a crisper verification algorithm, since we used encryption in counter mode, one can simply avoid encryption of the ID by using an 8-bit mask. In this case the receiver's algorithm from Algorithm 3 can simply proceed with the key allocated for a particular ID. Encryption of the counter can also raise some concerns in case that frames are lost, however since frame emission takes place at fixed intervals, e.g., 2 min, it is easy for the receiver to retrieve the current value of the counter by simply checking the elapsed time since the protocol started. Again, as the counter holds no critical information, it can be sent in plain-text as well (this is just a minor implementation decision).

4.3   Randomness

While strong randomness is vital for the session key initialization, an in-depth analysis of how to generate randomness is out of scope for the current work. Fortunately, there should be enough randomness in the values reported by the sensor, e.g., acceleration in particular, as these depend not only on tire condition, but also on the behavior of the driver. Thus, we can immediately garner whatever output from the sensor data on a randomness pool. We recommend for each sensor to keep a randomness pool that is a simple state variable that XORs over all values that are recorded by the sensor. This state value is used to refresh the authentication key at each renegotiation.

Algorithm 1. Sender's algorithm

```
 1: procedure BUILD AND SEND FRAMES
 2:     SetSessionKey()
 3:     sess_cnt ← 0
 4:     repeat
 5:         if sess_cnt > max_sess then
 6:             SetSessionKey()
 7:         end if
 8:         data ← ReadSensorData()
 9:         frame ← concat(data, sess_cnt)
10:         frame ← concat(frame, sess_id)
11:         if opt_conf then
12:             kstream ← Cipher(𝕂_conf,
                    sess_cnt)
13:             frame ← frame ⊕ kstream
14:         end if
15:         tag ← MAC(𝕂_aut, frame)
16:         frame ← concat(frame, tag)
17:         SendFrame(frame)
18:         sess_cnt ← sess_cnt + 1
19:     until true
20: end procedure
```

Algorithm 2. Frame Verification

```
 1: procedure CHECKFRAMEAUTHENTICITY(frame)
 2:     id ← extract(frame, ps_id, ln_id)
 3:     sess_cnt ← extract(frame, ps_cnt, ln_cnt)
 4:     if sess_cnt > sess_cnt[id] then
 5:         sess_id ← extract(frame,        ps_sid,
                ln_sid)
 6:         if sess_id = sess_id[id] then
 7:             tag ← extract(frame,        ps_tag,
                    ln_tag)
 8:             tag' ← MAC(𝕂_aut[id], frame)
 9:             if tag = tag' then
10:                 data ← extract(frame,
                        ps_data, ln_data)
11:                 return data
12:             end if
13:         end if
14:     end if
15:     return ⊥
16: end procedure
```

Algorithm 3. Receiver's algorithm

1: **procedure** RECEIVE AND VERIFY FRAMES
2:　　**repeat**
3:　　　　$frame \leftarrow ReceiveFrame()$
4:　　　　**if** opt_conf **then**
5:　　　　　　**for** $i \leftarrow 1, n$ **do**
6:　　　　　　　　$frame' \leftarrow frame \oplus kstream[i]$
7:　　　　　　　　$data \leftarrow$ CheckFrameAuthenticity($frame'$)
8:　　　　　　　　**if** $data \neq \perp$ **then**
9:　　　　　　　　　　$frame \leftarrow frame'$
10:　　　　　　　　　　**exit for**
11:　　　　　　　　**end if**
12:　　　　　　**end for**
13:　　　　**else**
14:　　　　　　$data \leftarrow$ CheckFrameAuthenticity($frame$)
15:　　　　**end if**
16:　　　　**if** $data \neq \perp$ **then**
17:　　　　　　$id \leftarrow extract(frame, ps\_id, ln\_id)$
18:　　　　　　$sess\_cnt[id] \leftarrow sess\_cnt[id] + 1$
19:　　　　　　$kstream[id] \leftarrow$ Cipher($\mathbb{K}_{conf}[id], sess\_cnt$)
20:　　　　**end if**
21:　　　　$data \leftarrow \perp$
22:　　**until true**
23: **end procedure**

---

5 Experimental Results

Our experimental results are concerned with two aspects: the computational performance of lightweight cryptographic designs and the energy consumption of the protocol, both with respect to the implementation on the SP37 sensor. We discuss these in what follows.

5.1 Lightweight Cryptographic Designs

The lightweight block ciphers that we chose for our implementation are the SPECK [2] and PRESENT [3] block ciphers. These ciphers were chosen because of their design simplicity which leads to low RAM and flash memory usage. The Katan32 block cipher used by Xu et al. [18] did not appear to be suitable on the SP37 sensor due to higher RAM and Flash memory requirements.

From the lightweight block-cipher family of SIMON and SPECK [2], we choose SPECK as it is designed for optimal performance in software while SIMON is optimal in hardware. SPECK supports a wide range for block and key sizes, starting from 32 bits to 128 bits for the block size, respectively from 64 bits to 256 bits for the key size. We started with an implementation of several SPECK configurations with the code from [4, 7]. At first, a software configuration larger than SPECK 48/96 was not usable due to RAM limitations. Consequently, we optimized the code in order to minimize RAM usage. This was possible by computing the key stream at the same step where it is used and not by computing and memorizing it in an array for later use (this was the general approach in the available implementations). Thus, the key expansion and the encrypt functions were reduced to a single function. After performing these optimizations, all configurations up to SPECK64/128 could be uploaded on our platform.

The PRESENT block cipher is also suitable for our TPMS application. Although it is optimal in hardware, it is also convenient for software implementations on low-end platforms. From the two available PRESENT configurations, consisting in 64 bit block size and 80 bit vs. 128 bit key, we chose the first one. We started by adapting the available software implementation from [13].

Measurements were done in terms of code size, data size and execution time as can be outlined in Table 2. For memory consumption, the measurements were done with and without the use of compiler optimizations. As can be easily observed, the SPECK block cipher is more suitable for our constrained platform than PRESENT, due to smaller memory needs and execution time.

Table 2. SPECK and PRESENT performances on Infineon SP37T with and without using compiler optimizations

Block cipher (block/key size)	Flash(bytes) w/wo opt	Flash(%) w/wo opt	Data(bytes) w/wo opt	Data(% out of RAM) w/wo opt	Duration(ms)
SPECK32/64*	1032/1371	16,8/22,3	100/117	39/45,7	6,6
SPECK32/64	566/642	9,2/10,4	0/21	0/8,2	2,5
SPECK48/72	843/1175	13,7/19,1	16/37	6,2/14,4	18,2
SPECK48/96	867/1203	14,1/19,5	20/41	7,8/16	19,3
SPECK64/96	841/1031	13,6/16,7	16/37	6,2/14,4	28
SPECK64/128	865/1059	14/17,2	20/41	7,8/16	29,1
PRESENT64/80	846/1159	13,7/18,8	27/51	10,5/19,9	303,3

5.2 Design Considerations for Energy Efficiency

One of the key concerns in implementing the protocol was energy efficiency. To obtain a minimal current consumption, the following key aspects were kept in mind: ensure minimal consumption of memory resources, ensure protection against battery drain attacks, ensure minimal usage of RF transmitter, parallelize sensor operations, use sensor specific methods for reduced energy consumption (e.g., power-down mode).

For ensuring minimal memory resources, the Speck 32/64 implementation was optimized in terms of RAM and code size. The key expansion step was done together with the encryption step for all results summarized in Table 2 (starting from the 2nd line). Second, the RF data transmission method was chosen considering minimal RAM usage. The dedicated ROM library function for RF transmission was not used because it would require a data buffer where all the RF data is stored before transmission. We did a manual configuration of the transmission procedure, where only the useful data was sent stepwise to the TDA5240.

Ensuring protection against battery drain attacks forced by LF triggers was a significant concern. The default sensor design allows LF telegrams to be received with the following functionalities: requesting sensors measurement, requesting for the sensor ID of a tire, configuring an operation mode or updating the configuration. The last two procedures can lead immediately to battery loss, e.g., forcing the sensor to enter in the diagnose mode will trigger a transmission every 500 ms. The first two triggers are not necessarily innocuous as they also lead to waking the sensor up from power-down mode. The driver would not recognize any change or misbehaviour until the battery will run out. As a consequence and since any unnecessary wake-up pattern will lead to battery loss if triggered for sufficiently many times, we decided to ignore LF requests completely. Thus, no wakeup from the power down mode of the 8051 microcontroller and peripherals is generated if an LF telegram is received by the sensor. If these triggers are still needed, a counter must be used to ensure that a maximum number of requests is not overdo. If a maximum value is reached, the TPMS sensor would ignore further requests until the counter reaches the value 0, by decrementing it at every cyclic transmission of the sensor. This would be a feasible solution for the first two kind of requests. For the last two, in case of switching into another operating mode or changing the frequency of transmission of the TPMS sensor, a security measure would be to display this request on the driver dashboard and to wait for his feedback. Of course, all this interaction will be authenticated with the same master key. Due to space constraints, we will not insist in designing subprotocols for these functionalities since they do not appear to pose additional challenges and do not appear to be compulsory for existing systems.

As stated in the RAM and code size minimization steps, the RF transmitter configuration and transmission was done manually and not by making use of an available ROM library function. This was not the only reason for taking this decision. Another reason is the fact that for achieving minimal current consumption during RF transmission, a control mechanism is needed in order to manage the consumption of the application. This mechanism is provided by the SP37 by a special function register bit, which can be used for indicating that the 8051 microcontroller and other peripherals can enter into an idle mode (a low-current consumption mode) until an event is triggered so that the normal operation can continue. During the RF transmission of one byte this mechanism was used in order to minimize the energy consumption. Starting from the fact that the RF transmission represents the highest current consumption, the values reported by the sensor and the sensor ID was scaled down to 8 bits for the temperature, acceleration and pressure values with only 7 bits for the sensor ID and 1 bit representing the battery status. This offers of course a baseline for energy consumption and one can increase them at the cost of more energy.

A decision also had to be taken for the measurement of battery voltage. There are two sets of ROM library functions which can be used for this purpose. One is a standalone function (which can be called any-time in the application code) and the other consists in three functions which must be called in a specific order during RF transmission. The last set is recommended in the SP37 ROM library guide [10] because of two optimization aspects: one is the execution time of the two sets and the other one, the parallelization of sensor operations. We opted for the more efficient method.

Besides the optimizations used during the RF transmission, the SP37 sensor has a specific power mode called power-down mode in which only a few peripherals are powered, excluding the microcontroller, which is also waiting for an event in order to wake up and execute the user code. It is important to notice that during most of its lifetime the SP37 sensor is in power down mode.

5.3   Energy Consumption

Our measurements included the three cases that can be distinguished: frames without security elements, authenticated frames and encrypted authenticated frames. The difference in energy consumption between the last two is not very high since most of the energy is spent in sending the frame while encrypting the frame does not increase its size. The measurements for standard frames and encrypted authenticated frames are depicted in Fig. 5.

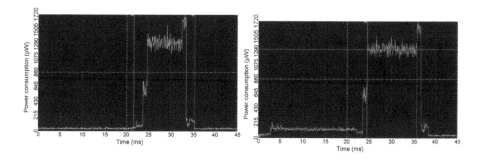

Fig. 5. Power consumption: without (i) and with (ii) encryption and authentication

When comparing the energy consumption for a normal frame with any of the secured frames two differences can be easily observed: the duration of the data processing time and the duration of the RF transmission window. The overall duration required for sending and computing a secured frame is almost double the duration of an unsecured one, 35 ms respectively 29 ms vs. 14 ms. However, in the RF transmission segment (where the highest power consumption levels are reached) the delay generated by the added security bits has a value of 3.4 ms which represents only 22 % from the total frame duration increase and only 9.7 % from the total frame duration of a secured frame. Consequently, this addition will not have a big impact on battery discharging. The power consumption during this segment is constant for all frame types at 1.32 mW. Looking at the data processing segment and comparing an unsecured frame with an authenticated one, the delay generated by the authentication has a value of 9.6 ms, which represents 64 % from the time required to send a regular frame and 33.1 % from the time for an authenticated frame. From the power consumption point of view, in case of an unsecured frame we have an average of 92 μW, which is comparable to the average value of an authenticated frame, i.e., 133 μW. Between an authenticated frame and an authenticated-encrypted frame there are minimal differences in term of delays, i.e., 6 ms, due to only two other Speck32/64 calls. The total energy consumption increases from 13.11μJ in case of the standard frames to 20.34μJ in case of the authenticated and encrypted frames. This is roughly by 50 % but it is mostly due to increasing the size of the frame with 32 bits for the authentication tag and not due to the cryptographic operations which cost in the order of 2.77μJ. With a larger data frame the added cost will be much lower than 50 % as the size of the authentication tag remains constant.

Since in a typical TPMS system the sensor is more than 90 % of the time in power down mode, these delays of 3.4 ms and 9.6 ms will not have a big impact on battery lifetime. By comparing our results to the power consumption measurements from Xu et al. [18], here we have a consumption of only 1.32mW during RF transmission, compared to about 450mW in [18]. The time delay introduced by processing and sending a secured frame of 13.1 ms in their work is comparable with our time delay in the same scope of 14 ms (however our platform has lower computational capabilities).

6   Conclusion

Our work shows cryptographic security to be achievable on real-world TPMS sensors at minimal computational costs and energy expenses. For real-world use it is preferable to rely on hardware cryptographic implementations, still, the software implementation that we use in our protocol design, proved to be energy efficient with the additional costs for cryptographic computations being at only 2.77μJ which is around 20 % from the total cost of a regular frame transmission at 13.11μJ. This cost can be actually nullified by a proper hardware implementation which is certainly to come for TPMS sensors. At the communication level, the size of the frame is expanded by the 32-bit authentication tag which (along with the costs of the underlying cryptography) increases consumption from 13.11μJ to 20.34μJ which is roughly 50 %. We underline that this cost is in fact an upper bound since the authentication tag is equal in size with the actual sensor data (32 bit) while with a larger data-field this percentage decreases as the authentication tag remains constant in size. Compared to the energy consumption reported by previous work [18] our result is two orders of magnitude lower, this is of course mainly due to the dedicated TPMS sensors from the deployment platform but also due to the lighter cryptographic constructions, i.e., SPECK.

Given that a system is only as secure as its weakest link, we consider that securing TPMS interfaces should be taken more serious by automotive manufacturers. Clearly, potential attacks on such systems can now lead to some inconveniences to the drivers but can have far more serious consequences if TPMS data is going to be used in more critical tasks.

References

1. Basin, D., Cremers, C., Meier, S.: Provably repairing the iso/iec 9798 standard for entity authentication. J. Comput. Secur. **21**(6), 817–846 (2013)
2. Beaulieu, R., Shors, D., Smith, J., Treatman-Clark, S., Weeks, B., Wingers, L.: National Security Agency. The Simon and Speck families of lightweight block ciphers. pp. 16–45 (2013)
3. Bogdanov, A.A., Knudsen, L.R., Leander, G., Paar, C., Poschmann, A., Robshaw, M., Seurin, Y., Vikkelsoe, C.: PRESENT: an ultra-lightweight block cipher. In: Paillier, P., Verbauwhede, I. (eds.) CHES 2007. LNCS, vol. 4727, pp. 450–466. Springer, Heidelberg (2007)
4. Cazorla, M., Marquet, K., Minier, M.: Survey and benchmark of lightweight block ciphers for wireless sensor networks. In: Samarati, P. (ed.) SECRYPT 2013 - Proceedings of the 10th International Conference on Security and Cryptography, Reykjavík, Iceland, 29–31 July 2013, pp. 543–548. SciTePress (2013)
5. Checkoway, S., McCoy, D., Kantor, B., Anderson, D., Shacham, H., Savage, S., Koscher, K., Czeskis, A., Roesner, F., Kohno, T., et al.: Comprehensive experimental analyses of automotive attack surfaces. In: USENIX Security Symposium, San Francisco (2011)
6. Dodis, Y., Reyzin, L., Smith, A.: Fuzzy extractors: how to generate strong keys from biometrics and other noisy data. In: Cachin, C., Camenisch, J.L. (eds.) EUROCRYPT 2004. LNCS, vol. 3027, pp. 523–540. Springer, Heidelberg (2004)
7. FrenchNationalResearchAgency. Speck sample source code. http://bloc.project.citi-lab.fr/library.html
8. Infineon. SP37T 1300kPa.Product brief. http://www.infineon.com/dgdl/SP37_1300kPa_PB.pdf?fileId=db3a3043382e83730138566f83105c7c
9. Infineon. SP37T Datasheet., 1.0 edn., January 2010
10. Infineon. SP37T ROM Library Guide., 1.0 edn., January 2010
11. Infineon. TDA5240 Datasheet., 4.0 edn., February 2010
12. Ishtiaq Roufa, R.M., Mustafaa, H., Travis Taylora, S.O., Xua, W., Gruteserb, M., Trappeb, W., Seskarb, I.: Security, privacy vulnerabilities of in-car wireless networks: a tire pressure monitoring system case study. In: 19th USENIX Security Symposium, Washington DC, pp. 11–13 (2010)
13. Klose, D.: Ruhr-University-Bochum. Present sample source code. http://www.lightweightcrypto.org/implementations.php
14. Koscher, K., Czeskis, A., Roesner, F., Patel, S., Kohno, T., Checkoway, S., McCoy, D., Kantor, B., Anderson, D., Shacham, H., et al.: Experimental security analysis of a modern automobile. In: 2010 IEEE Symposium on Security and Privacy (SP), pp. 447–462. IEEE (2010)
15. Stajano, F.: The resurrecting duckling. In: Malcolm, J.A., Christianson, B., Crispo, B., Roe, M. (eds.) Security Protocols 1999. LNCS, vol. 1796, pp. 183–194. Springer, Heidelberg (2000)
16. Toth, A.: Method and system for monitoring a parameter of a tire of a vehicle, 16 April 2014. EP Patent App. EP20,120,464,019
17. van Zyl, P., Goethem, S.v., Jansen, S., Kanarchos, S., Rexeis, M., Hausberger, S., Smokers, R.: Study on tyre pressure monitoring systems (tpms) as a means to reduce light-commercial and heavy-duty vehicles fuel consumption and co2 emissions. Final report, European Commission DG Clima (2013)
18. Xu, M., Xu, W., Walker, J., Moore, B.: Lightweight secure communication protocols for in-vehicle sensor networks. In: Proceedings of the 2013 ACM Workshop on Security, Privacy & Dependability for Cyber Vehicles, pp. 19–30. ACM (2013)

Umbra: Embedded Web Security Through Application-Layer Firewalls

Travis Finkenauer[✉] and J. Alex Halderman

University of Michigan, Ann Arbor, USA
{tmfink,jhalderm}@umich.edu

Abstract. Embedded devices with web interfaces are prevalent, but, due to memory and processing constraints, implementations typically make use of Common Gateway Interface (CGI) binaries written in low-level, memory-unsafe languages. This creates the possibility of memory corruption attacks as well as traditional web attacks. We present Umbra, an application-layer firewall specifically designed for protecting web interfaces in embedded devices. By acting as a "friendly man-in-the-middle," Umbra can protect against attacks such as cross-site request forgery (CSRF), information leaks, and authentication bypass vulnerabilities. We evaluate Umbra's security by analyzing recent vulnerabilities listed in the CVE database from several embedded vendors and find that it would have prevented half of the vulnerabilities. We also show that Umbra comfortably runs within the constraints of an embedded system while incurring minimal performance overhead.

Keywords: Embedded security · Firewall · Web security

1 Introduction

Embedded devices such as routers [16], printers [26], and supervisory control and data acquisition (SCADA) systems [8,53] are frequently managed through web interfaces, which potentially create an opening for remote attackers. Many of these systems are critical, such as SCADA systems that manage utilities and medical devices that support life directly [22]. These web interfaces often use Common Gateway Interface (CGI) binaries implemented in low-level languages, such as C, which introduces the possibility of memory corruption attacks and input validation vulnerabilities. In one recent example, researchers found that an embedded web interface's login page had remotely exploitable buffer overflow vulnerabilities in the username and password fields, which would allow an attacker to take control over the host system [6]. The same implementation was also vulnerable to several other textbook attacks, including shell injection and authentication bypass.

However, this is not a case of a single careless vendor that makes products with vulnerabilities; embedded devices in general tend not to have strong security. With the recent Misfortune Cookie vulnerability, over 200 models of

© Springer International Publishing Switzerland 2016
A. Bécue et al. (Eds.): CyberICS 2015/WOS-CPS 2015, LNCS 9588, pp. 112–126, 2016.
DOI: 10.1007/978-3-319-40385-4_8

routers from several vendors were found to be using an out-of-date web server that was vulnerable a memory corruption attack, allowing an attacker to gain complete control over the router [9]. Many vendors were using a decade-old version of the RomPager web server in their device firmware. Problems like these are all too common, and, coupled with the fact that embedded devices can act as a foothold into a target network [29], they make embedded web interfaces an attractive attack vector for prospective intruders.

Ideally, all the code in an embedded device would be subjected to a security audit. However, such audits are expensive and time consuming, require security expertise, and may not be feasible when embedded devices reuse off-the-shelf closed-source components [43]. As an alternative, we propose introducing a small layer of security software that can be integrated into many kinds of embedded devices and act as a "friendly man-in-the-middle" that enforces a security policy set by the developers of each device. Such an application-layer firewall can provide concentrated protection at the web interface's attack surface and greatly reduce overall vulnerability at low cost.

We present Umbra, our implementation of an application-layer firewall that can be easily integrated with preexisting embedded systems to provide additional security. Umbra is designed to work with existing web server binaries, to be simple to configure, and to work within the limited resources of embedded systems.

In order for a manufacturer-side security solution to garner adoption, it must have small perceived cost to developers. For example, enabling stack canaries only requires a compiler flag and has gained wide adoption; today's compilers often enable stack canaries by default [13,57]. In contrast, various heavy-weight approaches, such as dynamic taint tracking have not gained traction, because they introduce on the order of two times slowdown [7,15]. Since Umbra acts as a "shim" in front of existing web servers, manufacturers can keep their existing code and thus reduce the cost to adopting security. Also, embedded devices' code is often licensed from third-party vendors, so the embedded developer does not always have the source code for all parts of the firmware. Umbra works on systems where source code is not available.

Umbra needs to have information about the web application being protected. We define a policy language that allows embedded system developers to easily describe security properties for an HTTP interface, such as the set of allowed characters or maximum length for HTTP parameters. The Umbra shim is compiled together with these policies and enforces the specified properties.

We evaluate Umbra's functionality and performance. In a review of recent vulnerabilities in some of Umbra's target devices, we find that Umbra would have prevented or mitigated more than half of these issues. We also show that when running on a Raspberry Pi system with OpenWrt, Umbra adds only 5 ms (about 3 %) to average page download times, demonstrating that it comfortably runs within the resource constraints of embedded Linux systems.

Source Code Release. We are releasing our Umbra prototype as open-source software. It is available at https://github.com/umbra-firewall/umbra.

2 Related Work

There are various standalone application-layer firewalls that secure HTTP interfaces, including Barracuda Web Application Firewall [3], Cisco ACE Web Application Firewall [10], and HP TippingPoint [27]. Some of these devices even provide features such as outbound filtering of sensitive data, including credit card and social security numbers, which can aid organizations in being compliant with the Payment Card Industry Data Security Standard (PCI DSS) [47].

IronBee and ModSecurity are examples of host-based application layer firewalls. ModSecurity supports Apache, Nginx, and Microsoft IIS web servers, and IronBee supports Apache and Nginx [48,56]. These web servers are not commonly used in embedded systems because of their larger CPU, memory, and storage footprint compared to special-purpose embedded servers. Instead, embedded devices use servers such as lighttpd [33], uhttpd [45], or a custom HTTP server (e.g., [37]). Hence, these existing solutions are not appropriate for integration with embedded devices.

Many recent studies have demonstrated vulnerabilities in embedded devices—including traffic light cameras [23], server lights-out management controllers [6], and automobile controller-area network (CAN) buses [50], to name just a few—and the trend towards the "Internet of Things" suggests that there will be vastly more embedded devices in the future [36]. Many embedded devices get connected to the public Internet, where they can be mapped and probed with publicly available tools [19]. In one case, a vulnerability in just two UPnP libraries affected 2 % of public IPv4 addresses [42]. The security of embedded devices is a significant and growing issue, and the widespread vulnerability seen among today's devices demonstrates that even basic network protections are often absent.

3 Design and Implementation

Embedded systems may often be administered through a variety of protocols, including HTTP, SSH, Telnet, IPMI, and proprietary protocols [25,26,31,55]. HTTP also sometimes acts as the transport for other protocols (such as SOAP [34] and HNAP [11]) and REST style interfaces [46]. Since HTTP is widely used and subject to a range of common vulnerabilities, Umbra focuses on defending web interfaces, though the architecture could be extended to support other protocols.

In this work, we only consider attacks targeting embedded web interfaces, through either HTTP or HTTPS. Our threat model assumes that the attacker does not have valid credentials or physical access to the target. For example, the attacker can submit arbitrary content to forms or visit arbitrary URLs corresponding to the targeted device. We also consider attacks where a legitimate user may visit an attacker-controlled web page to allow for cross-site request forgery (CSRF) attacks.

Umbra works by acting as a transparent proxy between clients and the web server, as illustrated in Fig. 1. The pass-through is achieved by introducing a

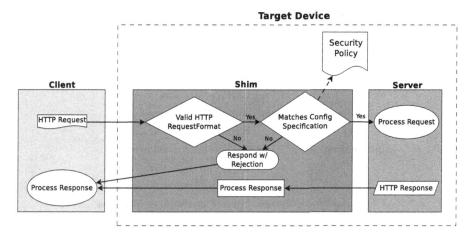

Fig. 1. A lightweight software "shim" runs on the embedded device and transparently proxies client requests, rejecting those that are malformed or that do not match a predefined security policy.

small software layer, which we call the Umbra *shim*, that runs on the embedded device and listens on the standard HTTP or HTTPS port. When the Umbra shim receives client requests, it checks to ensure that they comply with a *security policy*. This policy, defined in advance by the device manufacturer, specifies which security features should be applied and how the features should be enforced. For example, the policy might dictate the maximum allowed length for HTTP form inputs and specify a whitelist of permitted characters. (For details, see Sect. 3.2.) Umbra forwards requests that satisfy the policy to the original embedded web server and responds with rejections to requests that do not.

Umbra is designed to be integrated into device firmware by the manufacturer. To apply Umbra to an existing device, the manufacturer must:

1. Write a security policy tailored to the device's embedded web application.
2. Compile the Umbra shim for the embedded device. The policy gets compiled into the Umbra binary.
3. Configure the device's existing web server to listen on an alternate port and on the loopback interface.
4. Set the Umbra shim to run at boot time, listening on the default web port on the external interface.

Note that a device maker can add Umbra to its firmware without having to modify the source code for the existing web application.

3.1   Security Features

Our Umbra implementation is designed to protect against a range of common attacks, as summarized in Table 1. By adjusting the global settings in the security

Table 1. Umbra Security Features—Umbra's security features mitigate or protect against a variety of common attacks

Vulnerability	Security Features
XSS	Parameter whitelist
CSRF	CSRF protection
Authentication bypass	Authentication enforcement
	HTTP method whitelist
Information leak	Authentication enforcement
	HTTP method whitelist
	Directory traversal check
CGI memory corruption	Parameter character whitelist
	Parameter length check
	Header field length limit
Directory traversal	Directory traversal check

policy, it can be configured to have any combination of the security features described below:

CSRF Protection. Cross-site request forgery (CSRF) attacks occur when an attacker causes a victim to perform an unintended action while the victim is logged into a target website [4]. For example, the victim might visit an attacker-controlled web page that uses JavaScript to make a POST request to http://target-site.com/delete-account. Since the victim's browser is logged in to the target site, the request includes the victim's session cookies, and the site accepts this request as authorized.

Umbra prevents CSRF attacks by using a CSRF-prevention token [4], a well-known technique used by many web frameworks [5,17]. To implement this defense, Umbra generates a random CSRF-prevention token for each browser session, which it sends as a cookie in every HTTP response. The shim also modifies pages that are specified in the security policy as requiring CSRF protection. It injects JavaScript into these pages that modifies HTML forms to add a hidden field containing the same token. For pages that the security policy specifies as receiving a form action from a CSRF-protected form, Umbra verifies that the submitted data contains a token that matches the one in the client's cookie.

Pages that both submit and receive a CSRF protected form (e.g., pages with self-referencing forms) present a complication, since a client would never be able to navigate directly to the page with the correct CSRF token. For such pages, the shim only enforces the presence of a CSRF token parameter for HTTP POST requests, not GET requests.

Although this approach requires client browsers to have JavaScript enabled, this is a reasonable assumption, as many embedded web interfaces require JavaScript (e.g., [37,55]). A downside to this technique is that it only works when HTML forms send requests, and hence would not work when other methods are used to send HTTP requests, such as JavaScript's `XMLHttpRequest` or browser plug-ins. Device manufacturers would need to manually implement CSRF protection for these methods. We note that, as with other common CSRF defenses, an attacker could bypass the protection by exploiting a separate XSS vulnerability [12].

Page-Level Authentication Enforcement. A common vulnerability in embedded devices is where page-level authentication is not properly enforced. For example, in a set of five simultaneously-disclosed vulnerabilities found in D-Link IP cameras, four were due to incorrect authentication [49]. With another brand of IP camera, an attacker could visit most pages without any authentication [18].

To protect against such vulnerabilities, the Umbra shim enforces RFC 2617 HTTP Basic Authentication [21]. The suggested configuration would be to require authentication by default and specify pages that do not require authentication, such as a status page or login page. The shim reads credentials from a file specified as a command-line parameter. This file is reloaded on each page request, so the web application may change the credentials by modifying this file at run time.

Directory Traversal Protection. Another common class of attacks involves directory traversal vulnerabilities (e.g., [37]), where an attacker controls part of a file path and can inject a relative path to escape a directory. For example, an attacker may be able to inject a path such as "`../../passwords.txt`" to read the password file stored two directories above. To guard against this, the Umbra shim blocks HTTP requests with URLs that contain two periods in a row ("`..`").

The directory traversal protection does not currently attempt to check for directory traversal in HTTP parameters. Future versions of Umbra might add this as a per-parameter option, although this would introduce further complexity to the security policies.

HTTP Method Whitelist. HTTP allows for pages to be accessed via different methods, such as GET, POST, or HEAD. Different web applications may not account for pages being viewed with an unexpected method and may leak information unintentionally. In order to prevent this, Umbra security policies can specify which HTTP methods are allowed for each page.

HTTP Header Length Limits. The HTTP protocol includes headers that provide metadata about requests and responses, such as the client's user agent or the language of a response. Maliciously crafted headers have been used to exploit buffer overviews and command injection vulnerabilities in embedded web applications [14]. Umbra can be configured to limit the length of both HTTP header fields and values. If the length of any field name or value exceeds the corresponding maximum length, the shim will block the request.

Per-Parameter Limits. There are two options that can be enforced on a per-HTTP-parameter basis. These protections can help mitigate various input validation vulnerabilities—such as shell injection, SQL injection, and cross-site scripting—as well as memory corruption attacks. The first is *character whitelists*, which cause the shim to limit input characters to those from a specified set, such as lowercase letters and numbers. This is specified with a regular expression character class, such as [a-z0-9]. The second protection is *length enforcement*, in which the shim ensures that parameters do not exceed a given number of characters, such as the name and password field for a login page [6].

3.2 Security Policy Language

The embedded developer must specify the desired security policy for Umbra, and we provide a policy language for this purpose. The language is designed to make it easy to specify conservative settings globally and relax them for specific pages as necessary for compatibility. There are three sections in the configuration file: global configuration, default page policy, and per-page policy. Each section consists of a JSON object with the options specified as member pairs.

The global_config section includes directives for enabling and disabling security features. For example, to enable CSRF prevention, the user would add ''enable_csrf_protection'': true. This global configuration section also has global options that are not page specific, such as the maximum allowed header field lengths.

The default_page_config section sets the default policy for all pages. Each page-level option must have a default value specified here.

The page_config section sets policies for specific URI paths that override some or all of the default policy options. If the policy for certain options is not specified, then the default page policy will be used for those options. In this sense, each page inherits the default policy. For example, the default policy may be to enforce authentication for a page; however, the developer may want a status page to be visible without requiring authentication, so the developer could disable the authentication check for the status page.

In the per-page policy section, options for specific parameters can be specified, such as a character whitelist and length limits. This allows for parameter-level control of the security policy. For example, in Fig. 2, the favorite_vowel parameter has a max length of six and only accepts characters that are vowels.

The configuration is interpreted with Python, which outputs C code that is compiled into the Umbra shim. With this technique, there does not need to be C code that interprets the configuration at run time, keeping the resulting binary smaller and the C code simpler.

We give a simple example of a security policy in Fig. 2. The global configuration section enables several security features. The default page policy indicates that by default, GET and HEAD requests are allowed, authentication is required, no CSRF protection is used, and parameters are limited to a length of 30 and alphanumeric characters. There are two pages for which the default policy is overridden. For the root page (/), no authentication is required to view the

```
{
  "global_config": {
    "enable_request_type_check": true,
    "enable_param_len_check": true,
    "enable_param_whitelist_check": true,
    "enable_csrf_protection": true,
    "enable_authentication_check": true,
    "session_life_seconds": 300
  },
  "default_page_config": {
    "request_types": ["GET", "HEAD"],
    "requires_login": true,
    "has_csrf_form": false,
    "receives_csrf_form_action": false,
    "max_param_len": 30,
    "whitelist": "[a-zA-z0-9]"
  },
  "page_config": {
    "/": {
      "requires_login": false,
      "has_csrf_form": true
    },
    "/cgi-bin/favorites": {
      "request_types": ["POST"],
      "receives_csrf_form_action": true,
      "params": {
        "favorite_vowels": {
          "max_param_len": 6,
          "whitelist": "[aeiouy]"
        },
        "favorite_number": {
          "max_param_len": 3,
          "whitelist": "[0-9]"
        }
      }
    }
  }
}
```

Fig. 2. Sample Umbra Security Policy—This is an example of a security policy file. Path-specific rules for / and /cgi-bin/favorites override the global defaults.

page, and forms on the page will include the hidden CSRF token (see Sect. 3.1). The /cgi-bin/favorites page has a parameter that allows only vowels and another parameter that only allows numbers.

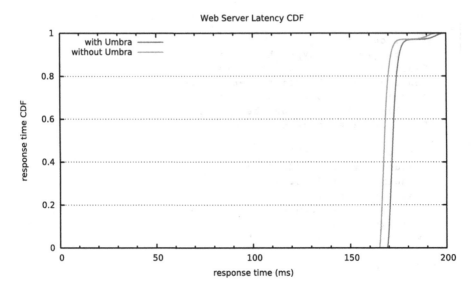

Fig. 3. Server Response Time—This graph shows the response time of the web server with and without Umbra; the average overhead is about 5 ms (3 %).

3.3 Implementation

We implemented our Umbra prototype for Linux, which is a popular platform for Internet-attached embedded devices. To provide high-performance non-blocking sockets, we use Linux's `epoll(7)` interface [20]. Since the shim needs to run within the footprint of embedded systems, we wrote it in C. We considered memory-safe languages such as Python and Go, but Python is not usually installed on embedded devices and requires a large runtime. While the Go compiler generates machine binaries, the Go runtime library is statically linked, leading to binaries that are prohibitively large.

The shim minimizes use of external libraries, only using an HTTP parsing library [30]. It also optionally links against OpenSSL to provide HTTPS support [44]. The complete Umbra implementation, including the shim and the policy interpreter, is 5676 lines of C and 631 lines of Python. When compiled as an ARM binary, the shim executable is 75 KB.

4   Evaluation

4.1   Performance

To measure the performance of Umbra, we used the Apache Benchmark tool, which records the time taken for an HTTP server to respond to requests [1]. We ran our benchmark on a Raspberry Pi Model B running OpenWrt Barrier Breaker 14.07. The requests were made from a laptop that was connected directly via a 100 Mbps Ethernet cable. We made 1000 requests to the web interface both with and without the Umbra shim.

The results of this benchmark are shown in Fig. 3. Umbra, on average, added only about 5 ms of overhead, or about 3 %. We configured Umbra to check header length, HTTP request method, directory traversal, and authentication. We had Apache Benchmark send the correct HTTP Basic Authentication credentials.

Umbra comfortably ran within the Raspberry Pi's footprint. The shim compiled to a 75 KB dynamically linked ARM binary. In comparison, the BusyBox binary in the firmware image is 370 KB. The OpenWrt firmware image itself is 40 MB, with 33 MB available, so the executable can easily fit within the firmware image. During the benchmark, the Raspberry Pi reported 2–3 % CPU utilization and peaked at a virtual memory size of 1.2 MB.

4.2   Security

In order to estimate the security provided by Umbra, we surveyed vulnerabilities that were assigned Common Vulnerability and Exposure (CVE) identifiers since 2012 from eight embedded device manufacturers: Brother, Cannon, Cisco, D-Link, Linksys, Lorex, Netgear, Supermicro, TP-LINK, Trendnet, and Xerox. There were 284 vulnerabilities across all these vendors. We randomly selected 100 of them and classified each based on the information in the public CVE database and public exploit code [40].

For each vulnerability, we first determined whether the vulnerability was for an embedded web server. We found that 40 of the 100 vulnerabilities were related to embedded web interfaces. For each embedded web interface related vulnerability, we manually determined: the class of vulnerability, the Umbra feature that

Table 2. Evaluating Vulnerability Protection—We rate the level of protection Umbra would have provided against a sample of real-world vulnerabilities.

Vulnerability	Protection Level				Total
	None	Partial	Full	Unknown	
Bypass	1	0	4	0	5
Command injection	0	0	2	0	2
CSRF	0	0	5	1	6
Directory traversal	0	0	1	0	1
Denial of service	3	1	1	1	6
Information leak	1	0	3	0	4
Memory corruption	2	0	1	0	3
Other	0	0	0	1	1
SQL injection	0	0	0	1	1
XSS	2	3	3	3	11
Protect Totals	9	4	20	7	40

would mitigate or prevent the vulnerability (if any), and the level of protection provided by Umbra. We determined the level of protection based on whether or not there exists an Umbra configuration that would prevent the vulnerability without breaking functionality. We classified the level of protection as either *none* (would provide no protection), *partial* (would prevent some parts of the vulnerability or make it more difficult to exploit), *full* (would completely eliminate the vulnerability), or *unknown* (there was not enough public information to determine whether Umbra could have prevented the vulnerability).

A summary of the types of vulnerabilities and the amount of protection provided by Umbra is shown in Table 2. At least half of the surveyed vulnerabilities would have been prevented by Umbra. Umbra would fully prevent 4 of the 5 authentication bypass vulnerabilities, 5 of the 6 CSRF vulnerabilities, and 3 of the 4 information leak vulnerabilities. This indicates that Umbra is an effective tool for mitigating these common classes of vulnerabilities.

Umbra would have worked less well for defending against denial of service and XSS vulnerabilities. Umbra only prevented 1 of the 6 denial of service vulnerabilities and 3 of the 11 XSS vulnerabilities in our sample. XSS vulnerabilities are difficult to prevent using a "pass-through" system like Umbra, because the system does not have context for the data—only the information provided in the security policy. Umbra's main defense against XSS vulnerabilities is the parameter character whitelist, where the attacker is limited by which characters may be passed through HTTP parameters. This may be enough to stop some XSS attacks but not all. For example, with an improperly escaped parameter that allows quotes, an attacker could close an HTML attribute and create a new attribute corresponding to a JavaScript callback. In other instances, XSS may be done through alternative vectors. For example, in CVE-2014-4645, an attacker could inject arbitrary HTML or JavaScript by altering the attacker machine's

Table 3. Security Feature Applicability—We show how many times each Umbra security feature prevented different types of vulnerabilities in our sample.

Vulnerability	Security Feature						Total
	Auth	CSRF	Dir. Traver	Header Length Check	Param. White	Param. Length	
Bypass	4	0	0	0	0	0	4
Command injection	0	0	0	0	2	0	2
CSRF	0	5	0	0	0	0	5
Directory traversal	0	0	1	0	0	0	1
Denial of service	0	0	0	1	0	0	1
Information leak	2	1	0	0	0	0	3
Memory corruption	0	0	0	0	0	1	1
Other	0	0	0	0	0	0	0
SQL injection	0	0	0	0	0	0	0
XSS	0	0	0	0	3	0	3
Feature Totals	6	6	1	1	5	1	20

hostname [39]. In some of these cases, the developer must properly escape the data in the web application to prevent the vulnerability.

The Umbra security features that would have prevented each of the sampled vulnerabilities are shown in Table 3. The authentication, CSRF prevention, and parameter whitelist features provided the largest security impact, accounting for 17 of the 20 vulnerabilities that would have been prevented by Umbra.

5 Future Work

In future work, we plan to investigate applying similar techniques to protect other management protocols commonly used in embedded devices, such as IPMI and SNMP. Both of these protocols are common in larger networks and provide a well-known attack surface [38,41].

Future versions of Umbra might consider other implementation languages that offer better memory safety. One potential candidate is Rust, a systems-oriented language that provides memory safety and protection against other security bugs [51]. When we wrote the original version of Umbra, the Rust language was not yet stable, but there has since been a stable release [52].

An alternative to adopting a safer language would be to apply formal verification to the shim C code. Recent efforts have produced formally verified versions of an optimizing C compiler [35] and an operating system kernel with 8700 lines of C code [32], so verifying the 5617-line Umbra shim should be tractable.

One downside to Umbra is that the developer needs to define the security policy manually. Instead, the system could be extended to infer a security policy from examples of valid inputs during a "training" period, as is done by security modules such as AppArmor [2] and Grsecurity [54]. This would simplify integrating Umbra with existing devices and increase the likelihood of adoption.

Although Umbra mitigates several significant classes of vulnerabilities affecting embedded web interfaces, one common problem that it does not yet address is flawed TLS implementations. Embedded devices often do not use HTTPS, implement it incorrectly, or use self-signed or default TLS certificates [24]. Umbra could be extended to upgrade all connections to HTTPS and to automatically request a browser-trusted certificate from a robotic CA such as Let's Encrypt [28].

Lastly, to spur Umbra adoption and improve the security of embedded devices generally, we hope to work with embedded vendors to help them integrate Umbra into their products. If several manufacturers integrate Umbra, there will be competitive pressure for other vendors to adopt similar security mechanisms.

6 Conclusion

Web interfaces in embedded devices are a common source of security vulnerabilities. We have shown that Umbra, a light-weight application-layer firewall, can prevent about half of known vulnerabilities in embedded web interfaces while adding negligible run-time overhead. Unlike existing application-layer firewalls,

Umbra can run comfortably in the constrained memory and CPU footprint of an embedded device. Embedded systems present many security challenges, but Umbra offers a promising approach to helping them achieve defense-in-depth.

Acknowledgments. This material is based upon work supported by a gift from Super Micro Computer, Inc. We would particularly like to thank Arun Kalluri, Joe Tai, Linda Wu, Mars Yang, Tau Leng, and Charles Liang from Supermicro. Additional support was provided by the National Science Foundation under grants CNS-1345254, CNS-1409505, and CNS-1518888.

References

1. Apache Software Foundation: ab–Apache HTTP server benchmarking tool, April 2015. http://httpd.apache.org/docs/2.4/programs/ab.html
2. AppArmor Security Project: Getting Started, September 2011. http://wiki.apparmor.net/index.php/GettingStarted
3. Barracuda Networks: Barracuda web application firewall (2015). https://www.barracuda.com/products/webapplicationfirewall
4. Barth, A., Jackson, C., Mitchell, J.C.: Robust defenses for cross-site request forgery. In: 15th ACM Conference on Computer and Communications Security, pp. 75–88. CCS (2008)
5. Bigg, R., et al.: Ruby on Rails security guide (2015). http://guides.rubyonrails.org/security.html
6. Bonkoski, A., Bielawski, R., Halderman, J.A.: Illuminating the security issues surrounding lights-out server management. In: 7th USENIX Workshop on Offensive Technologies. WOOT (2013)
7. Bosman, E., Slowinska, A., Bos, H.: Minemu: the world's fastest taint tracker. In: Sommer, R., Balzarotti, D., Maier, G. (eds.) RAID 2011. LNCS, vol. 6961, pp. 1–20. Springer, Heidelberg (2011)
8. Certec EDV: Atvise SCADA (2014). http://www.atvise.com/en/products-solutions/atvise-scada
9. Check Point: Misfortune cookie. http://blog.checkpoint.com/2014/12/18/misfortune-cookie-the-hole-in-your-internet-gateway-3/
10. Cisco Systems: Cisco ACE web application firewall, May 2008. http://www.cisco.com/c/en/us/products/collateral/application-networking-services/ace-web-application-firewall/data_sheet_c78-458627.html
11. Cisco Systems: Home network administration protocol (HNAP) whitepaper, January 2009. http://www.cisco.com/web/partners/downloads/guest/hnap_protocol_whitepaper.pdf
12. Coen, T.: Bypass CSRF via XSS. Software talk, March 2015. http://software-talk.org/blog/2015/03/bypass-csrf-via-xss/
13. Cowan, C., et al.: StackGuard: automatic adaptive detection and prevention of buffer-overflow attacks. In: 7th USENIX Security Symposium (1998)
14. D-Link: DIR-645: Rev. Ax–Command injection–Buffer overflow: FW 1.04b12, January 2015. http://securityadvisories.dlink.com/security/publication.aspx?name=SAP10051
15. Davi, L., Sadeghi, A.R., Winandy, M.: ROPdefender: a detection tool to defend against return-oriented programming attacks. In: 6th ACM Symposium on Information, Computer, and Communications Security, pp. 40–51. ASIACCS (2011)

16. DD-WRT Wiki: Web interface. http://www.dd-wrt.com/wiki/index.php/Web_Interface

17. Django Software Foundation: Cross site request forgery protection (2015). https://docs.djangoproject.com/en/1.8/ref/csrf/

18. Doyle, J.: Lorex IP camera authentication bypass (CVE-2012-6451), December 2012. https://www.fishnetsecurity.com/6labs/blog/lorex-ip-camera-authentication-bypass-cve-2012-6451

19. Durumeric, Z., Wustrow, E., Halderman, J.A.: ZMap: fast internet-wide scanning and its security applications. In: 22nd USENIX Security Symposium (2013)

20. epoll(7): process trace. Linux Programmer's Manual

21. Franks, J., Hallam-Baker, P., Hostetler, J., Lawrence, S., Leach, P., Luotonen, A., Stewart, L.: HTTP authentication: basic and digest access authentication. RFC 2617 (Draft Standard), June 1999, updated by RFC 7235. http://www.ietf.org/rfc/rfc2617.txt

22. Fu, K., Blum, J.: Inside risks: controlling for cybersecurity risks of medical device software. Commun. ACM **56**(10), 21–23 (2013)

23. Ghena, B., Beyer, W., Hillaker, A., Pevarnek, J., Halderman, J.A.: Green lights forever: analyzing the security of traffic infrastructure. In: 8th USENIX Workshop on Offensive Technologies. WOOT (2014)

24. Heninger, N., Durumeric, Z., Wustrow, E., Halderman, J.A.: Mining your Ps and Qs: detection of widespread weak keys in network devices. In: 21st USENIX Security Symposium, August 2012

25. Hewlett-Packard: HP Jetdirect print servers–Using Telnet to configure the HP Jetdirect print server. http://h20564.www2.hp.com/hpsc/doc/public/display?docId=emr_na-bpj05732

26. Hewlett-Packard: HP embedded web server user guide, August 2007. http://h20628.www2.hp.com/km-ext/kmcsdirect/emr_na-c01151842-2.pdf

27. Hewlett-Packard: TippingPoint next-generation firewall (NGFW) technical specifications (2015). http://www8.hp.com/us/en/software-solutions/ngfw-next-generation-firewall/tech-specs.html

28. Internet Security Research Group: Let's Encrypt (2015). https://letsencrypt.org/

29. Jones, N.: Exploiting embedded devices, June 2012. http://pen-testing.sans.org/resources/papers/gpen/exploiting-embedded-devices-129676

30. Joyent: HTTP parser, April 2015. https://github.com/joyent/http-parser

31. Ketkar, C.: Standard versus proprietary security protocols. Justice League Blog, May 2014. http://www.cigital.com/justice-league-blog/2014/05/28/standard-versus-proprietary-security-protocols/

32. Klein, G., et al.: seL4: Formal verification of an OS kernel. In: 22nd Symposium on Operating Systems Principles. pp. 207–220. SOSP, October 2009

33. Kneschke, J.: Lighttpd: Fly light, March 2014. http://www.lighttpd.net/

34. Lafon, Y., Mendelsohn, N., Karmarkar, A., Nielsen, H.F., Hadley, M., Gudgin, M., Moreau, J.J.: SOAP version 1.2 part 2: Adjuncts (2nd edn.). W3C recommendation, April 2007. http://www.w3.org/TR/soap12-part2/

35. Leroy, X., Blazy, S., Dargaye, Z., Jourdan, J.H., Tristan, J.B.: CompCert, June 2015. http://compcert.inria.fr/

36. Lewis, D.: Security and the Internet of Things. Forbes, September 2014. http://www.forbes.com/sites/davelewis/2014/09/16/security-and-the-internet-of-things/

37. Linksys: GPL code center (2014). http://support.linksys.com/en-us/gplcodecenter

38. Medin, T.: Invasion of the network snatchers: Part I. SANS Penetration Testing, May 2013. http://pen-testing.sans.org/blog/2013/05/31/invasion-of-the-network-snatchers-part-i

39. MITRE Corporation: CVE-2014-4645, June 2014. http://cve.mitre.org/cgi-bin/cvename.cgi?name=CVE-2014-4645

40. MITRE Corporation: Common vulnerabilities and exposures, April 2015. https://cve.mitre.org/

41. Moore, H.D.: Penetration tester's guide to IPMI and BMCs. Rapid7Community, July 2013. https://community.rapid7.com/community/metasploit/blog/2013/07/02/a-penetration-testers-guide-to-ipmi

42. Nachreiner, C.: H.D. Moore unveils major UPnP security vulnerabilities. WatchGuard Security Center, January 2013. http://watchguardsecuritycenter.com/2013/01/31/h-d-moore-unveils-major-upnp-security-vulnerabilities/

43. Open Crypto Audit Project: Welcome to the Open Crypto Audit Project, June 2014. https://opencryptoaudit.org/

44. OpenSSL Project: Welcome to the OpenSSL project (2015). https://www.openssl.org/

45. OpenWRT Project: Web server configuration uHTTPd (2014). http://wiki.openwrt.org/doc/uci/uhttpd

46. Orchard, D., McCabe, F., Newcomer, E., Haas, H., Ferris, C., Booth, D., Champion, M.: Web services architecture. W3C note, February 2004. http://www.w3.org/TR/2004/NOTE-ws-arch-20040211/

47. PCI Security Standards Council: Payment Card Industry (PCI) data security standard requirements and security assessment procedures version 3.1, April 2015. https://www.pcisecuritystandards.org/documents/PCI_DSS_v3-1.pdf

48. Rectanus, B.: IronBee reference manual (2014). https://www.ironbee.com/docs/manual/

49. Rocha, M., Riva, N., Falcon, F., Santamaria, P.: D-Link IP cameras multiple vulnerabilities, April 2013. http://www.coresecurity.com/advisories/d-link-ip-cameras-multiple-vulnerabilities

50. Rosenblatt, S.: Car hacking code released at Defcon. CNET, August 2013. http://www.cnet.com/news/car-hacking-code-released-at-defcon/

51. Rust Core Team: The Rust programming language. http://www.rust-lang.org/

52. Rust Core Team: Announcing Rust 1.0. Rust Programming Language Blog, May 2015. http://blog.rust-lang.org/2015/05/15/Rust-1.0.html

53. Siemens: WinCC/Web navigator: Operator control and monitoring via the web. http://w3.siemens.com/mcms/human-machine-interface/en/visualization-software/scada/wincc-options/wincc-web-navigator/pages/default.aspx

54. Spengler, B.: Grsecurity ACL documentation v1.5, April 2003. https://grsecurity.net/gracldoc.htm

55. Supermicro: Supermicro intelligent management (2015). http://www.supermicro.com/products/nfo/IPMI.cfm

56. Trustwave SpiderLabs: ModSecurity: Open source web application firewall (2015). https://www.modsecurity.org/

57. Wagle, P., Cowan, C.: StackGuard: simple stack smash protection for GCC. In: GCC Developers Summit, pp. 243–255, May 2003

Towards Standardising Firewall Reporting

Dinesha Ranathunga[1]([✉]), Matthew Roughan[1], Phil Kernick[3],
and Nick Falkner[2]

[1] ARC Centre of Excellence for Mathematical and Statistical Frontiers,
University of Adelaide, Adelaide, Australia
dinesha.ranathunga@adelaide.edu.au
[2] School of Computer Science, University of Adelaide, Adelaide, Australia
[3] CQR Consulting, Unley, Australia

Abstract. Rubin and Greer stated that "The single most important factor of your firewall's security is how you configure it." [17]. However, firewall configuration is known to be difficult to get right. In particular domains, such as SCADA networks, while there are best practice standards that help, an overlooked component is the specification of firewall reporting policies. Our research tackles this question from first principles: we ask what are the uses of firewall reports, and we allow these to guide how reporting should be performed. We approach the problem by formalising the notion of *scope* and *granularity* of a report across several dimensions: time, network elements, policies, *etc.*

Keywords: SCADA security · Firewall autoconfiguration · Zone-Conduit model · Firewall reporting · Report granularity · Granularity dimension

1 Introduction

"The only thing worse than no coffee is bad coffee."

The quote is germane because the only thing worse than no security is bad security. The appearance of security permits behaviour that would be more carefully scrutinised in an insecure domain. For instance, we might allow unpatched systems behind a firewall, confident in the blanket of protection provided.

In the context of complex networks, it is terribly easy to either misconfigure firewalls or, for some part of the security setup to otherwise malfunction, either breaking the network or reducing its security.

There are many workable steps to guard against such failure, but one of the most important is to constantly examine the security mechanisms of the network. This can be performed externally, and by using reports from the devices involved.

However, even in domains such as Supervisory Control and Data Acquisition (SCADA) networks, which control the distributed assets of many critical systems such as power generation and water distribution, the standards for reporting and analysing firewall data are scant and vague. At the same time, SCADA networks

© Springer International Publishing Switzerland 2016
A. Bécue et al. (Eds.): CyberICS 2015/WOS-CPS 2015, LNCS 9588, pp. 127–143, 2016.
DOI: 10.1007/978-3-319-40385-4_9

often incorporate highly vulnerable devices. The Programmable Logic Controllers (PLCs) that control physical devices such as gas valves have highly constrained memory and computational power. Today, they often include network functionality such as a TCP/IP stack, but exclude sophisticated security functionality. Thus, firewalls are a critical component of SCADA networks. As Rubin and Greer note [17] it is vital that these firewalls are configured correctly.

Most firewalls have the ability to generate reports in highly flexible and diverse ways (*e.g.,* logs, traps, alarms and alerts). But we lack clear direction in what they *should* report. This paper starts the discussion on how reporting policy should be specified by

i. Looking at the ways firewall reports can be used, and how that impacts reporting requirements.
ii. From this, formalising notions of the *scope* and *granularity* of reports.
iii. Considering which use cases are actually reasonable uses of firewall resources.

We find that reporting at the right granularity is key to saving valuable firewall and network resources while achieving the required use case outcomes. In some cases a low (*i.e.,* coarse) granularity such as the reporting of configuration changes at a firewall level is sufficient. In other cases a higher (*i.e.,* refined) reporting granularity in the likes of recording individual IP packets is required. The volume of firewall reports generated usually increases with granularity and can have a detrimental effect on a SCADA firewall's primary function- traffic filtering. Identifying reporting granularity requirements can help justify whether a potential use case is best served if it is conducted by a SCADA firewall or not.

We also find that reporting needs to be coupled with security policy specification to be of use. This important principle has been overlooked in the best practices [2,20]. Coupling reporting and policy also provides security managers with a *single source of truth* for easy reference.

2   Background

Firewall configuration is a critical activity, yet hard to get right. It involves training in proprietary and device specific configuration languages, and the production of long and complex device configurations.

The problem of firewall configuration is well studied. Fang [10] and Lumeta [21] are interactive management and analysis tools that run queries on firewall rules to check for errors. Tools such as these have been used to analyse working firewalls configurations and have shown that critical errors are very common, even in quite simple networks [15,22,23]. We argue that this difficulty extends to firewall reporting, and that this component is also important to get right.

Firewall vendors have introduced many products and security management tools with varying levels of sophistication [3,4,6,8]. However, what these tools have typically done is to increase the range of options. They provide more power, but we still lack guidelines on how to best utilise this power.

In the context of SCADA networks, critical systems are protected by firewalls, and so best practice guidelines have been prepared to help. They suggest a number of high-level policy abstractions for SCADA networks [1]. In particular, we refer to the *Zone-Conduit abstraction* as a way of segmenting and isolating the various sub-systems. Firewall reporting is not considered in detail, however. We will demonstrate that it is useful to link firewall reporting to policy, so we include a brief description of this abstraction.

A *zone* is a logical or physical grouping of an organisation's systems with similar security requirements so that a single policy can be defined for all zone members. A *conduit* provides the secure communication path between two zones, enforcing the policy between them [1]. Security mitigation mechanisms (*e.g.,* firewalls) implemented within a conduit helps it to resist Denial of Service (DoS) attacks, and preserve the integrity and confidentiality of network traffic. A conduit could consist of multiple links and firewalls but, logically, is a single connector.

3   Firewall Reporting Use Cases

Firewalls can generate logs, alerts, traps, and provide other information for instance via SNMP (Simple Network Management Protocol) polling. We term all these informational content together as *reporting*.

Most firewalls allow a panoply of highly flexible and configurable reports. It is hard to even categorise all of the possibilities without some framework. It is useful here to consider the classical hierarchy of knowledge that *data* → *information* → *knowledge* → *decisions*. If the data does not inform decisions its value is zero, so simply collecting data is insufficient motivation for the cost of collection. Hence we base our framework on *use cases*. That is, we frame our discussion of what to report based on how the data will be used.

We reviewed the literature on firewall reporting in both SCADA and Corporate domains [9,18,19] and classified the various uses of the reports. Out of necessity, we grouped certain activities together, and simplified the nomenclature. Our resulting classification is as follows:[1]

Accounting measures network usage, for instance, to monitor network bandwidth usage for network planning.

Network-based Intrusion Detection (ID) is the near real-time monitoring of network traffic to identify traffic from unauthorised sources [19]. Near real-time implies without a significant delay (allowing transmission and automated processing delays), usually up to a few minutes [19]. Network-based ID particularly helps administrators to secure a SCADA network by blocking the attack before it causes damage to critical systems.

For example, some firewalls can monitor traffic that passes key network locations, and generate alarms when known attack signatures are present. Other firewalls might send traffic data to an ID system for analysis.

---

[1] At this point we classify existing activities and do not consider which of these cases is a sensible use of firewall resources.

Post-mortem analysis is the analysis of an *incident* after the fact. Analysis aims to identify root causes in order to prevent future occurrences. In a cyber-physical domain, analysis may be mandatory to meet regulatory compliance.

Security policy verification checks a firewall rule base for invalid rules. Configuration inefficiencies in firewalls are largely due to obsolete rules (*e.g.,* rules pertaining to a decommissioned server) and incorrect rules (*e.g.,* rules with source and destination IP address in wrong order) [15,22]. Efficient firewall configurations can be maintained by identifying such invalid rules.

Troubleshooting operational issues is the debugging of network errors associated with firewalls, for instance, to identify the root cause(s) of connection problems through a firewall.

Given the primary function of a firewall is traffic filtering, we need to carefully consider what secondary reporting functions should be conducted by a firewall. To do so, we need to identify the reporting granularities associated with each use case above. We discuss these requirements in detail next.

4   Report Granularity and Scope

Firewall reports can be thought of as a form of *lossy data compression*. A firewall will internally register myriad events and data. A report, whether it be an alarm or log-message or polled counter, is a compressed form of this information.

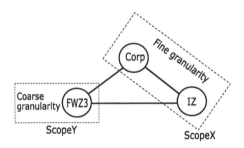

Fig. 1. Illustration of scope vs granularity.

Ideally, we would lose as little information as possible in compressing the data. Even the most effective compression mechanism (*e.g.,* JPEG images) allow some loss, but try to ensure that it is not important information. In the context of firewalls, we aim to initiate a discussion of what is important through discussing the *resolution* or *granularity* of reports[2]. Granularity refers to the finest level of the discrimination we can make. For instance, in an image, resolution or granularity is the pixel size – we can't separate objects in an image that are

---

[2] Although we view the two terms as close to synonymous in this context, resolution is overloaded with meaning and so we prefer the term granularity.

smaller. The first concern when compressing an image would be how many pixels do we need, and so this is a first step in considering firewall reports.

Related to granularity is *scope*. In image terms, this is analogous to field-of-view, *i.e.*, how widely is the data collected. We can talk about both scope and granularity with the same terminology, though the details can vary across the network as shown in Fig. 1.

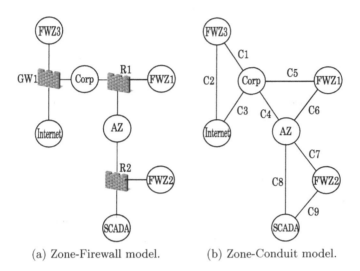

(a) Zone-Firewall model.   (b) Zone-Conduit model.

Fig. 2. Security models of a SCADA network adapted from a case study [15].

To help refine our discussions, Fig. 2 depicts the *Zone-Firewall* and *Zone-Conduit* models of an example SCADA network from an actual case study [15].

Most vendor firewalls support different reporting *verbosity* levels, *e.g.*, debug, info, warning [3,4,8,14]. However, the terminology (for instance *warning* level) is not universal. We aim here for *vendor-independent* notions of reporting, and so will avoid these terms.

The terms also obscure the multiple dimensions of firewall reporting: for instance, the level could refer to nature of events with respect to the network, policy definitions, or time. Hence, in the next section, we will tease these aspects of reporting detail by considering granularity and scope with respect to the multiple aspects of a network that firewalls observe.

4.1   Granularity Dimensions

Network Granularity is the level of detail resolved in a network. Firewall reports may need to resolve network-specific detail, often at a network-wide, Zone-Conduit, interface, prefix or IP address level. We describe these levels of detail in order of increasing granularity next.

(i) **Network-wide-level** refers to an entire network. At this level we might only distinguish between events internal, and external to the network. This might be important for intrusion detection or post-mortem analysis, and for general accounting of network usage.

(ii) **Zone-Conduit-level** resolves information per zone. For instance, in intrusion detection, we might like to understand which components of the network (*e.g.,* SCADA or Corporate) were potentially compromised, and the zone concept requires that all network elements in a zone are treated equally (*i.e.,* even if only one IP address is *observed* to be attacked, we assume all might have been, at least through proxy attacks).

(iii) **Prefix-level** resolves information per block of IP addresses. Where zones are not used, we might naturally wish to group data for analysis by subnet.

(iv) **Interface-level** resolves information per firewall interface. Large firewall installations could have multiple interfaces serving a zone, and/or there is the question of where traffic triggers an event: when it enters a firewall, or leaves it. This level of resolution is needed when such fine discrimination is important, for instance, in troubleshooting firewall problems.

(v) **IP-address-level** resolves information per network host (*e.g.,* a server). This is the finest network-granularity usually possible, though sometimes virtual machines could be hosted by separate ports at a single IP address.

We seek to define granularity in terms of a hierarchy in which the information present in a coarser granularity can be derived from the finer. This hierarchy is shown in Fig. 3, and note that it should recur in other granularity dimensions.

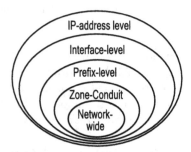

Fig. 3. Network granularity hierarchy: Coarse granularities are subsets of the finer.

Policy Granularity is the level of detail resolved in a security policy. Firewall reports may need to resolve policy detail, often at a global, zone, service, rule or sub-rule level. We describe these below.

(i) **Global-level** resolves rule-set wide information for a policy. *i.e.,* it separates events or traffic into *in-policy* and *out-of-policy* traffic. Out-of-policy traffic includes 'defective' traffic (*e.g.,* packets with ill-formed headers). Such data can help track the amount of attack traffic aimed at a network.

(ii) **Zone-policy-level** refines the global-level by resolving traffic that is in- and out-of-policy at the zone level, so that we can see, for instance the amount of attack traffic breaching the outer level of a defence-in-depth.

(iii) **Service-policy-level** level of detail resolves policy details per service either allowed or explicitly denied in a firewalls security policy.

(iv) **Rule-level** refines the Service-policy-level by noting that a "service" might be defined by several rules. One common example is a service such as WWW, which could include HTTP and HTTPS. Another is a service that requires requests to be allowed in one direction, and responses in the other.

Traffic Measurement Granularity is one of the common reports firewalls may produce concerns the traffic they observe, either generally, or because it matches some particular pattern (*e.g.,* it is invalid, or matches a particular type of attack) or translation (*e.g.,* IP header changes by NAT, or IP payload encryption by IPSec in a VPN tunnel). We describe here the granularity with which traffic can be reported.

(i) **Counter-level** resolves traffic measurement details into certain bins, and then counts the amount of traffic into these bins. The granularity of the bins is defined by the previous two dimensions of network- and policy-level.

For instance, in policy verification, the key interest is in whether a policy rule has hits (*i.e.,* if IP packet matches have been recorded for the corresponding ACL rules).

The nature of the information recorded in each bin might vary: commonly we might measure packets, bytes, or connections (or all three). However, we lose all of the meaning within the packets.

(ii) **Connection-level** records traffic per connection. It is very similar to flow-level, which we discuss in more detail below.

(iii) **Flow-level** resolves traffic measurements per IP flow: *i.e.,* by grouping a series of connected packets, typically those with the same IP protocol, IP source and destination addresses, and TCP source and destination ports.

For instance, in accounting for network usage, it may be necessary to resolve the source IP from the destination IP address of a flow. This would resolve the upload and download traffic of a host or subnet. Such flows are almost analogous to connections, but are easier to collect.

(iv) **Packet-header-level** records each packets' headers. It includes information such as the *flags* and *fragment-offset* fields in the IP header, which indicate whether IP fragments can produce a complete datagram.

(v) **Packet-level** requires us to store whole packets, or at least a substantial part of each packet. This allows us to reconstruct, for instance, the details of a particular attack.

The traffic granularity discussion illustrates one important issue. Traffic measurements are collected using many different *mechanisms*, and the mechanism is often related to the type of measurement. For instance, SNMP is often used to collect counter-level data, and NetFlow to collect flow-level data.

However, this is just how it is done now. We aim to define universal concepts, and leave the mechanisms of their implementation to the engineers building devices. The goal of device and vendor independence requires this approach of decoupling what we want to measure, from how it is measured.

Performance Measurement Granularity is another of the common reports firewalls may produce concerns performance metrics. Of the many measurements attributable to a firewall or its interface performance, the memory and CPU utilisation are most significant. Both metrics can help identify ongoing attacks (*e.g.,* DoS) or other problems. Similarly, packet queue-length and packet loss measurements can indicate attacks through overloaded queues resulting from high traffic, *e.g.,* as might result from a DoS attack.

We describe here the granularity with which performance can be reported.

(i) *Firewall-level* records performance measurements per individual firewall. For instance, post-mortem analysis might use firewall CPU and memory utilisation to help resolve the root cause of a network problem.
(ii) *Process-level* records performance measurements per firewall software process. For instance, when a new policy is pushed to a firewall, the policy processing module may fail to load the policy, if the memory required for the policy exceeds the module's allowance [5]. Module's CPU and memory utilisation reports can help troubleshoot firewall problems in this scenario.
(iii) *Interface-level* records performance metrics specific to a firewall interface. For instance, in troubleshooting firewall errors, it may be necessary to resolve reverse DNS lookup errors per firewall interface.

Temporal Granularity is the level of detail (*e.g.,* measurements or counts) resolved per set of time instances. In this context, granularity is not exactly the right concept, but we will explain below.

(i) *Per-T* records detail per time interval T. The measurements could be counter measurements of traffic, configurations changes and so on. Common intervals T vary from
    – daily;
    – hourly; and
    – minutes;
    and potentially finer intervals. However, the mechanisms used to support granularities down to minutes are often not suitable (*e.g.,* SNMP polling) for measurements at per-second granularity and finer, so we qualitatively separate these into the following category.
(ii) *Near-real-time* means reporting data as soon as possible given the limitations of processing and network speed. Delays of up to seconds are reasonable, but not minutes. While the previous granularity can be reported through *pull* mechanisms, nearly all near-real-time support is provided by *push* mechanisms, *e.g.,* traps or notifications or alarms.

Note that it is non-trivial to set up accurate distributed clocks, but doing so should be seen as vital for any level of temporal granularity in order that any data collected is meaningful.

Operational Measurements is another of the common reports firewalls can produce concerns the events they observe. Granularity does not seem to be a useful concept in this domain because there is no reason we would ever store data at a coarser granularity than its origin. The standard means to describe the level of detail in event logs are vague terms such as *debug, error, warning, informational.* They specify the "level" of events to be reported, not the level of detail of the actual reports, but this notion of level is too context dependent to be universally agreed. A warning in one domain is an error in another.

Errors can also be ambiguous to interpret. Some report abnormal behaviour that require no response action (*e.g.,* traffic with a broadcast destination address dropped). Others relate to a significant breakdown in operation that needs urgent attention. We increase clarity by classifying the latter type of errors as *failures.*

We studied corporate firewall logs and identified some common events that occur in real firewall deployments. Logs from five such firewalls were analysed. These aggressively reported on traffic denials at the external firewall interfaces.

Of over 4.5 million log messages in a month, 97.58 % were traffic denial events (both in- and out-of-policy); 1.18 % were power-state changes; 0.78 % were VPN-state changes; 0.42 % were *failures*; and 0.03 % related to firewall-user activity.

Motivated by our findings, and avoiding bland ambiguous terms in favour of precision, we classify events by their nature[3]:

(i) **State transitions:** reports of state changes of the firewall and its components (*e.g.,* interface power-up, software process startup- such as for a HTTP or VPN server).

(ii) **User activity:** reports of user login activity, commands executed by a user logged into firewall including actions to change its configuration, and their consequences, including any errors or warnings.

(iii) **Failures:** reports of breakdown of normal operation (*e.g.,* VPN tunnel failure), that require immediate action. These are not regular state changes and hence are excluded from *state transitions.*

(iv) **Diagnostics:** reports of self-tests deployed on the firewall and their outcomes (*e.g.,* test failover interface).

(v) **Table dumps:** tables of comprehensible information (*e.g.,* active NAT translations) or potential events, internal to a firewall.

As an illustration of the concepts, Fig. 4 is an example summary of the firewall reporting requirements against network-granularity for the use cases discussed. It shows that in each use case a *Zone-Conduit level* network-granularity is required.

---

[3] Note that some types of events are already implicitly included in traffic or performance measurements, for instance, denied packet counts.

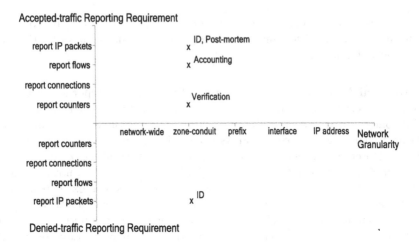

Fig. 4. Traffic reporting requirement vs network granularity: depicts the *zone-conduit level* network-granularity required for each reporting use case.

4.2   Relation Between Reporting Granularity Dimensions

Reporting granularity dimensions may not be entirely orthogonal. We describe the relation that exist between some dimensions below.

Traffic measurement and Time: Packets, flows and connections can arrive at variable rates in time to a firewall. So, the traffic granularity required for each use case can restrict the temporal granularity achievable (and vice versa). For instance, if a use case requires reporting every IP packet, that typically implies reporting at a per millisecond temporal granularity. Conversely, if a firewall reports per millisecond, a packet or flow level of granularity can be achieved.

Traffic measurement and Policy: Traffic granularity requirements can also restrict the policy granularity achievable (and vice versa). For instance, reporting every IP packet implies a rule-level policy granularity. Conversely, if reporting at a rule-level, a packet or flow or connection-level traffic granularity is achievable.

Traffic management and Network: Traffic granularity requirements can also restrict the network granularity achievable (and vice versa). For instance, reporting every connection implies an address-level network granularity. Conversely, if reporting at an address-level, a connection or flow or packet-level traffic granularity is achievable.

For all reporting use cases, the network granularity required is *Zone-Conduit level*. But the relation between traffic and network granularity implies that the actual network granularity achieved is dependent on the traffic granularity of a use case. For instance, intrusion detection requires reporting every IP packet. Adhering to this requirement, a finer *address-level* network-granularity is achieved. A similar network-granularity is obtained for all other use cases.

5   Reporting Cost

Report generation costs CPU, memory and network resources. The cost can potentially impact the performance of a firewall, and compromise its primary function- traffic filtering, so it is an important factor to consider.

The cost depends on several factors: the granularity and scope; whether the reports are distributed or centralised; and the retention period. We have already discussed granularity and scope in detail: finer granularity measurements cost more. We discuss the other two issues below.

5.1   Distributed vs Centralised Analysis and Retention

Firewalls can be configured to report to several destinations including internal storage, NAS (Network-Attached Storage), a report server or historian, a Telnet or SSH session, or an email account [3,4,8].

Distributed collection and retention – by which we mean that the reports are collected and stored at the firewall – has a low network communications cost, but the trade-off is that it requires local storage. Firewalls rarely have very large internal storage, so it must be frequently overwritten or cleared [4].

Moreover, the data lacks use in this form. For example, accurate ID and troubleshooting require correlating reports from multiple sources (firewalls, routers, servers, *etc.*) and to manually extract these from each device is cumbersome.

At the other end of the spectrum lies centralised collection. In this strategy network devices perform minimal analysis of data: they just collect it and pass it to a single repository. Reports can then be analysed together. However, centralised collection creates potentially large volumes of network traffic.

Centralised collection can also introduce security vulnerabilities in a network. The centralised server, by its nature, must collect data across zones with different levels of security. However, many reporting mechanism (for instance syslog) are based on UDP, so a central syslog server would inherit any UDP vulnerabilities. Therefore, a central syslog server should not be located in a high-security zone (*e.g.,* in a SCADA zone) [2]. Another vulnerability stems from unsafe storage of sensitive information (*e.g.,* firewall-admin passwords) in the reports.

However, these vulnerabilities can be minimised with a carefully constructed collection strategy. For example, a syslog server can be placed in a DMZ and polled from the internal networks. Reports can also be sanitised to ensure that an attacker cannot obtain sensitive information. Doing so would allow each use case to reap the benefits of centralised collection, and reduce associated risks. However, this does require a careful and considered report architecture.

In reality, the two polarised extremes of decentralised and centralised are rare. There is actually a spectrum (Fig. 5) where some processing and analysis is distributed but eventually summary data is brought to one or small number of data historians. For example, firewalls typically perform significant processing of network traffic prior to sending back some notifications to a central historian.

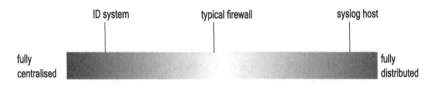

Fig. 5. Spectrum of centralised vs distributed report collection.

5.2 Report Retention

Reported information needs to be retained for some time determined by the requirements of the use case. There are cyber-security industry standards [11,12] for data retention. The rationale for the lengths suggested are, however, not clear, and the standards also make a distinction between *reportable events* and other, without clearly specifying what is reportable.

Given the progressively declining electronic storage costs, and the original data collecting cost, we argue that, from a cyber-security industry point of view, it is more cost-effective today to retain firewall reports (almost) perpetually.

If storage really becomes a problem, then progressive reduction in granularity can be a useful tool. For instance see RRDtool [13].

However, we do consider minimum retention periods for each use case here.

Accounting for network usage reports are useful until the end of an usage evaluation period. Once processed and usage information is extracted, these reports can be purged. They should be retained for a minimum of 90 days [12].

Intrusion detection: Some attacks (*e.g.,* DoS, Port scans) can last longer than others. So, at a minimum, reports must be retained until the attack has passed. Post-attack retention also helps identify the types of attacks common in a network, so better defence mechanisms can be formulated for the future. Industry recommends retaining these reports for a minimum of 90 days [12].

Policy verification reports are useful until a verification period ends. Post report-processing, invalid rules are located and rectified, so reports can be purged. Industry recommends retaining these reports for a minimum of 90 days [12].

Post-mortem analysis reports should allow tracing back of, for instance, the origins of a SCADA network attack that circumvented intrusion detection systems. Doing so, may require processing of historical records that date back several years. These reports should be retained for a minimum of 3 years [11].

Troubleshooting reports are useful to monitor firewall configuration errors in near-real time. Once the error is rectified, they may be archived for future reference. Industry recommends retaining these reports for a minimum of 90 days [12].

6 What *Should* Firewalls Report?

The previous sections discussed what a firewall *could* report, and the use of that data. However, the ability to generate data does not mean we should. There is a cost to data collection, and some functions are better supported elsewhere.

For instance, firewalls have a limited perspective of a network so effective Intrusion Detection (ID) requires additional sensors (for instance at hosts and on wireless networks [19]). However, given such sensors why use the firewall at all? Collecting data at the firewall could compromise its main function through the cost of data collection, which may be amplified by a DoS attack. Moreover, a firewall, by its nature, is a visible target. It is far better to use passive (invisible) sensors for ID.

The conclusion is that a firewall is a poor source of data for ID.

Post-mortem analysis has fine granularity requirements, similar to ID, but lacks the near-real-time requirement. Hence, this use case is a marginally more acceptable use of firewall resources, but should not be implemented lightly.

Network usage accounting also requires traffic reporting but only at *flow-level* traffic-granularity. During a DoS attack, many flows can amplify the effect of the attack. But, if accounting focuses on accepted traffic, this effect is mitigated.

Policy verification is key to maintaining robust and efficient firewall configurations. The granularity requirements for this use case are quite coarse, and other devices cannot provide accurate information on packets that are matched by a firewall's policy, so this type of use case should definitely be supported.

Similarly, troubleshooting requires coarse information that can only be collected by the firewall, *e.g.,* an accurate change history can only be obtained from the firewall itself. Hence, firewall reporting should be enabled for this use case.

7 Implementation

We make the ideas discussed so far concrete, by presenting our implementation next. A goal is to extend *ForestFirewalls*: a high-level security policy specification system built using the Zone-Conduit model [16]. It aims to improve the efficiency and reliability of the SCADA firewall configuration process. This paper concentrates on reporting, so we describe the mechanism for the two use cases that require firewall reporting: (i) *policy verification* and (ii) *troubleshooting*.

Current firewall configuration platforms present "policy" and reporting as separate functions. Decoupling can be useful in some contexts to separate *structure* from *function*, *e.g.,* to separate security policy from the underlying network.

However, reporting and security policy are *inter-dependent* network functions. Scope and granularity are intimately related to the use of data, which, in turn, is related to the corresponding policies. Decoupling the two allows bad decisions to be made: for instance, addition of policies that aren't verified.

The Object Oriented Programming [7] paradigm makes it clear that *encapsulation* of related concepts and code together is vital for reliable and maintainable systems. A useful policy specification platform should encapsulate related specifications together. This implies that security policy and reporting specifications should be encapsulated together. Doing so, gives SCADA security managers a *single source of truth* to see 'who gets in and who doesn't' along with audit trails required to check the configuration. We show how this works in the following.

7.1 Reporting Policy for Verification

The granularity and scope requirements for a typical policy verification scenario are given in Table 1. We then list, in Table 2, the resulting reporting *attributes* grouped by granularity dimension. These are specified in the system as follows:

```
rule_group security_policy_rules {<rule1>, <rule2>,..., <ruleN>}

reporting_rule verify_a_rule { use_case=verification;
    granularity.policy={rule_or_group={<rule1>}};
    granularity.traffic={measurement={counter}; counter_type={connection};};
    granularity.temporal={per_hour};}

policy <policy-name>  { security_policy_rules; verify_a_rule; }
```

A `rule_group` contains a set of security policy rules, and a `reporting_rule` object defines a set of reporting requirements. The `policy` object encapsulates the security policy rules and the reporting rule together. This facilitates reuse both of policies and reporting rules (which could come from a library), but encapsulates them together in the final specification.

7.2 Reporting Policy for Troubleshooting

A summary of the granularity requirements for this use case is given in Table 3. The list of specification attributes is given in Table 4. We use these attributes to specify troubleshoot reporting for one or more firewalls as:

Table 1. Summary of reporting granularity requirements for policy verification.

Granularity dimension	Required granularity	Scope
Network	zone-conduit	network-wide
Policy	rule	global
Traffic-measurement	connection-count	counter
Temporal	per-hour	per-day
Performance	process	firewall

Table 2. Reporting policy attributes derived for policy verification.

Reporting attribute	Example value
use_case	verification;
granularity.network	{zone_or_group={SCADA}; traffic_direction={inbound};}
granularity.policy	{rule_or_group={rule1}; policy_action={permit};}
granularity.traffic	{measurement={counter}; counter_type={connection};}
granularity.temporal	{per_hour}
granularity.performance	{process}

Table 3. Reporting granularity requirements for troubleshooting firewall errors.

Granularity Dimension	Required granularity	Scope
Network	Zone-Conduit	network-wide
Policy	rule	global
Temporal	near real-time	per-day
Performance	interface	firewall

Table 4. Reporting policy attributes for troubleshooting firewall errors.

Reporting attribute	Example value
use_case	troubleshoot;
granularity.network	{zone_or_group={SCADA}; traffic_direction={inbound};}
granularity.policy	{rule_or_group={rule1}; policy_action={permit};}
granularity.temporal	{near_realtime}
granularity.performance	{measurement={interface};}

```
rule_group security_policy_rules {<rule1>, <rule2>,..., <ruleN>}

zone_group FIREWALL_ZONES {<zone1>, <zone2>,..., <zoneM>}

reporting_rule debug_firewalls { use_case=troubleshoot;
     granularity.network={zone_or_group={FIREWALL_ZONES};
                         traffic_direction={inbound, outbound}};
     granularity.policy={rule_or_group={security_policy_rules}};
     granularity.performance={measurement={interface};
        performance_type={memory, CPU, packet_loss, queue_length}};
     granularity.temporal={near_realtime};}

policy <policy-name>  { security_policy_rules;  debug_firewalls; }
```

As before, the **reporting_rule** object for the use case includes the attributes, *e.g.*, *interface-level* performance statistics and *near real-time* temporal-granularity. The reporting rule is encapsulated in the **policy** statement.

8   Lessons Learned

There are several takeaways from our study:

1. A SCADA firewall should not cater for every use case. For some use cases, it is better to employ additional dedicated infrastructure to meet requirements, and allow firewalls to focus on their primary function: *traffic filtering.*
2. Firewall reporting should be configured at the right granularity for its use. Data that is collected but not used is just wasting resources.
3. Reporting and policy need to be coupled. Both are inter-dependent network functions and there is little sense in deploying one without the other.

4. Firewall vendors need to support standard firewall features to consistently map high-level reporting policy to firewall capabilities. These include: performance, operational and traffic measurements, and policy actions.

9   Conclusion and Future Work

The standards and best practices for reporting and analysis of firewall data lack clarity in what firewalls *should* report.

Our research utilises the use cases of firewall reports and specifies reporting in terms of scope and granularity. From this we identify reporting requirements with respect to several dimensions: time, network elements, policies, *etc.*, and evaluate costs. We provide clarity on what a SCADA firewall *should* report, and demonstrate our high-level reporting implementation.

Acknowledgements. This project was supported by the Australian Government through an Australian Postgraduate Award, Australian Research Council Linkage Grant LP100200493, and CQR Consulting.

References

1. ANSI, ISA-62443-1-1. Security for industrial automation, control systems part 1–1: Terminology, concepts, and models (2007)
2. Byres, E., Karsch, J., Carter, J.: NISCC good practice guide on firewall deployment for SCADA and process control networks. National Infrastructure Security Coordination Centre (2005)
3. Check Point. NGX R65 CC Evaluated Configuration User Guide. Check Point, software technologies Ltd., USA (2008)
4. Cisco Systems. Cisco ASA 5500 Series Configuration Guide using the CLI. Cisco Systems Inc., 170 West Tasman Drive, San Jose, CA 95134–1706, USA (2010)
5. Cisco Systems. ASA 8.3 and later: Monitor and troubleshoot performance issues. White paper, Cisco Systems, March 2014
6. Cisco Systems. Cisco ASA 5585-X adaptive security appliance architecture. White paper, Cisco Systems, May 2014
7. De Champeaux, D., Lea, D., Faure, P.: Object-oriented System Development. Addison Wesley, Reading (1993)
8. Juniper Networks. Firewall Filter and Policer Configuration Guide. Juniper Networks Inc., 1194 North Mathilda Avenue, Sunnyvale, California 94089, USA (2011)
9. Kent, K., Souppaya, M.: Guide to computer security log management. NIST Spec. Publ. **800**(92), 16–16 (2006)
10. Mayer, A., Wool, A., Ziskind, E.F.: A firewall analysis engine. In: IEEE Symposium on Security and Privacy, pp. 177–187 (2000)
11. NERC. Cyber security- Incident reporting and response planning. Critical Infrastructure Protection Standards, 008(3) (2009)
12. NERC. Cyber security- Systems security management. Critical Infrastructure Protection Standards, 007(3a) (2013)
13. Oetiker, T.: RRDtool. http://oss.oetiker.ch/rrdtool/
14. Purdy, G.N.: Linux Iptables Pocket Reference. O'Reilly Media Inc., USA (2004)

15. Ranathunga, D., Roughan, M., Kernick, P., Falkner, N., Nguyen, H.: Identifying the missing aspects of the ANSI/ISA best practices for security policy. In: Proceedings of CPSS, pp. 37–48. ACM (2015)

16. Ranathunga, D., Roughan, M., Kernick, P., Falkner, N., Tune, P.: ForestFire-walls: Getting firewall configuration right in critical networks. http://tinyurl.com/pzqtzkm

17. Rubin, A., Geer, D.: A survey of Web security. Computer **31**(9), 34–41 (1998)

18. Scarfone, K., Hoffman, P.: Guidelines on firewalls and firewall policy. NIST Spec. Publ. 800(41), 1–48 (2009)

19. Scarfone, K., Mell, P.: Guide to Intrusion Detection and Prevention Systems (IDPS). NIST Spec. Publ. **800**(94), 16–16 (2007)

20. Stouffer, K., Falco, J., Scarfone, K.: Guide to Industrial Control Systems (ICS) security. NIST Spec. Publ. **800**(82), 16–16 (2008)

21. Wool, A.: Architecting the Lumeta firewall analyzer. In: USENIX Security Symposium, pp. 85–97 (2001)

22. Wool, A.: A quantitative study of firewall configuration errors. IEEE Comput. **37**(6), 62–67 (2004)

23. Wool, A.: Trends in firewall configuration errors: Measuring the holes in Swiss cheese. IEEE Internet Comput. **14**(4), 58–65 (2010)

CyberICS 2015 Short Papers

Forensics in Industrial Control System: A Case Study

Pieter Van Vliet[2], M.-T. Kechadi[1], and Nhien-An Le-Khac[1(✉)]

[1] School of Computer Science and Informatics, University College Dublin,
Belfield, Dublin 4, Ireland
{tahar.kechadi,an.lekhac}@ucd.ie
[2] Rijkswaterstaat Security Centre, Ministry of Infrastructure
and the Environment, Derde Werelddreef 1, Delft, The Netherlands
pieter.van.vliet01@rws.nl

Abstract. Industrial Control Systems (ICS) are used worldwide in critical infrastructures. An ICS system can be a single embedded system working stand-alone for controlling a simple process or ICS can also be a very complex Distributed Control System (DCS) connected to Supervisory Control And Data Acquisition (SCADA) system(s) in a nuclear power plant. Although ICS are widely used today, there are very little research on the forensic acquisition and analyze ICS's artefacts. In this paper we present a case study of forensics in ICS where we describe a method of safeguarding important volatile artefacts from an embedded industrial control system and several other sources.

Keywords: Industrial control system · Forensic artefacts · Forensic process · Case study

1 Introduction

Industrial Control Systems (ICS) are used worldwide in critical infrastructures. The term "critical infrastructure" conjures up images of highways, electrical grids, pipelines, government facilities and utilities. But the U.S. government definition also includes economic security and public health. The Department of Homeland Security defines critical infrastructure as "Systems and assets, whether physical or virtual, so vital to the United States that the incapacity or destruction of such systems and assets would have a debilitating impact on security, national economic security, national public health or safety, or any combination of those matters." [1].

In fact ICS is a broad term used in a variety of industries. ICS is not a single system but is a general term. As mentioned in the abstract, an ICS system can be a single embedded system like a Programmable Logic Controller (PLC) working stand-alone for controlling a simple process like an automatic door in an office building or an elevator in the same office building. ICS can also be a very complex Distributed Control System (DCS) connected to Supervisory Control And Data Acquisition (SCADA) system(s) [6] in a nuclear power plant.

On the other hand, there is little knowledge of ICS in the "forensic computer investigator world" resulting in a serious need for computer forensics to become more

© Springer International Publishing Switzerland 2016
A. Bécue et al. (Eds.): CyberICS 2015/WOS-CPS 2015, LNCS 9588, pp. 147–156, 2016.
DOI: 10.1007/978-3-319-40385-4_10

informed. Cybercrime related issues such as espionage and terrorism are challenges, but forensic investigations involving a fire in a chemical plant or explosion in electrical grid systems are increasing challenges for digital investigation units.

In most ICS systems a big part of the system are normal computers. Also the network diagrams and protocols are mostly just like normal ICT with conventional network setup and well-known protocols. For this part of the system traditional investigation methods are sufficient for digital investigation on the ICS system. Normal hard disk investigation, log analysis and network tools can be used to investigate what is running on the system and reveal the cause of the incident. However, standard forensics methodologies do not have inherent data collection capabilities for Programmable Logic Controller (PLC), Remote Terminal Unit (RTU), Intelligent Electronic Device (IED), or some other field-level device that is empowered to communicate through these communications mechanisms. In any ICS investigation, regardless of the age or uniqueness of the environment, collecting information from these field devices is a difficult task. Unlike normal ICT systems, ICS systems are designed with another perspective. ICS systems are designed with Safety in mind, rather than Security. The ICS timeline is also quite different in relation to ICT systems. An ICS system is designed for much longer periods of time. It is common for an ICS system to run for 20 or 30 years without update or upgrade.

With the experience of decades of forensic investigator career including many investigations related to ICS systems, authors discovered the lack of a framework for ICS forensics to safeguard the important information from the ICS system. Safeguard this information is a difficult task for computer forensics. PLC and DCS systems are embedded systems with their own operating systems and program languages. Dedicated hardware and many protocols are in use. Most digital forensic investigations techniques only cover conventional computer forensics and network investigations. Therefore, in this paper, we present an ICS Forensic process including important steps for acquiring important digital evidence for digital forensic investigation purposes. Not only the technical part of "how to safeguard" the important information is investigated, also the different jargon, perspective, timelines, goals and mind-set is described. We also focus on a case study of forensics in ICS system. The rest of this paper is organised as follows: Sect. 2 shows the related work of digital forensics for ICS systems. We discuss on ICS forensics challenges in Sect. 3, we also present an ICS process in this section. We describe and discuss a case study of ICS forensics in Sect. 4. Finally, we conclude and discuss on future work in Sect. 5.

2 Related Work

Forensic ICS in literature are very often only related to SCADA systems. Some research topics contains more or less information about other devices like PLC, DCS, Industrial protocols (Modbus [7], Profibus [8] etc.) or security related issues on industrial control systems.

In 2013 Wu et al. [1] proposed SCADA Forensics Architecture and the increasing threat of sophisticated attacks on critical infrastructures, the limitations of using traditional forensic investigative processes and the challenges facing forensic investigators and there are no methodologies or data acquisition tools to extract data from embedded devices such as PLCs. There are data acquisition tools compatible with some field devices with the use of cables and flashing equipment, although this type of equipment is usually used for system servicing and repairs. This makes it difficult to obtain less common models of PLCs and RTUs and forensically sound access to the RAM and ROM on these devices is difficult to achieve without first turning the device off.

Barbosa [2] described Anomaly Detection in SCADA Systems, A Network Based Approach. He presented an extensive characterization of network traces collected in SCADA networks used in utility sector: water treatment and distribution facilities, and gas and electricity providers and note that despite the increasing number of publications in the area of SCADA networks, very little information is publicly available about real-world SCADA traffic. The number of attacks reported to the United States' Department of Homeland Security (DHS) grew from 9 in 2009, to 198 in 2011 and 171 in 2012.

van der Knijff [3] discussed on the difference between Control systems and SCADA forensics and the forensic knowledge and skills that are needed in the field of hardware, networks and data analysis. Assistance from experienced field engineers during forensic acquisition seems inevitable in order to guarantee process safety business continuity and examination efficiency. For specific control system components, there are currently no dedicated forensic tools to support acquisition and analysis of data. Instead of expensive and time-consuming physical examination methods, it is more practical to use existing tools and knowledge from the control system industry.

In 2008 U.S. Department of Homeland Security [4] provided a guidance for creating a cyber-forensics program for a control systems environment. This guidance described the challenges with collection, data analyses and reporting to industrial control systems. It identifies cautionary points that should be considered carefully when developing a cyber-forensics program for control systems. Many traditional device and control systems technologies do not provide for the collection of effective data that could be used for post-incident security analysis. An investigation harvesting evidence from core components that augment base operating systems should only be done with a full understanding of how the operating system has been changed. In addition, any auditing activity needs be carefully tested and deployed to assess any taxation on system resources. This guidance also describes what elements are important during investigations:

- Reference clock system
- Activity logs and transaction logs
- Other sources of data
- General system failures
- Real time forensics
- Device integrity monitoring
- Enhanced all-source logging and auditing

There is a project operating called the CRISALIS project [9]. CRISALIS aims at providing new means to secure critical infrastructure environments from targeted attacks, carried out by resourceful and motivated individuals. At the time of writing this paper the project is still ongoing and there is no working product available.

There are also open source tools for network security monitoring like the open-source Security Onion Linux suite [10], including Wireshark [11], NetworkMiner [12], etc. for network monitoring and intrusion detection. Passive network security monitoring is recommended as a key element to incident response. This will fit for the ICS environment because it is non-intrusive, so there is no risk of it disrupting critical processes or operations.

3   ICS Forensics

3.1   ICS Forensic Challenges

Forensic acquisition tools are widely available for conventional IÇT systems like hard disks, volatile memory (RAM) and common consumer electronics like mobile phones and navigations systems. Similar tools do not exist for most ICS devices. Besides, in ICS systems, safety is the main goal rather than Security. If ICT people talk about Security and Safety in ICT systems they do mean:

- Firewalls to prevent hackers from entering the system since confidential information must be protected.
- Antivirus and Antimalware for protecting the users and the systems against viruses.
- Anti-spam to protect the users against spam in their mail.

However, If ICS people talk about Security and Safety in ICS systems they do mean:

- Protect the system against dangerous issues like wrong values in PLC's.
- Flow control and temperature sensors in the chemical plant.
- Voltage and current control in electrical grid installations.

Not only the other interpretation or different jargon can be an issue, also the difference between ICT people who are working mainly in the office or data centers and the ICS people working on the field inside the plant or control room. There is a big gap between the two different departments; other goals and other problems are creating completely different priorities on a daily base.

3.2   ICS Forensic Process

The purpose of our approach is to safeguard the important information from the ICS system. Depending if we talk about a running system which is still intact and connected to other devices like a distributed control system, or if we talk about a standalone control system like a single PLC or a post mortem investigation after a big incident like a fire or explosion in a chemical plant, several information sources are available to acquire important digital evidence for digital forensic investigation purposes. For this reason we have to setup an ICS Forensic process. Inside this process, we split up the information from two different sources:

- Network data
- Device data

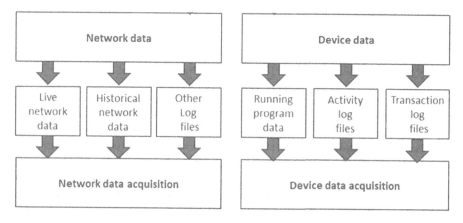

Fig. 1. ICS forensic process

Network data acquisition: For network data acquisition network investigation (depending on our investigation) we have to decide on what level (or levels) we need to analyze the network traffic (Fig. 1).

Network Levels: A typical distributed ICS system has at least three different levels of network types:

- Device level such as sensor, programmable logic controller (PLC), actuator.
- Cell Level that is responsible to control the device controllers.
- Plant Level that is responsible to control the cell controllers.

Beside, network data can also be historical information like backup files, logging databases etc. Sources of network data can be listed as:

- Live Network Data (raw network data, arp tables, flow records, etc.)
- Historical Network Data (host based logs, database queries, firewall-logs, etc.)
- Other Log Files (backup archives, access point logs, historians, etc.)

Not all tools or methods are safe to use in ICS environments. ICS systems often monitor or control processes in which a failure may have disastrous consequences (or may be otherwise very undesirable). For this reason active probing (like scanning for open ports and then opening arbitrary TCP connections) should generally be avoided.

Device data acquisition: Device data acquisition forensic tools do not exist for most ICS devices. Product specific service tools for programming a PLC, saving the program and servicing log files from a PLC to a service computer do exist. The question is can we use those service tools in a forensic matter to save important data from the PLC for later analyses? The sources of device data can be listed as:

- Running Program Data such as RAM dump, CHIP images, Memory cards…
- Activity Log Files such as RAM dump, active processes, control room logs, etc.
- Transaction Log Files such as Serial communication logs, Error logs, Event logs, etc.)

4 Case Study

This case study relates to an ICS investigation of an incident in a Wind Turbine in October 2013. In this incident two service engineers died during a fire in the nacelle of a 70 m high wind turbine in a 12 wind turbines farm the Netherlands. During this investigation we found out how crucial some ICS systems related forensic investigations depend on volatile memory inside the PLC. During the fire all electronics from the nacelle were severely destroyed by the fire. The only device what was still intact was the ground controller inside the turbine tower on the ground level of the tower section. After the fire we removed the controller from the base of the turbine (Fig. 2).

In close assistance with the Netherlands Forensic Institute, Department Digital Technology and the wind turbine manufacturer, we decided not to power-on the Cotas ground controller (Fig. 3) because without all normal connected devices it would probably overwrite existing log entries with error messages due the missing devices. The wind turbine manufacturer later confirmed this. The battery pack attached to the ground controller contains two 1.5 V batteries for power supply the battery operated RAM with 3 V. During measurement we found out the battery power was dropped down to 2.2 V.

At this stage it was not sure if this low voltage preserved all RAM content. Without opening the existing battery compartment, two extra battery pack holders ware connected in parallel with fresh batteries. This solution made it possible to replace the batteries one by one when needed if the voltage drops down again. To prevent data overwriting when powering up the ground controller again, the strategy was chosen in close assistance with the Netherlands Forensic Institute and the wind turbine manufacturer, to swap the PLC controller with a similar ground controller from a wind turbine in the same wind turbine farm as the destroyed one.

At this stage it was possible to make a copy of the RAM memory from the device. We used the service software and hardware from the wind turbine manufacturer. First

Fig. 2. Fire in wind turbine

(a) Battery pack connected   (b) Front picture ground controller

Fig. 3. Cotas ground controller

we tested the software on another ground controller which was still in use in the same plant. After a successful test on this other ground controller we did the same on the ground controller from the destroyed turbine. The hardware was a serial to infrared converter to connect to the ground controller and setup a serial connection to the ground controller and download the configuration and log files from the ground controller. All configurations, alarm, system, production and warning logs including entries within the accident period were present so the 2.2 V had preserved all RAM content. The only line what did overwrite an entry in the log file was a normal start-up. During start up both ground controllers we did check the systems clock time with a real-time DCF clock to find out if there was a difference between the system time of the ground controller and the real time. For later analyses it was very important to know the exact time difference inside the log files and the real time (Table 1). A portable DCF [5] clock is an easy way to do this.

After successfully download all configuration and log files from the ground controller we calculated a SHA-256 hash value from all downloaded files to verify that the saved data set has not been altered later during the investigation process.

Now we did successfully download all the important files from the ground controller it was possible to investigate the log files from this unit. The service software from the wind turbine manufacturer did have an option to save the files as .xml files and we were able read the content. The time and date inside this log files is not the real time, you have to convert all time lines with the difference measured during the start-up and the check we did with the DCF-clock.

Table 1. Time difference measurements with a DCF-clock

Ground controller	Date-time controller	Date-time DCF-lock	Difference
15190 (turbine 12)	12-12-2013 10:48:05	12-12-2013 10:23:47	00:24:18
15183 (turbine 2)	12-12-2013 11:07:01	12-12-2013 10:42:42	00:24:19

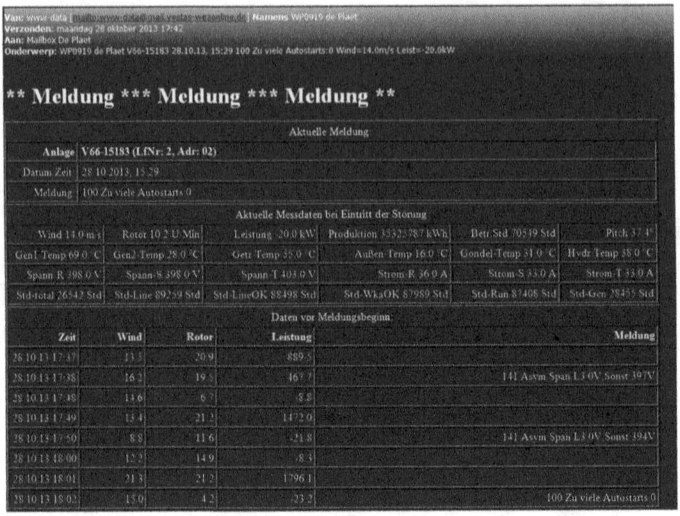

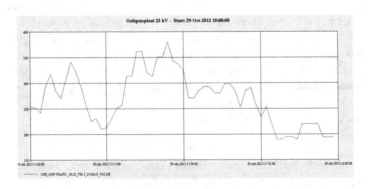

Fig. 4. Email from the SCADA server

Besides investigating the ground controller from the destroyed turbine, we also checked for other sources of digital evidence outside the turbine. One of the other sources was the connected SCADA server from the windmill park. Inside one of the other turbines there was a SCADA server installed in 2002. This server was a small industrial personal computer running on MS-DOS operating system. I did use a standard forensic method to make a forensic copy of the hard disk inside this SCADA server using a Tableau write-blocker and the forensic software FTK-imager. This SCADA server created reports of events, measurements and alarms. One of the events is shown below (Fig. 4), this is an email from the SCADA server to the miller regarding an alarm.

One other source of digital evidence was the grid operator Stedin. The grid operator was able to deliver grid information about the time around the incident. The grid operator Stedin generated a report from the grid with a time sample of 10 s (Fig. 5).

Fig. 5. Overview from grid operator

5   Conclusions and Future Work

Investigating ICS systems is not only about finding evidence of cybercrime related activities. Most investigations are incident related, like fire or explosions inside areas with ICS systems. Understanding the way how ICS systems are working, technical and tactical, is a must if you are involved with this kind of investigations. A big part of ICS systems is not different from normal conventional digital forensic work. Some parts of an ICS system are more difficult be course embedded systems like PLC's are different devices with their own communication protocols, connection interfaces, operating systems and program languages. Almost all manufactures of PLC's do have service tools that are able to safeguard RAM from the device, not always in a forensic certified way, but with some help of other tools you can get close to a forensically sound procedure in a manner that ensures it is "as originally discovered" and is reliable enough to be admitted into evidence.

In the future more research is desirable in reference systems and network flow. Anomaly detection [2] in ICS related networks is a very promising technique in securing ICS systems against cybercrime related crime. Especially ICS systems do have a static network flow and predictable behavior. Also in post mortem investigations like after an incident this predictable behavior can be a great help as long as you have a reliable source from the past. Anomaly detection technique can only work well if you know what is normal. Sources form the past can come from historians, pcap's, firewall log files, SCADA systems, etc. Also others sites with the same ICS system installed can be a good reference model for post mortem anomaly detection. Indeed, when dealing with the analysis of very forensics data extracted from ICS systems, data mining framework and knowledge map techniques [13–15] will be considered.

If you have a big and complex ICS system with remote sites and SCADA systems connected, it is not always necessary to investigate the whole system. Depending on your investigation you can make the system smaller and only investigate the PLC memory. Smaller do not always means simple, again a simple standalone PLC, without any connection to a SCADA system or any other device like a HMI, can still be a complex device. For example, if you don't know how to connect your tools to an embedded device like this, or if you are not familiar with the programming language in use. On the other hand, investigating the PLC RAM directly will give you more information about the PLC process. Most of the remote SCADA systems only record parts of the log files generated by the PLC. Some log files are not interesting for the process and will not be transmitted to the SCADA systems. In this case the only place where you can find all the needed information is inside the RAM on the PLC itself. Working together in close assistance with the manufacturer can help you to take the best actions and deliver the needed tools during your investigation.

References

1. Wu, T. et al.: Towards a SCADA forensics architecture, Newport (2013)
2. Barbosa, R.: Anomaly detection in SCADA systems, Enschede (2014)

3. van der Knijff, R.: Control systems/SCADA forensics, what's the difference, The Hague (2014)
4. U.S. Department of Homeland Security, Creating Cyber Forensics Plans for Control Systems, Idaho (2008)
5. http://en.wikipedia.org/wiki/DCF77
6. Boyer, S.: SCADA Supervisory Control and Data Acquisition, 2nd edn. ISA, Research Triangle Park (1999)
7. Modbus. http://en.wikipedia.org/wiki/Modbus. Accessed 4 Feb 2015
8. Profibus. http://en.wikipedia.org/wiki/Profibus. Accessed 4 Feb 2015
9. CRISALIS, Critical Infrastructure Security Analysis (2015). http://www.crisalis-project.eu/
10. Security Onion Linux suite. http://www.securityonion.net. Accessed 17 May 2015
11. Wireshark. https://wiki.wireshark.org/CaptureSetup/Ethernet
12. Hjelmvik, E.: SCADA network forensics, Stockholm (2014)
13. Aouad, L.M., Le-Khac, N.-A., Kechadi, T.: Lightweight clustering technique for distributed data mining applications. In: Perner, P. (ed.) ICDM 2007. LNCS (LNAI), vol. 4597, pp. 120–134. Springer, Heidelberg (2007)
14. Le-Khac, N.-A., Aouad, L.M., Kechadi, M.-T.: A new approach for distributed density based clustering on grid platform. In: Cooper, R., Kennedy, J. (eds.) BNCOD 2007. LNCS, vol. 4587, pp. 247–258. Springer, Heidelberg (2007)
15. Le-Khac, N.-A., Aouad, L.M., Kechadi, M.-T.: Distributed knowledge map for mining data on grid platforms. IJCSNS Int. J. Comput. Sci. Netw. Secur. 7(10), 98 (2007)

An Attack Execution Model for Industrial Control Systems Security Assessment

Ziad Ismail[1,2(✉)], Jean Leneutre[2], and Alia Fourati[1]

[1] EDF R&D, 1 Avenue du Général de Gaulle, 92140 Clamart, France
alia.fourati@edf.fr
[2] Télécom ParisTech, 46 rue Barrault, 75013 Paris, France
{ismail.ziad,jean.leneutre}@telecom-paristech.fr

Abstract. The improved communication and remote control capabilities of industrial control systems equipment have increased their attack surface. As a result, managing the security risk became a challenging task. The consequences of attacks in an industrial control system can go beyond targeted equipment to impact services in the industrial process. In addition, the success likelihood of an attack is highly correlated to the attacker profile and his knowledge of the architecture of the system. In this paper, we present the Attack Execution Model (AEM), which is an attack graph representing the evolution of the adversary's state in the system after each attack step. We are interested in assessing the risk of cyber attacks on an industrial control system before the next maintenance period. Given a specific attacker profile, we generate all potential attacker actions that could be executed in the system. Our tool outputs the probability and the time needed to compromise a target equipment or services in the system.

Keywords: Industrial control systems security · SCADA security · Attack graph

1 Introduction

In industrial control systems (ICSs), unpatched vulnerabilities continue to pose a serious threat to the security and safety of these systems. In 2014, most incidents reported by ICS-CERT targeted the energy sector [1]. The impact of cyber attacks on industrial control systems extends in scope, severity and damage than their counterparts in traditional IT systems. The introduction of new communication mediums between the system operator and industrial equipment and the use of off-the-shelf operating systems have increased the attack surface of these systems. The notion that control networks of industrial systems are "air gapped" (isolated from unsecured networks such as the internet) does not hold anymore [2] and the increased number of cyber attacks targeting these systems is a clear indication. In order to assess the potential impact of a cyber attack, utilities need to identify all possible actions that can be undertook by an adversary to compromise critical equipment and services in the control system.

© Springer International Publishing Switzerland 2016
A. Bécue et al. (Eds.): CyberICS 2015/WOS-CPS 2015, LNCS 9588, pp. 157–167, 2016.
DOI: 10.1007/978-3-319-40385-4_11

Our main objective is to assess the risk of cyber attacks on industrial control systems before the next maintenance period. The asset owner has to quantify the risk unpatched vulnerabilities pose to the system. A good assessment of the probability of successfully exploiting vulnerabilities in industrial control systems should take into account attackers' profiles that include their skills, access levels on machines, and their knowledge of the topology of the control system. In order to identify the critical vulnerabilities, we need to model the different ways an attacker can proceed to compromise equipment. Attack graphs are a promising solution to this problem. In this type of graphs, attack paths represent the sequence of actions an attacker has to execute in the system in order to compromise a specific target. The objective of the asset owner is to evaluate the probability that an attacker with a certain profile compromises critical equipment in the system within a certain time frame and harden security on these equipment accordingly.

With the increased complexity of interconnections between industrial equipment, an automated tool able to assess the impact of attacks on control system equipment and their associated control processes is needed. To achieve this objective, the tool needs to satisfy the following requirements: (i) model interdependencies that may exist between physical equipment and the services they offer to the system, (ii) model interdependencies between services, (iii) model the time required to execute each attack action, and finally (iv) take into account the attacker profile (knowledge of the architecture of the system, skill level, etc.) and the accumulated knowledge an attacker acquires while compromising equipment (credentials, additional knowledge of the topology).

The remainder of the paper is organized as follows. We discuss related work in Sect. 2. In Sect. 3, we present our motivations of some key aspects of our attack graph model. Section 4 defines the components of the network and service layers of our model. We present the attack execution model in Sect. 5. In Sect. 6, we discuss briefly the attack executions generation process in our tool. Finally, we conclude the paper in Sect. 7.

2   Related Work

Patching vulnerable equipment in the ICS is a challenging task. It is important from the point of view of the system administrator to assess the potential impact of exploiting a set of vulnerabilities on the system. Attack graphs were proposed as a potential solution to this problem. However, most attack graphs generation techniques focus on model scalability [3–5]. In this category of work, Lippmann et al. propose Predictive graphs [6]. The authors focus on identifying redundant structures in the attack graph that need to be explored only once. Another limitation of the classic attack graphs generation techniques is that they fail to assess the impact of an attack on the services (which can be interdependent) running in the system. Kheir et al. [7] propose a privilege-based service dependency model. Even though the proposed model offers a good representation of services dependencies, it does not show how to generate attack paths that can be used to compromise a service. To conduct this type of analysis, service dependency models need to be combined with attack graphs. A first attempt was conducted by Albanese et al. [8]. However, the authors combine services dependencies with other types of dependencies that can exist in the system rendering the generation of this generalized dependency graph a challenging task.

In the state of the art, there are a number of works that integrate the notion of time in the attack process. Leversage et al. [9] propose a state-space model in order to compute the Mean Time-to-Compromise (MTTC) for a given system. However, the attack paths are not automatically generated and need to be manually entered into the model. LeMay et al. propose a tool ADVISE [10] based on an attack execution graph to check whether a given state or an event in the system can be reached by the attacker within a certain time frame. ADVISE focuses on architectural-level vulnerabilities and therefore uses a very abstract view to represent potential attack steps. These attack steps need to be manually defined and the security of the system is evaluated against a certain attacker profile. In his anticipation games [11], Bursztein presents a dual-layer structure timed game in which he models the interactions between an attacker and a defender trying to compromise and defend a set of dependent services respectively. The tool implementing anticipation games uses heuristics to generate the optimal strategy for each player when the number of states explodes. However, in our case, we are interested in all attack executions that lead to the compromise of a machine or service within a specific time frame.

3   Towards a Time-Based Stochastic Attack Behavior

In general, traditional attack graphs generation techniques focus on model scalability and a certain abstraction of the components of the system is usually performed [3–5]. As a result, in some cases, the generated attack graph can miss important set of executions that are in practice the most interesting. We present our motivations to model events that represent key elements to consider to derive the time required to compromise a target machine. The time it takes an attacker to compromise an equipment depends on four main atomic events: arrival time of the attacker, probing time, access time, and time to exploit vulnerabilities. In addition to the characteristic of a vulnerability, the time needed to execute an attack depends on the profile of the attacker. We are interested in evaluating the impact of different types of attackers on the ICS. Given a time period $[0, M]$, we try to find which equipment an attacker can compromise and how deep in the network he can successfully infiltrate.

In the attack process, the first event to consider is the arrival time of the attacker. This metric relates to the arrival rates of attackers and depends among other factors on their types, motivations, and skills. Arrival rates can be statistically inferred from historical data that depend on the frequency of attacks targeting the system and their severities. A good assessment model of the attack time should take into account the time required to probe the network to discover the different types of connections and services between machines. The objectives and motivations of attackers will dictate how long, how often and how deep they try to scan the network to discover connected equipment. The longer it takes an attacker to find its target, the more probable his actions will be detected by intrusion detection systems and network administrators. We will refer by t_s, the time elapsed to scan the network. Once a vulnerable machine is discovered, the attacker tries to exploit it. For each type of vulnerabilities and each attacker profile, the effort and time needed to develop and execute an exploit are different. We refer by $t_e(\gamma)$, the time required to exploit vulnerability γ.

Finally, when there are multiple vulnerable services on the same machine, important questions arise: Which one the attacker will decide to compromise first? What are the required conditions to execute the exploit? etc. In practice, we can focus on leveraging our knowledge of the preferences of the attacker (given his profile) in order to build a stochastic behavior of the evolution of the state of the system. This can have an important impact on reducing the complexity of building the model.

4   Control System Layers

In our model, we represent the control system in two layers: the network layer and the service layer. The network layer consists of the physical equipment and their interconnections. The service layer consists of services used to execute industrial processes. In this section, we will give formal definitions of the principal components of each of these layers.

4.1   Network Layer

The network layer represents configuration and topological information about the system. Each node in this layer refers to a machine in the network. The state of the attacker on each machine depends on his actions. We represent the network as a directed graph $\mathcal{H} = \langle \mathcal{T}, \mathcal{Y}, l_y \rangle$ where $\mathcal{T}$ represents the set of vertices and $\mathcal{Y}$ is a subset of $\mathcal{T}^2$ and referred to as the edges of $\mathcal{H}$. The communication from a vertex i to a vertex j is represented by the edge y_{ij}. $l_y : \mathcal{Y} \rightarrow \{n, m\}$ is an edge labeling function where n refers to a network-based communication and m refers to a manual human-based communication. In fact, in some cases, a human operator manually intervenes to transmit information and configuration files between two machines in the system. This scenario occurs in general when a machine needs files from another machine and there are no network-based communications between the two equipment. All vertices $i \in \mathcal{T}$ will be referred to as nodes in the remaining of this paper. More formally:

Definition 1. *A **node** i in the graph $\mathcal{H}$ represents a machine in the network and is represented by the tuple $= \langle \Gamma_i, \Delta_i, W_i^n, \{\alpha_i^h, \beta_i^h, \mu_i^h\} \rangle$.*

$\Gamma_i = \{\gamma_k\}$ represents the set of vulnerabilities γ_k on node i. In our model, a vulnerability $\gamma_i \in \Gamma$ represents a weakness in the hardware or software on a node. For each attacker, we associate two atomic propositions for each vulnerability γ_k:

is_discovered to indicate whether the vulnerability has been discovered by the attacker, and **is_exploited** to indicate if that vulnerability has been successfully exploited. $\Delta_i = \{\delta_k\}$ represents the set of services running on node i. Multiple services can run on a machine (depending on its role, computation capacity, etc.). In addition, multiple machines can be used to run a particular service. In this case, in order to compromise the service, the attacker needs to compromise it on one of the supporting machines. W_i^n represents the security asset of node i and is used when evaluating the financial impact of an attack on the node in addition to its impact on system operation and the environment. Finally, a host-based IDS could be installed on the node to detect malicious activities, and when it exists, it is characterized by its detection rate μ_i^h, its false positives rate α_i^h, and false negatives rate β_i^h. Similarly, when a network-based IDS is deployed, we associate for each edge y_{ij} monitored by the IDS the parameters μ_{ij}^n, α_{ij}^n, and β_{ij}^n representing the detection rate, the false positives rate, and the false negatives rate of the network-based IDS respectively.

4.2 Service Layer

The service layer represents dependencies between the services in the system. Each node in the system is responsible for providing a service or a set of services and multiple nodes can interact to provide a particular service. After each action executed by the adversary, the state of the services in this layer is synchronized with the state of the nodes in the network layer. The dependency graph $\mathcal{D}$ between the services is represented by a tuple $\mathcal{D} = \langle \Delta, \rightarrow \rangle$ where Δ refers to the set of services in the system, and $\rightarrow$ is a binary relation representing a dependency between two services. In general, we can have disjoint dependent set of services and cyclic dependencies between services could exist. We define a service in the system as follows:

Definition 2. *A **service** δ_i is an atomic function required to execute a specific industrial process and is defined by the tuple $\langle \{(l_i, k_i^c)\}, W_i^s \rangle$.*

$\{(l_i, k_i^c)\}$ refers to the set of access levels and credentials required to use/access service δ_i. In fact, different persons can access a service each with a different role in the network. For each role, the access level and the set of required credentials to access the service can be different. In addition, if the service requires interactions between multiple machines, using/accessing the service on each of the supporting machines may require different access levels and credentials. W_i^s represents the impact (economical, environmental, etc.) for the system operator resulting from a successful compromise of the service δ_i. It is an intrinsic value related to the service. However, using the service dependency graph $\mathcal{D}$, it is possible to compute the total impact of compromising service δ_i on the system by parsing $\mathcal{D}$ and identifying all the services that depend on δ_i.

5   Attack Execution Model

The pace of progress of the attacker in compromising machines in the system depends on his profile. To execute each attack step, the attacker needs to have acquired a set of knowledge items which is defined as follows:

Definition 3. *The set of knowledge items $\mathcal{K}$ is represented by the tuple $\langle K^a, K^c, K^t \rangle$.*

$K^a = \langle \mathcal{T}, \mathcal{Y} \rangle$ refers to information about machines (including their vulnerabilities, running services, etc.) and their interconnections. $K^c = \{(\tau_i, c_i) | \tau_i \in \mathcal{T}\}$ refers to the set of credentials on machines the attacker has acquired. For example, the knowledge of a password on a given machine can provide the attacker with the required credentials to gain access to that machine. Finally, K^t refers to the set of specific tools and expertise needed to exploit the vulnerabilities in the network.

The profile of the attacker plays an important role in assessing the potential impact of attacks on the system. We formally define an attacker as follows:

Definition 4. *An **attacker** is any type of adversaries targeting the system and is represented by the tuple $\langle \pi, s, A, R \rangle$.*

π refers to the type of the attacker and is one among the set $\Pi = \{script\ kiddie,\ hacker,\ hacktivist,\ nation\ state,\ insider\ attacker\}$. s refers to the skill level of the attacker. A refers to the possible actions that can be executed by the attacker where $A \subset \{scan,\ access,\ exploit\}$. The adversary's attack preferences R is an ordered set of priorities (depth of a scan, cost of an attack, its payoff, etc.) taken into account when executing an attack step. This information is used, in conjunction with other parameters, to assist in the attacker decision-making process regarding the choice of the next attack step when multiple possibilities exist.

Given all this information, we define our attack execution model as follows:

Definition 5. *An **attack execution model** is represented by the tuple $\langle \mathcal{G}, \Xi \rangle$.*

Let $\mathcal{G}$ be a labeled supergraph represented by the tuple $\langle \mathcal{V}, \mathcal{E}, \Sigma_{\mathcal{V}}, \Sigma_{\mathcal{E}}, l_{\mathcal{V}}, l_{\mathcal{E}} \rangle$. $\mathcal{V} = \{v_1, v_2, ..., v_N\}$ refers to the set of supervertices where each supervertex v_i represents a state of the system. In each supervertex v_i, let X_i represent the set of subvertices $\{x_1^i, x_2^i, ..., x_{N_i}^i\}$ each representing a state of the attacker (knowledge of the topology of the system, exploited vulnerabilities, acquired credentials, etc.) when the system state is v_i. At any given time t, the attacker state represents the adversary's access levels on equipment, acquired credentials, and knowledge about the topology and configuration of the control system. $\mathcal{E}$ is a subset of $\{\bigcup_i X_i\}^2$. An element of the set of ordered pairs of subvertices $\mathcal{E}$ is defined as $e_{ij} = (i, j)$. Let $\Sigma_{\mathcal{V}}$ and $\Sigma_{\mathcal{E}}$ be two finite alphabets of supervertex and edge labels respectively. $\Sigma_{\mathcal{V}}$ represents a description of the set of states the system can transition to following an action by the adversary. $\Sigma_{\mathcal{E}} = \{scan,$

network access, human-based access, exploit}. $l_\mathcal{V} : \mathcal{V} \to \Sigma_\mathcal{V}$ and $l_\mathcal{E} : \mathcal{E} \to \Sigma_\mathcal{E}$ are two mapping functions for supervertex and edge labeling respectively. The system and attacker states evolve depending on the actions of the attacker. The evolution of these states is described using a set of rules Ξ.

5.1   Rule-Based Attack Execution

In general, in an ICS, equipment often have limited resources. In addition, processes executed within the system are mission critical and a failure could result in a severe impact on the infrastructure's equipment, operations, and personnel. Therefore, any action executed by an attacker in the system should take into account these constraints. In order to represent the evolution of the attacker in the system, we adopt the notion of atomic attack executions. An atomic attack execution is a single action of the attacker that given a set of preconditions, the state of the attacker in the system changes. More formally:

Definition 6. *An **atomic attack execution** is a couple (ξ_i, τ_i) where ξ_i is a rule executed on node $\tau_i \in \mathcal{T}$.*

At $t = 0$, the attacker may possess a set of initial knowledge items k_i^0. This set contains information about the topology and the configuration of the network, access levels and credentials at the attacker's disposal, and a set of offensive tools used in the attack process. The attacker can choose to compromise equipment located on specific attack paths, leveraging his knowledge of critical assets' locations while decreasing the probability of being detected.

Ξ is the set of rules used to describe the evolution of the state of the attacker in the system. There are four types of rules: scan, network access, human-based access, and exploit. Each rule needs a set of preconditions to be executed, and its execution results in a set of postconditions. In the rest of this section, we formally define the rules governing the evolution of the state of the attacker in the system.

Scan. In order to compromise a target equipment, an attacker needs to identify the possible paths that could lead to his target. We define the scanning rule ξ_{scan} as follows:

$$\xi_{scan} : \textbf{Pre} \ \langle \mathcal{T}, R, \mathcal{K} \rangle \xrightarrow{t_s, c} \textbf{Post} \ \langle \Gamma, K^a \rangle \tag{1}$$

Taking into account the attacker's preferences (how often and how deep to scan, the probability of being detected, etc.) and his set of acquired knowledge items, scanning the network from a node $\tau_i \in \mathcal{T}$ results in the discovery of new equipment and their vulnerabilities. For this rule, we associate a time t_s representing the time the attacker spends to perform the scan and its associated cost c.

Network Access. We define an access from an equipment to another connected equipment in the network as follows:

$$\xi_{network\_access} : \mathbf{Pre} \ \langle \mathcal{T}, \mathcal{L}, \mathcal{K}, \mathcal{T} \rangle \xrightarrow{c_n, \rho_n} \mathbf{Post} \ \langle \mathcal{L}, K^a, K^c \rangle \tag{2}$$

The attacker tries to access a remote equipment in the system using his access level $l_i \in \mathcal{L}$ on a compromised machine and a set of knowledge items. If this type of access is allowed in the access control policy, the result of the execution of this rule is the set of access levels granted to the attacker on the remote equipment and an access to system configuration files. A cost c_n and a payoff ρ_n are associated to the execution of this rule.

Human-Based Access. In an industrial environment, an equipment could require configuration files generated on another equipment. In general, the operator transmits these files manually using USB flash drives or other storage mediums. We formally define this type of access rules as follows:

$$\xi_{human-based\_access} : \mathbf{Pre} \ \langle \mathcal{T}, \mathcal{L}, \mathcal{K}, \mathcal{T} \rangle \xrightarrow{t_h, c_h, \rho_h} \mathbf{Post} \ \langle \mathcal{L}, K^a, K^c \rangle \tag{3}$$

The key difference of executing this rule compared to the network access rule (Eq. 2) is taking into account the time t_h corresponding to the average time elapsed between two consecutive manual human intervention to transmit information from the compromised to the remote equipment.

Exploit. The pre/post-conditions model is used to represent the prerequisites and the consequences of exploiting a vulnerability. In particular, a vulnerability γ_i^j is represented by the tuple $\langle \varphi_{pre}, \varphi_{post} \rangle$. $\varphi_{pre} = \{b, s, k_c, k_t\}$ refers to the set of preconditions required to exploit the vulnerability. b is a binary value referring whether the vulnerability can be exploited locally (0) or remotely (1). s refers to the minimum attacker skill level required to exploit γ_i^j. $k_c \subset K^c$ and $k_t \subset K^t$ refer to the set of knowledge items the attacker needs to possess in order to successfully exploit the vulnerability. $\varphi_{post} = \{k_a', k_c'\}$ refers to the set of postconditions representing the consequences of successfully exploiting the vulnerability. k_a and k_c refer to the additional knowledge of the topology and the configuration of the network, and the access level and credentials acquired after exploiting the vulnerability respectively.

The rule to exploit a vulnerability $\gamma_i^j = \langle \varphi_{pre}, \varphi_{post} \rangle$ is defined as follows:

$$\xi_{exploit} : \mathbf{Pre} \ \varphi_{pre} \xrightarrow{t_e, c_e, \rho_e} \mathbf{Post} \ \varphi_{post} \tag{4}$$

We associate to the exploit rule of a vulnerability the time t_e needed to develop and execute the exploit and its development and execution cost c_e. The payoff ρ_e represents the gain the attacker gets if the exploit was successfully executed, which depend on the equipment security asset and the set of compromised services.

5.2   Attack Executions

An attack execution is a sequence of atomic attack executions corresponding to rules executed by the attacker and is defined as follows:

Definition 7. *An **attack execution** $p_i \in \mathcal{P}$ is a tuple $\langle (\Xi_i, \tau_i), q_i, > \rangle$.*

These rules have localities that determine on which nodes they are executed. We define a strict order $>$ on atomic attack executions. We associate a probability q_i to the attack execution p_i referring to the probability that the attacker executes the sequence of atomic attack steps resulting in p_i.

Definition 8. *The **strategy objective** of the defender is a critical set of equipment and services that needs to be protected within [0,M]. It is formally defined as a tuple $\langle \mathcal{T}_i, \Delta_i \rangle$.*

The defender is interested in protecting a set of equipment in the system and a set of services responsible of executing critical industrial processes. Using the attack execution model, the defender is able to verify whether his security objectives are satisfied at any given time of the attack process.

6   Attack Executions Generation Algorithm

The attack graph is generated using a depth-first strategy. At first, the profile of the attacker includes, among other factors, his initial knowledge of the architecture of the system and access levels on equipment. After each attack step, the knowledge of the attacker is updated with new information about the architecture of the system or his privilege level increases on an equipment and new information such as credentials is acquired after exploiting a vulnerability. In our model, we distinguish between two types of vulnerabilities: a local vulnerability that requires a local access on the equipment to be exploited and a remotely exploitable vulnerability. Since in general we do not know if a certain knowledge item such as a password will be useful for the attacker in future attack steps, we explore all possible attack paths. In addition, in order to find the most probable attack path with minimum time to achieve the attacker's objective, all possible combinations of attacker actions are explored. However, this increases the complexity of the generation algorithm and we are quickly limited by the number of equipment of the control system that we can model. For example, for an architecture of 80 equipment with four levels, each separated by a gateway, when each equipment is connected to five other equipment, we are able to generate all attack paths within 5 to 6 min when considering that the state of the system does not change. This limitation can be overcome using some pruning techniques applied during the process of generating the attack graph to reduce its size. For example, we can limit the number of actions an attacker can do at any given time depending on his partial knowledge of the architecture of the system by prioritizing among his possible immediate actions. The prioritization decision-making depends on the profile of the attacker and his objective. Finally, by analyzing the attacker's state, we can reduce the attack graph size and improve the generation time by finding whether the attacker can carry out the same future actions after compromising an equipment from different attack paths.

7   Conclusion

The life cycle of industrial control systems vary from several years to several decades. It is important to conceive a model that allows asset owners to quantify the risk that unpatched vulnerabilities pose to their systems. In this paper, we presented the attack execution model, which is a type of attack graphs that given the architecture of the system and an attacker profile, generates all attack executions that could be carried out by the attacker in the system before the next maintenance period. We focus on the time the attacker needs to achieve his objective and the success likelihood of the attack. In our future work, using the output of our attack graph, we plan to investigate optimal patching strategies of the vulnerabilities that have been exploited by the adversary in order to reduce the risk of attacks on the industrial control system while minimizing the overall cost of patch deployment. In addition, modifying the model in order to study the interactions between the attacker and the defender is an interesting extension to this work. For example, after each attack step, we try to find the best response of the defender taking into account the different operational and economical constraints in the control system and study the potential behavior of the attacker in this case.

References

1. ICS-CERT: NCCIC/ICS-CERT Monitor September 2014-February 2015. https://ics-cert.us-cert.gov/sites/default/files/Monitors/ICS-CERT_Monitor_Sep2014-Feb2015.pdf
2. Byres, E.: The air gap: SCADA's enduring security myth. Commun. ACM **56**(8), 29–31 (2013)
3. Ammann, P., Wijesekera, D., Kaushik, S.: Scalable, graph-based network vulnerability analysis. In: Proceedings of the 9th ACM Conference on Computer and Communications Security, CCS 2002 pp. 217–224 (2002)
4. Ingols, K., Lippmann, R., Piwowarski, K.: Practical attack graph generation for network defense. In: 22nd Annual Computer Security Applications Conference, ACSAC 2006, pp. 121–130 (2006)
5. Jajodia, S., Noel, S.: Topological vulnerability analysis. In: Jajodia, S., Liu, P., Swarup, V., Wang, C. (eds.) Cyber Situational Awareness. Advances in Information Security, vol. 46, pp. 139–154. Springer, US (2010)
6. Lippmann, R.P., et al.: Validating and restoring defense in depth using attack graphs. In: Proceedings of Military Communications Conference (MILCOM) (2006)
7. Kheir, N., Cuppens-Boulahia, N., Cuppens, F., Debar, H.: A service dependency model for cost-sensitive intrusion response. In: Gritzalis, D., Preneel, B., Theoharidou, M. (eds.) ESORICS 2010. LNCS, vol. 6345, pp. 626–642. Springer, Heidelberg (2010)

8. Albanese, M., Jajodia, S., Pugliese, A., Subrahmanian, V.S.: Scalable analysis of attack scenarios. In: Atluri, V., Diaz, C. (eds.) ESORICS 2011. LNCS, vol. 6879, pp. 416–433. Springer, Heidelberg (2011)
9. Leversage, D., Byres, E.: Estimating a system's mean time-to-compromise. IEEE Secur. Priv. **6**(1), 52–60 (2008)
10. LeMay, E., Ford, M., Keefe, K., Sanders, W., Muehrcke, C.: Model-based security metrics using adversary view security evaluation (advise). In: Proceedings of the 2011 Eighth International Conference on Quantitative Evaluation of SysTems, QEST 2011, pp. 191–200. IEEE Computer Society, Washington, DC (2011)
11. Bursztein, E.: Anticipation Games. Ph.D. thesis, Ecole Normale Supérieure de Cachan (2008)

Author Index

Armando, Alessandro   48

Bayou, Lyes   63

Coletta, Alessio   48
Coppolino, Luigi   31
Cuppens, Frédéric   63
Cuppens-Boulahia, Nora   63

D'Elia, Danilo   3

Espes, David   63

Falkner, Nick   127
Finkenauer, Travis   112
Fourati, Alia   157

Gondree, Mark A.   16
Groza, Bogdan   95

Halderman, J. Alex   112

Ismail, Ziad   157

Jäger, Michael   31

Kechadi, M.-T.   147
Kernick, Phil   127
Kuntze, Nicolai   31
Kylänpää, Markku   79

Le-Khac, Nhien-An   147
Leneutre, Jean   157

Nguyen, Thuy D.   16

Ranathunga, Dinesha   127
Rantala, Aarne   79
Rein, Andre   31
Rieke, Roland   31
Roughan, Matthew   127

Solomon, Cristina   95

Van Vliet, Pieter   147